DIRECTING STAFF EDITION

> RESTRICTED
> The information given in this document is not to be communicated either directly or indirectly to the Press or to any person not authorised to receive it.

BRITISH ARMY OF THE RHINE

BATTLEFIELD TOUR

OPERATION VARSITY

OPERATIONS OF XVIII UNITED STATES CORPS (AIRBORNE) IN SUPPORT OF THE CROSSING OF THE RIVER RHINE, 24 and 25 MARCH 1945

The Naval & Military Press Ltd

Published by

The Naval & Military Press Ltd
Unit 5 Riverside, Brambleside
Bellbrook Industrial Estate
Uckfield, East Sussex
TN22 1QQ England

Tel: +44 (0)1825 749494

www.naval-military-press.com
www.nmarchive.com

In reprinting in facsimile from the original, any imperfections are inevitably reproduced and the quality may fall short of modern type and cartographic standards.

BATTLEFIELD TOURS

Headquarters, British Army of the Rhine, compiled Battlefield Tours during 1947 covering the following operations in the Campaign in North-West EUROPE (June 1944–May 1945):—

Name of Operation	*Action covered*
GOODWOOD	Operations of 8 Corps East of the River ORNE (NORMANDY) 18–22 July 1944, with particular reference to 11th Armoured Division.
BLUECOAT	Operations of 8 Corps South of CAUMONT (NORMANDY) 30–31 July 1944, with particular reference to 15th (Scottish) Infantry Division.
TOTALIZE	Operations of 2 Canadian Corps astride the road CAEN–FALAISE (NORMANDY) 7–8 August 1944, with particular reference to 51st (Highland) Infantry Division.
NEPTUNE	Assault crossing of the River SEINE by 43rd (Wessex) Infantry Division 25–28 August 1944
VERITABLE	Operations of 30 Corps between the Rivers MAAS and RHINE 8–10 February 1945, with particular reference to 15th (Scottish) Infantry Division.
PLUNDER	Assault crossing of the River RHINE by 12 Corps 24–25 March 1945, with particular reference to 15th (Scottish) Infantry Division.
VARSITY	Airborne operations of XVIII United States Corps (Airborne) in support of the crossing of the River RHINE 24–25 March 1945, with particular reference to 6th British Airborne Division.

A similar book was written on each of these operations, of which four hundred copies were printed, one hundred of these containing notes for Directing Staff. A further fifty Directing Staff copies and two hundred and fifty Spectator's copies have been distributed to various libraries, original speakers and certain other individuals.

Directorate of Military Training, War Office, or Headquarters, British Army of the Rhine can supply information as to where these books are kept.

FOREWORD

By

Lieutenant General Sir Richard L. McCREERY, KCB, KBE, DSO, MC
General Officer Commanding-in-Chief the British Army of the Rhine

Battlefield Tours of Operations VERITABLE, PLUNDER and VARSITY have been prepared to provide material for the study of operations of a different character and under different conditions from the NORMANDY battles which were the subject of the British Army of the Rhine Battlefield Tour in June 1947.

Operations PLUNDER and VARSITY are complementary to each other and should whenever possible be studied together. Operation VARSITY is of particular interest, as it was the first occasion on which Airborne Forces were dropped within the range of our own supporting arms.

We have again been fortunate in obtaining the personal accounts of Army and Royal Air Force officers who took part in Operations PLUNDER and VARSITY. The personal accounts of operation VERITABLE were obtained by permission of the Staff College CAMBERLEY from their Battlefield Tour held in the Summer of 1947. These personal accounts introduce, as far as this is possible, the atmosphere of war.

When a battlefield is revisited at a later date, in full possession of all the information and with a clear picture of the situation, it is comparatively easy to say what should have been done. In war, the situation is rarely clear, the information is never complete, and actions must be considered in the light of the situation as it was known to the Commanders at the time. The view of the commander on the spot in each of the various situations is supplied in the personal accounts.

These past operations must be studied with an eye to the future if full benefit is to be derived from them. In studying the problems, constant consideration must be given to the conditions which are likely to be met and the material and equipment which is likely to be available in the next war. It is certain, however, that whatever form land warfare may take in the future, certain fundamental factors which constantly stand out in these operations, such as morale, training, junior leadership and surprise will retain their pre-eminent importance.

R. L. McCreery

Lieutenant General

OBJECT OF THE BOOK

This book describes the operations of XVIII United States Corps (Airborne) in support of the Second British Army crossing of the River RHINE, on 24 March 1945. It is especially concerned with the part played by 6 British Airborne Division in those operations on 24 and 25 March.

It forms the necessary background to a detailed study of the battle carried out on the ground.

CONTENTS

PART I—PLANNING THE OPERATION

		Page
Section I.	Introduction	1
	A. General	1
	B. 21 Army Group Plan	1
	C. Advance Planning	1
Section II.	Topography	3
Section III.	The Enemy	5
	A. General	5
	B. Enemy layout	5
	C. Enemy opposition to Operation VARSITY	5
Section IV.	Plan for Operation PLUNDER	7
	A. Task of Second British Army	7
	B. Second Army Outline Plan	7
	C. 12 Corps Intention	7
	D. Troops available to 12 Corps	7
	E. Formation Tasks	7
	F. 15 (S) Div Plan	8
Section V.	Command and co-ordination of Operations PLUNDER and VARSITY	9
	A. Ground	9
	B. Air	9
	C. Airborne	9
	D. Combined Command Post	9
Section VI.	Plan for Operation VARSITY	11
	A. Object	11
	B. Decisions affecting XVIII US Corps (Airborne)	11
	C. Troops available	11
	D. Task of 17 US Airborne Div	11
	E. Task of 6 Brit Airborne Div	11
	F. Plan of 6 Brit Airborne Div	11
	G. Role of 6 Gds Armd Bde	12
	H. Plan for Seaborne Tail of 6 Brit Airborne Div	13
	J. Subsequent Operations of XVIII US Corps (Airborne)	13
Section VII.	Planning by Air Forces	15
	A. Introduction	15
	B. Airborne Plan	16
	C. Air Support	17
	D. Final Preparation and Timings	18
Section VIII.	Fire Plan	19
	A. Chain of Command and Planning	19
	B. Allotment of Artillery for Operation VARSITY	19
	C. Tasks and Timings	20
	D. Safety Precautions and their effect	21
	E. Liaison and Communications	21

		Page
Section IX.	Communications	23
	A. General	23
	B. Communications for planning and launching	23
	C. Communications for Operations	23
	D. Air Support Communications	24
Section X.	Administrative Planning	25
	A. General	25
	B. Seaborne Tail	25
	C. Maintenance by Air	25
	D. Maintenance by ground resources	26
	E. Administrative Communications	26
	F. Administrative Services	26
	G. Reinforcements	26

PART II—ACCOUNT OF THE BATTLE

Section I.	Introduction	29
Section II.	Operations 24 March	31
	A. Flight of 6 Brit Airborne Div to the Objective	31
	B. Action of 6 Brit Airborne Div after Landing	33
	C. 6 Brit Airborne Div Administration	35
	D. 17 US Airborne Div	36
	E. 12 Corps	36
	F. Enemy	37
	G. Air Support	37
	H. Summary	37
Section III.	Operations 25 March	39
	A. Corps Commander's Orders for 25 March	39
	B. 6 Brit Airborne Div	39
	C. 17 US Airborne Div	39
	D. 12 Corps	40
	E. Enemy	40
	F. Summary	40
Section IV.	Subsequent Operations	41

PART III—PERSONAL ACCOUNTS OF ACTIONS FOR STUDY

Section I.	Introductory Lecture	45
Section II.	Itinerary	51
Section III.	Personal Accounts	53
Section IV.	Notes for the guidance of conducting officers	77

MAPS
PART I

		Facing Page
No. 1.	General Situation 23 March 1945	1
No. 2.	Appreciated enemy positions opposite 12 and XVIII Corps	3
No. 3.	Appreciated enemy AA positions on 18 and 23 March	5
No. 4.	12 Corps Plan	7
No. 5.	Objectives, DZs, LZs etc. of XVIII Corps	11
No. 6.	Routes by airborne forces	15
No. 7.	"Fly-in" and "Fly-out" routes	17
No. 8.	Gun areas	19
No. 9.	Fire support in 6 Brit Airborne Div area	21

PART II

		Facing Page
No. 10.	Plot of glider landings	31
No. 11.	Operations 24 and 25 March	33
No. 12.	Actual enemy positions East of River RHINE	37

PART III

No. 13.	Battlefield Tour—Operation VARSITY (Itinerary)	51
No. 14.	Action of 3 Para Bde and 8 Para Bn	59

With Appendices

No. A1.	Transit Camps and Airfields used by 6 Brit Airborne Div	89
	Map of General Area (1 : 25,000)	End pocket

DIAGRAMS

PART I

No. 1.	Airborne Chain of Command	14
No. 2.	Artillery Communications	Facing Page 23
No. 3.	XVIII Corps Communications (other than artillery)	„ 23
No. 4.	6 Brit Airborne Div Communications (down to Battalion HQ) (other than artillery)	„ 23
No. 5.	Air Support Communications	„ 23

PART II

No. 6.	Communications of FVCP and ASSU at HQ 6 Brit Airborne Div	38

With Appendices

No. 7.	Communications for Transit Camps and Airfields in Airborne Base	92

APPENDICES

A.	Order of Battle	81
B.	Equipment and Organisation (Allied and German)	85
C.	List of Reference Maps	87
D.	Organisation of the Airborne Base	89
E.	Casualties : Equipment and Personnel	93
F.	Extracts from 6 Brit Airborne Div Operation Order No. 1	95

PHOTOGRAPHS

No. 1.	Airborne 75 mm stowed in glider	
No. 2.	6 Airlanding Bde gliders	
No. 3.	HALIFAX/HAMILCAR combinations marshalled at WOODBRIDGE	
No. 4.	View of 3 Para Bde DZ	
No. 5.	HORSA gliders of 6 Airlanding Bde	
No. 6.	German 88 mm AA guns near HAMMINKELN	
No. 7.	HORSA gliders of 12 DEVON	
No. 8.	WACO gliders of 17 US Airborne Div	Following Page 109
No. 9.	Prisoners captured by 1 Cdn Para Bn	
No. 10.	HORSA gliders	
No. 11.	Mortar and Intelligence Sections of 9 Para Bn	
No. 12.	A HAMILCAR glider	
No. 13.	View of autobahn East of HAMMINKELN	
No. 14.	Part of 6 Airlanding Bde on LZ	
No. 15.	HAMILCAR glider on Div HQ LZ	
No. 16.	LIBERATOR bombers flying in first re-supply drop	

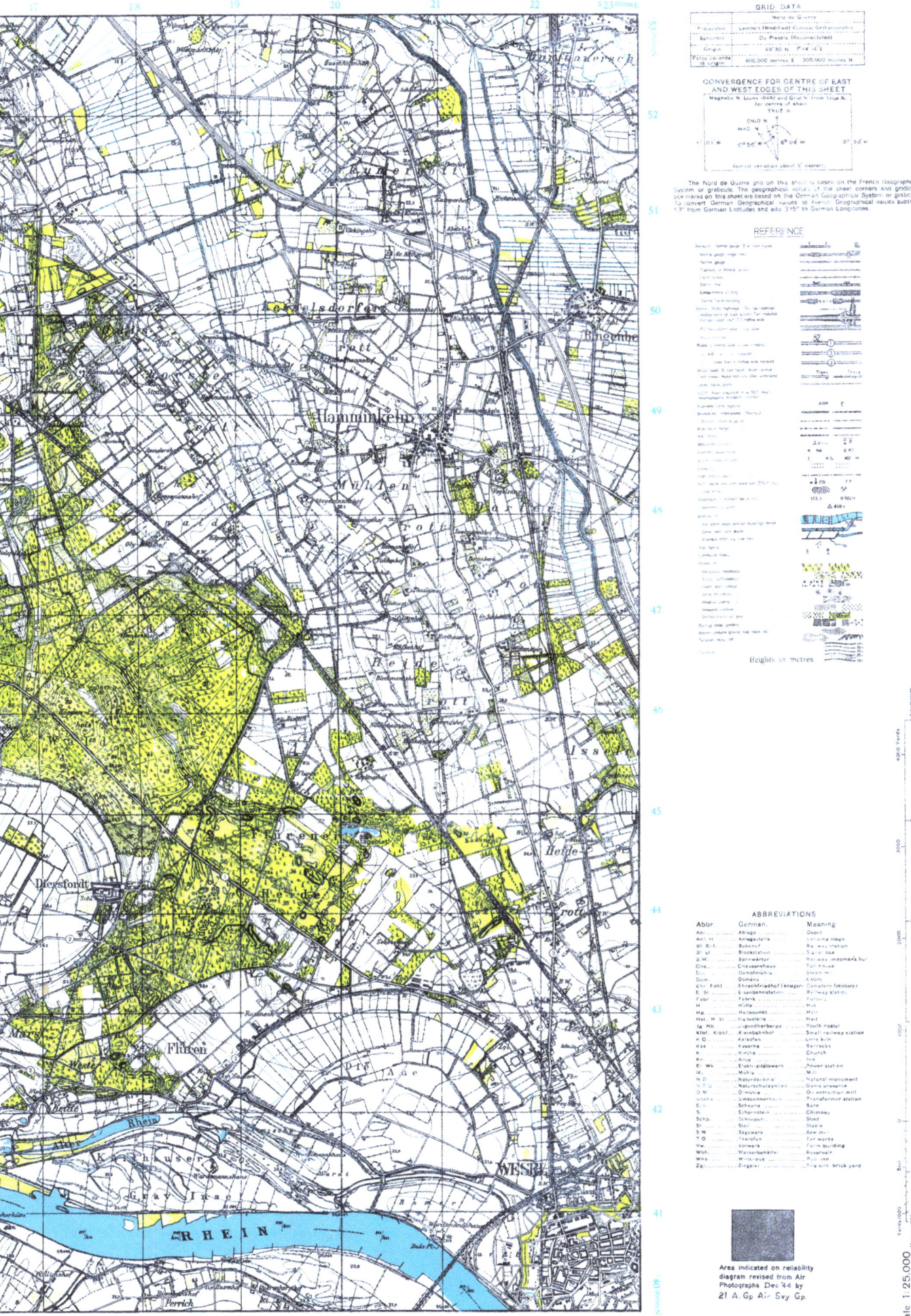

Operation Varsity 24 & 25th March 1945 — spread 1

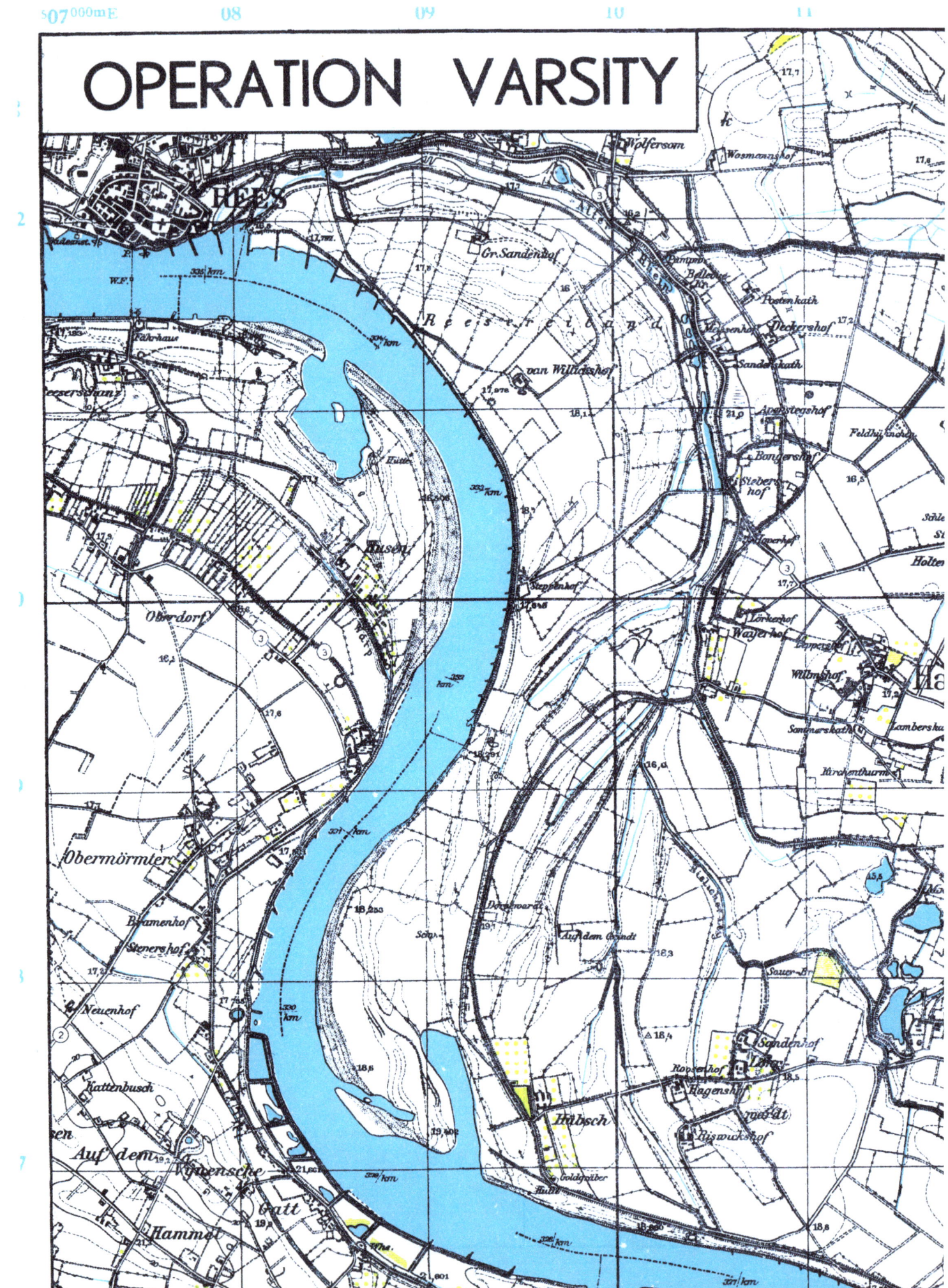

Operation Varsity 24 & 25th March 1945 — spread 1

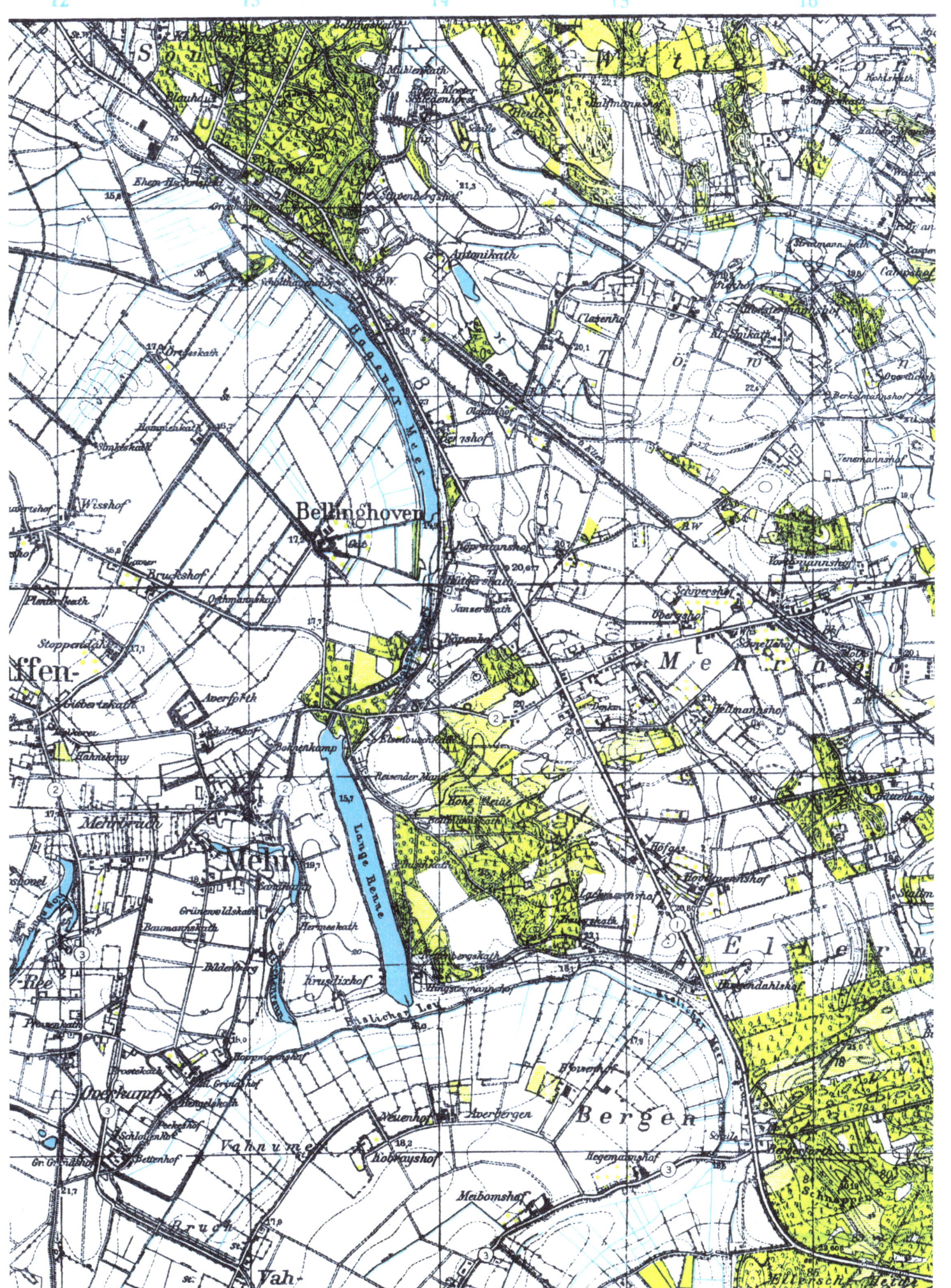

Operation Varsity 24 & 25th March 1945 — spread 2

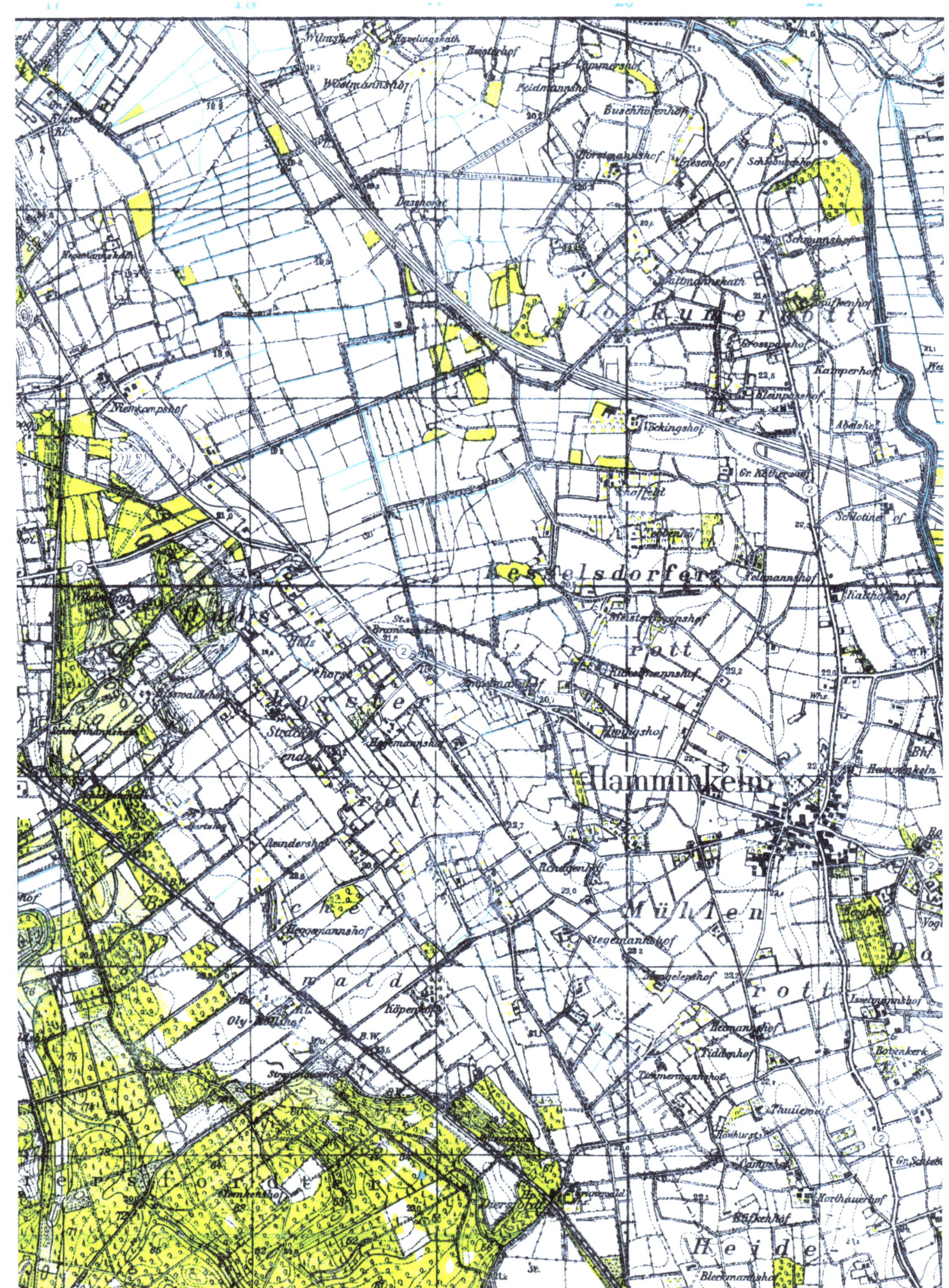

Operation Varsity 24 & 25th March 1945 — spread 2

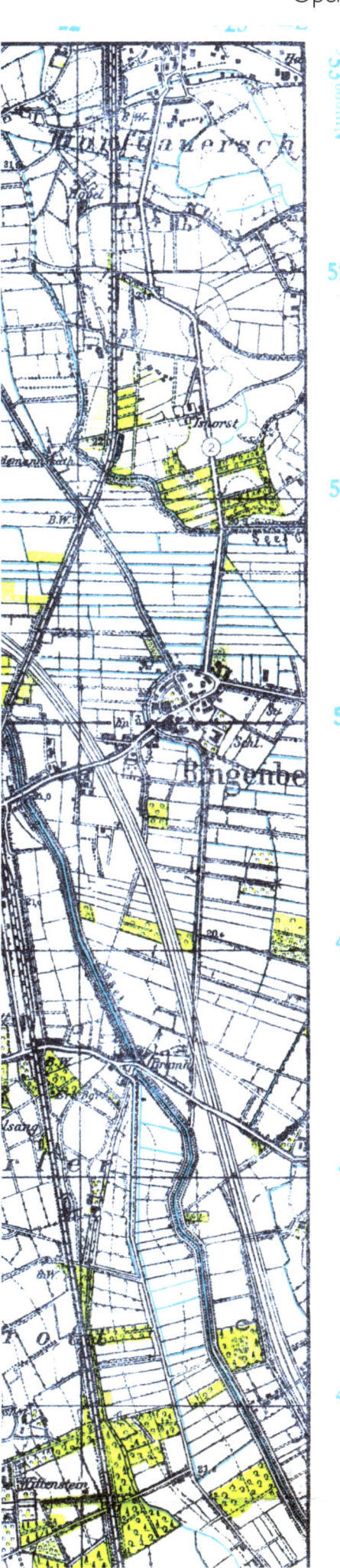

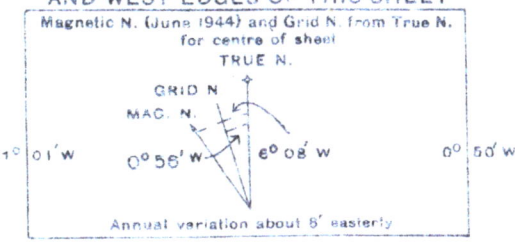

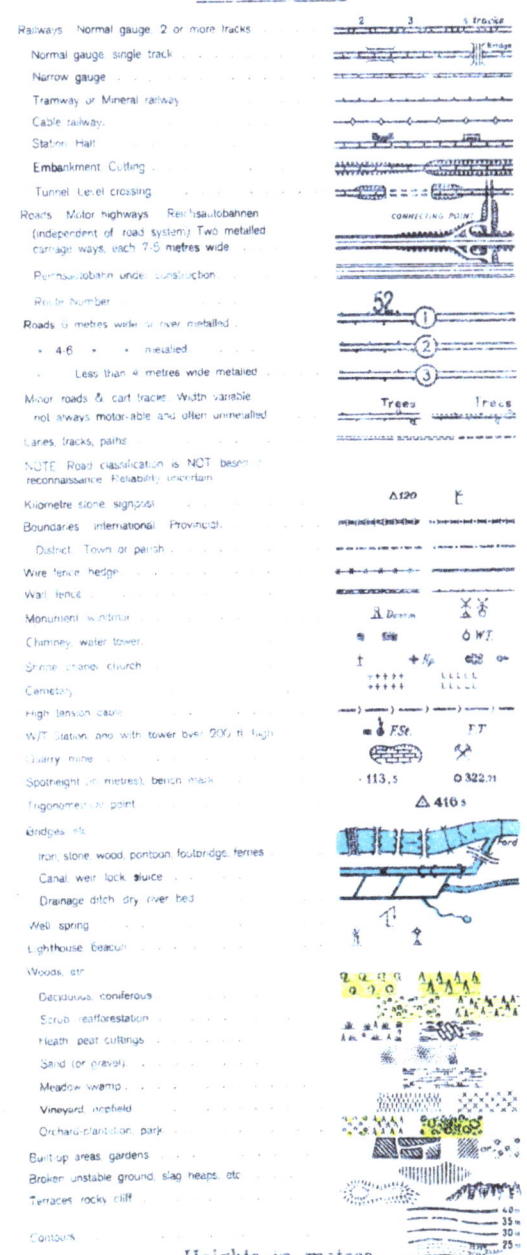

Operation Varsity 24 & 25th March 1945 — spread 3

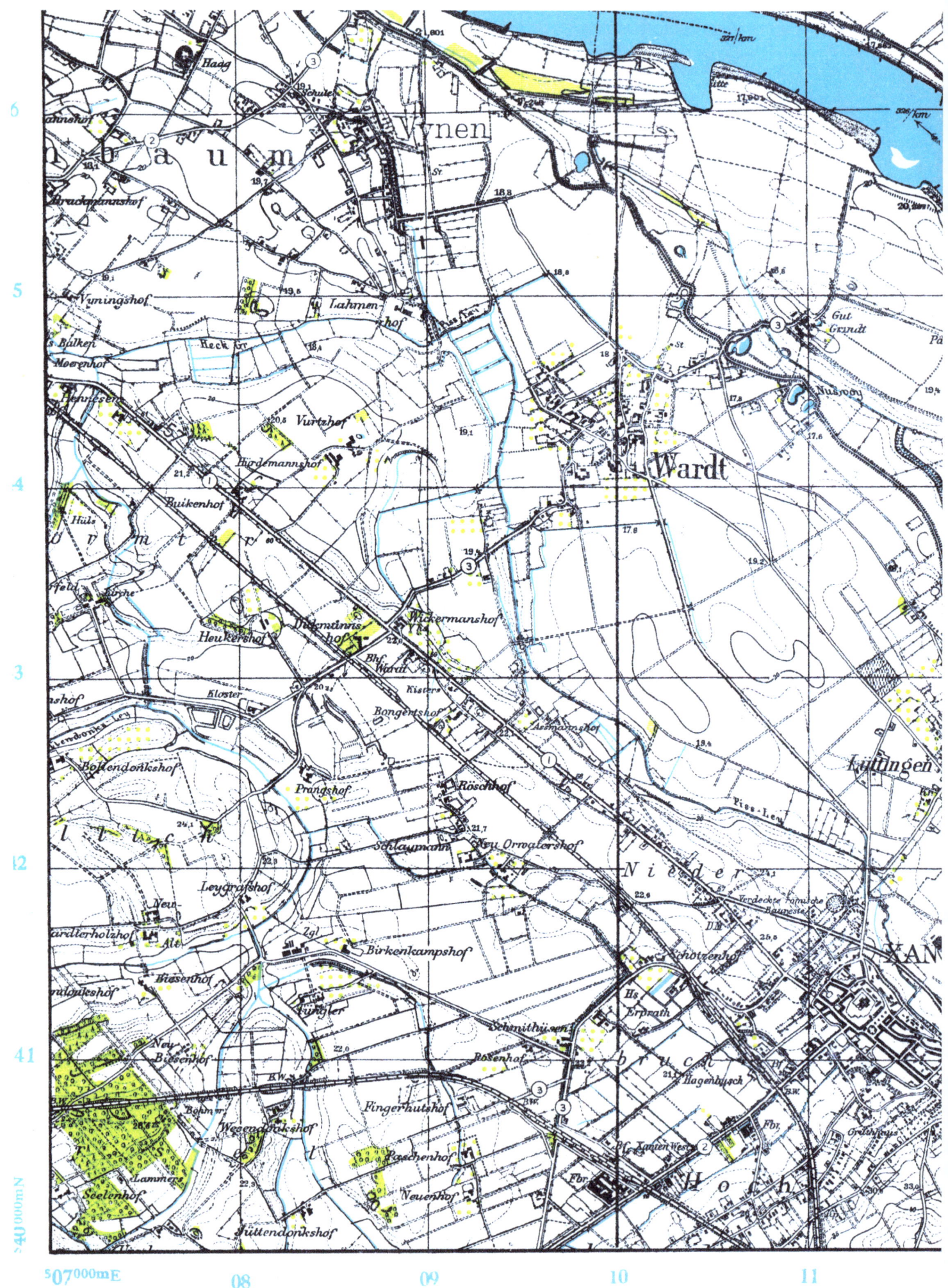

Operation Varsity 24 & 25th March 1945 — spread 3

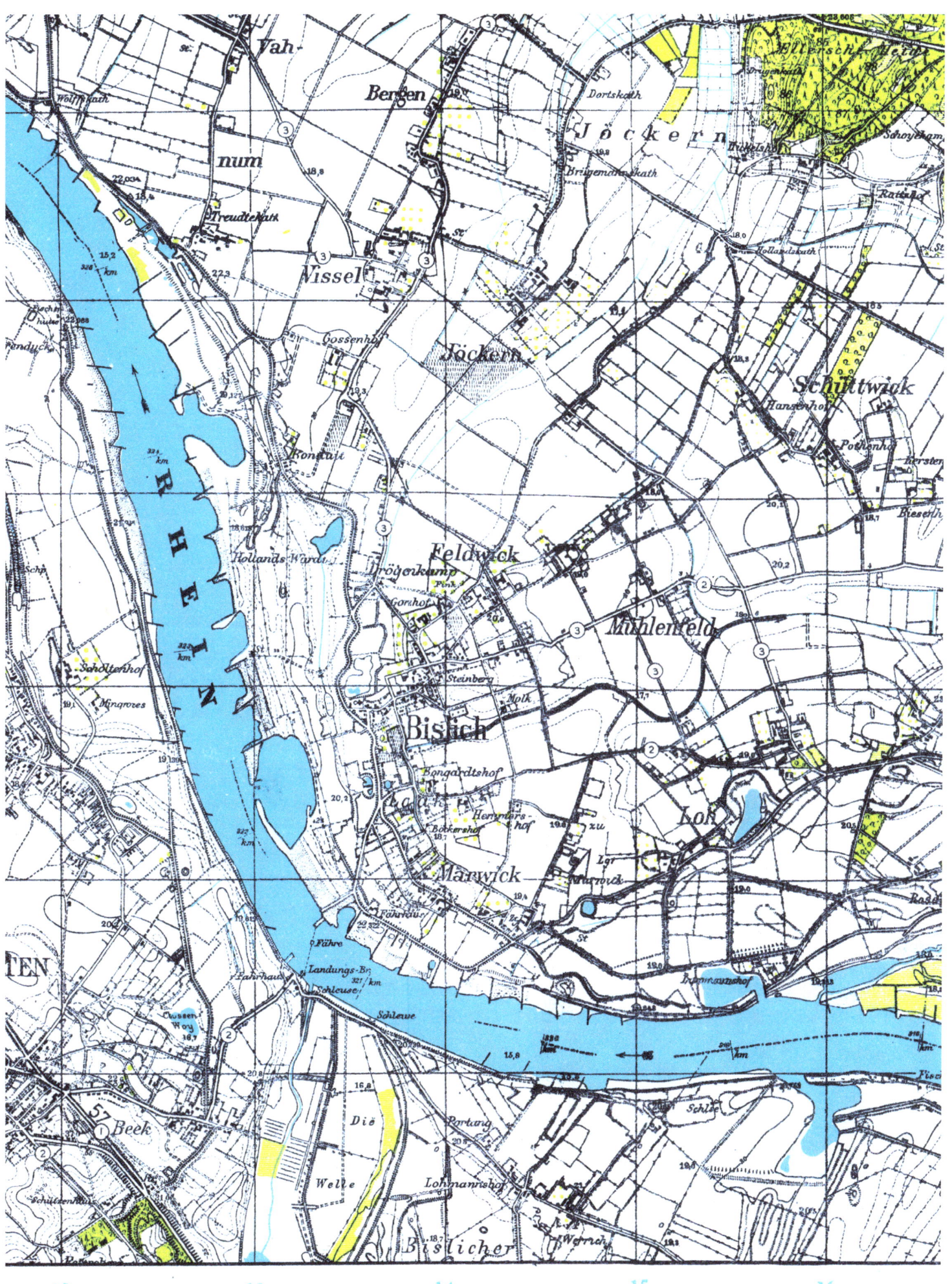

Operation Varsity 24 & 25th March 1945 — spread 4

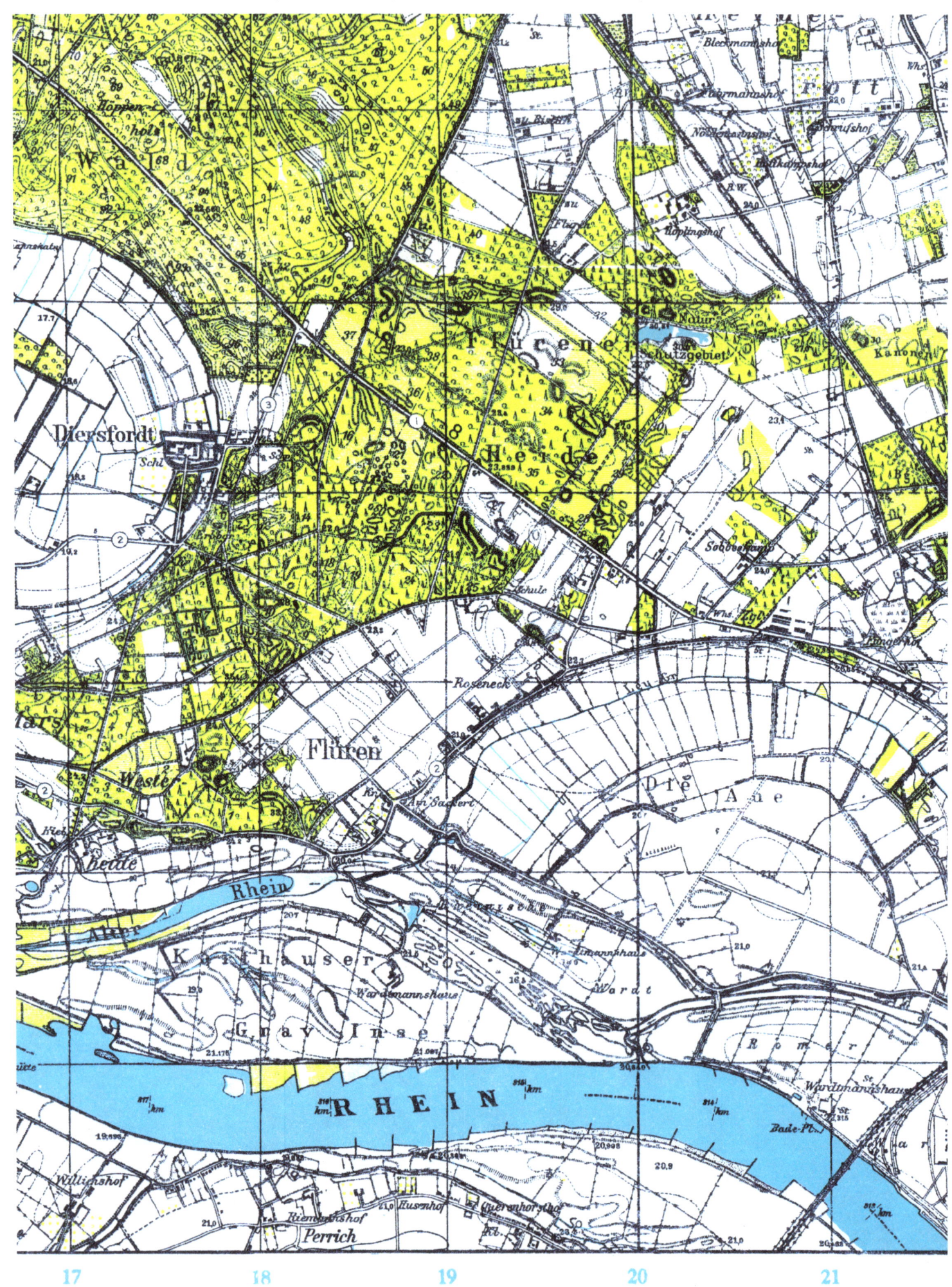

Operation Varsity 24 & 25th March 1945 — spread 4

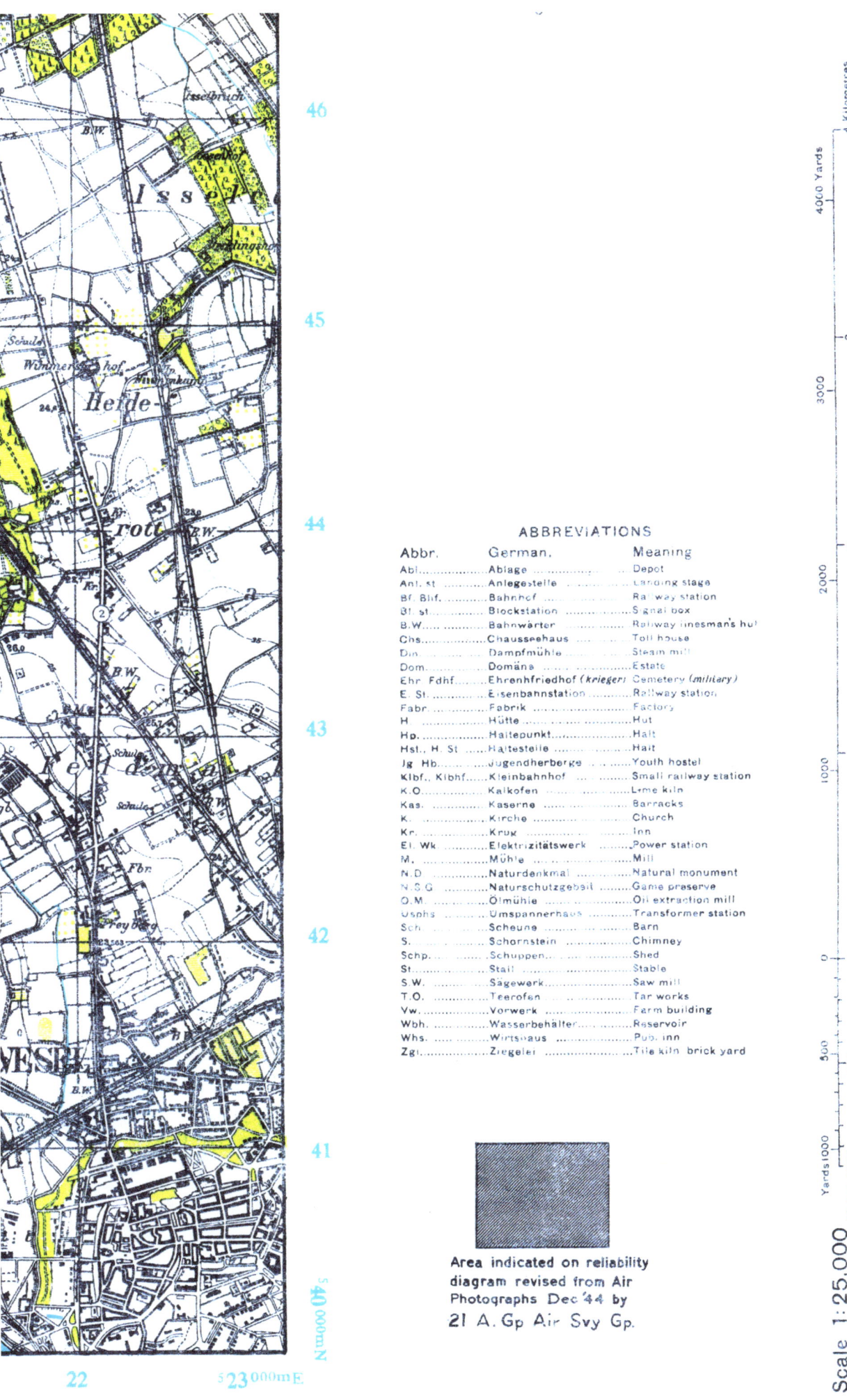

ABBREVIATIONS

Abbr.	German.	Meaning
Abl.	Ablage	Depot
Anl. st	Anlegestelle	Landing stage
Bf., Bhf.	Bahnhof	Railway station
Bl. st.	Blockstation	Signal box
B.W.	Bahnwärter	Railway linesman's hut
Chs.	Chausseehaus	Toll house
D.m.	Dampfmühle	Steam mill
Dom.	Domäne	Estate
Ehr. Fdhf.	Ehrenfriedhof (krieger)	Cemetery (military)
E. St.	Eisenbahnstation	Railway station
Fabr.	Fabrik	Factory
H.	Hütte	Hut
Hp.	Haltepunkt	Halt
Hst., H. St.	Haltestelle	Halt
Jg Hb.	Jugendherberge	Youth hostel
Klbf., Kl.bhf.	Kleinbahnhof	Small railway station
K.O.	Kalkofen	Lime kiln
Kas.	Kaserne	Barracks
K.	Kirche	Church
Kr.	Krug	Inn
El. Wk	Elektrizitätswerk	Power station
M.	Mühle	Mill
N.D	Naturdenkmal	Natural monument
N.S.G	Naturschutzgebeit	Game preserve
O.M.	Ölmühle	Oil extraction mill
Usphs	Umspannerhaus	Transformer station
Sch.	Scheune	Barn
S.	Schornstein	Chimney
Schp.	Schuppen	Shed
St.	Stall	Stable
S.W.	Sägewerk	Saw mill
T.O.	Teerofen	Tar works
Vw.	Vorwerk	Farm building
Wbh.	Wasserbehälter	Reservoir
Whs.	Wirtshaus	Pub, inn
Zgl.	Ziegelei	Tile kiln, brick yard

Area indicated on reliability diagram revised from Air Photographs Dec '44 by 21 A. Gp Air Svy Gp.

Scale 1:25,000

Field Survey Squadron R.E Feb 1948

PART I

Planning the Operation

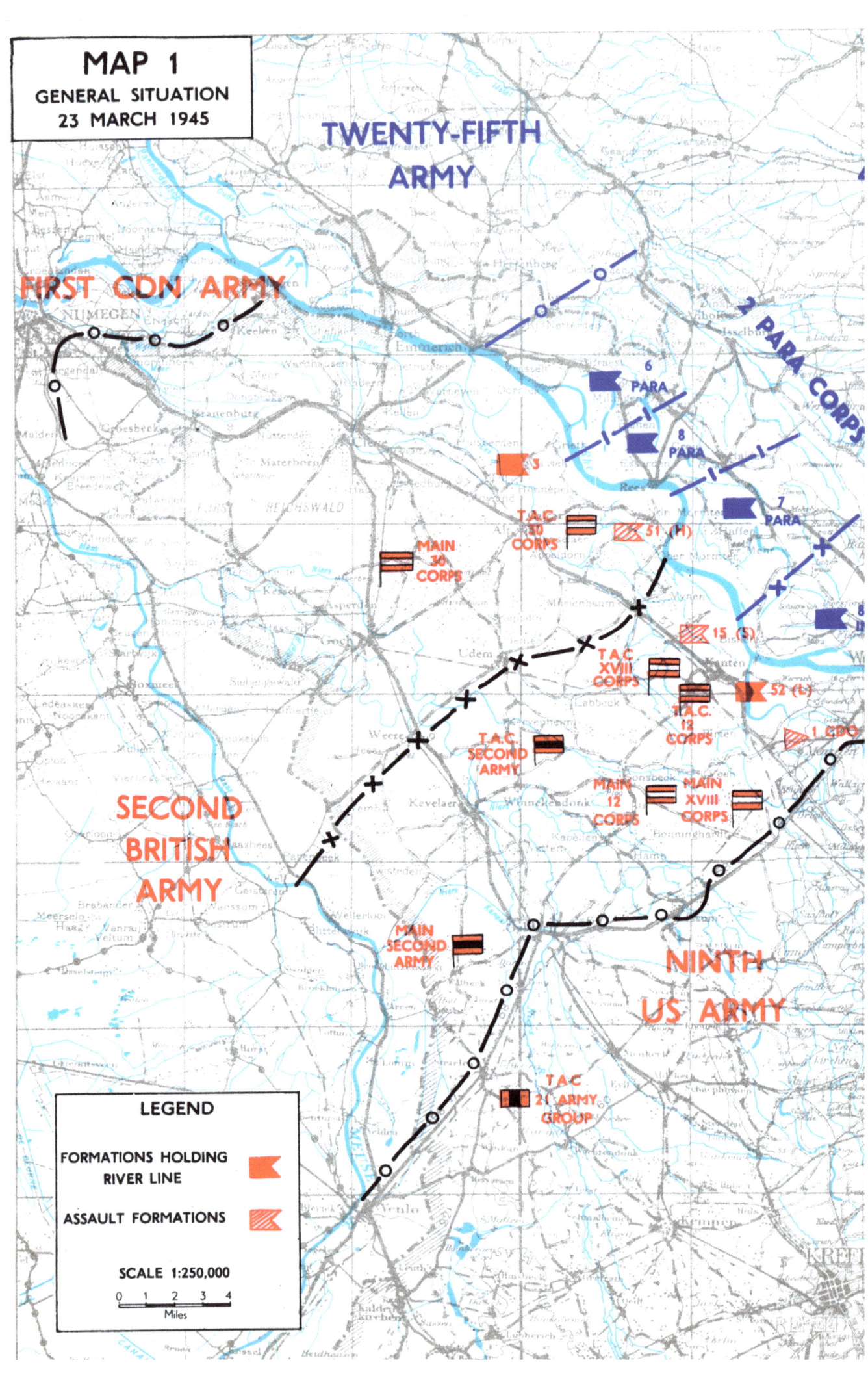

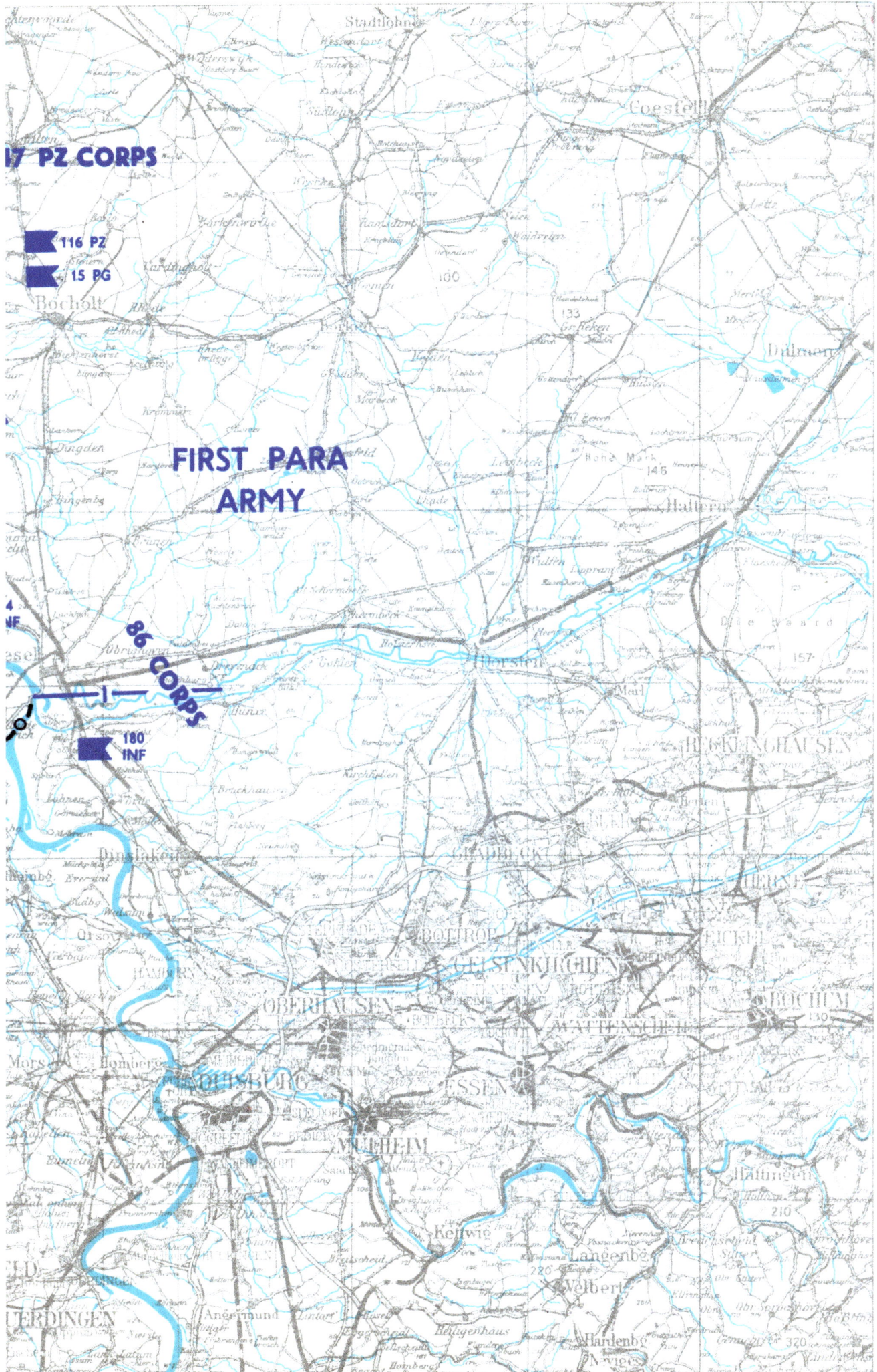

SECTION I

INTRODUCTION

A. GENERAL

On 16 December 1944 the Germans under Field Marshal von RUNDSTEDT launched a large scale offensive in the ARDENNES, and it was not until about a month later that the situation had again been stabilised. The Allied armies were then able to continue their fight towards the River RHINE and by the third week in March they had closed to it throughout its length.

21 Army Group was positioned North of the RUHR and clearly its next task was to assault across the RHINE with the least possible delay.

B. 21 ARMY GROUP PLAN

On 9 March Field Marshal MONTGOMERY, Commander-in-Chief 21 Army Group issued orders for the coming operation.

"My intention was to secure a bridgehead prior to developing operations to isolate the RUHR and to thrust into the Northern plains of GERMANY.

"In outline my plan was to cross the RHINE on a front of two armies between RHEINBERG and REES using Ninth American Army on the Right, and Second Army on the Left. The principal initial object was the important communications centre of WESEL. I intended that the bridgehead should extend to the South sufficiently far to cover WESEL from enemy ground action, and to the North to include bridge sites at EMMERICH : the depth of the bridgehead was to be made sufficient to provide room to form up major forces for the drive to the East and North East."

24 March was given as the target for D-Day.

The whole 21 Army Group operation was known as PLUNDER.

C. ADVANCE PLANNING

Since as early as October 1944 consideration had been given to the problem of making an assault crossing of the River RHINE in this sector, and a very great deal of detailed research was carried out.

HQ Second Brit Army had produced their planning study early in February 1945, and HQ 12 Corps had used this as a basis upon which to plan the details of the ground assault : other corps which would not be available for planning until only a few weeks before D-Day would thus find many of the details already worked out.

In the earliest planning stages, use of an airborne force to assist the operation had been visualised, and investigation into this aspect of the problem had also been proceeding. The airborne operation was known as VARSITY.

The following are some of the principal dates which mark the progress of the planning for Operation PLUNDER and VARSITY :—

Date	Event
7 November 1944	First Staff Study for Operation VARSITY issued by HQ First Allied Airborne Army.
December 1944	HQ 6 Brit Airborne Div completed study of plans for an operation similar to VARSITY.
16 December 1944	Start of German offensive in the ARDENNES.
16 January 1945	The ARDENNES "gap" closed.
4 February 1945	HQ Second Brit Army issued Planning Study for Operation PLUNDER.
5 February 1945	HQ 12 Corps began planning for operation PLUNDER.
9 February 1945	Commanding General, XVIII US Corps (Airborne) received first instructions for Operation VARSITY from Commander-in-Chief 21 Army Group.
10 February 1945	Final revised airborne plan for Operation VARSITY issued by HQ First Allied Airborne Army.
13 February 1945	HQ XVIII US Corps (Airborne) began planning for Operation VARSITY. 17 US Airborne Div withdrawn from active operations and began planning and training for Operation VARSITY.

24 February 1945	6 Brit Airborne Div returned to UK from HOLLAND.
28 February 1945	First air co-ordinating conference held at SHAEF(Air) by Deputy Supreme Commander.
1 March 1945 (approx)	17 US Airborne Div given tasks for Operation VARSITY. 6 Brit Airborne Div started planning and training for Operation VARSITY.
7 March 1945	HQ 12 Corps first planning conference.
9 March 1945	Orders for Operation PLUNDER issued by Commander-in-Chief, 21 Army Group.
11 March 1945	All enemy cleared from West of River RHINE in 21 Army Group sect.
20 March 1945	Final air plan completed and submitted to SHAEF.
24 March 1945	D-Day, Operations PLUNDER and VARSITY.

SECTION II

TOPOGRAPHY

The area in which XVIII US Corps (Airborne) was to land forms part of the RHINE Flood Plain and is mostly flat agricultural land. It does, however, contain the one commanding feature on the East bank of the RHINE which overlooks the crossing places used by 12 Corps, and rises to a height of about 65 feet above river level. This is the wooded high ground known as the DIERSFORDTER WALD : through it runs the main lateral road from WESEL to REES and EMMERICH.

The DIERSFORDTER WALD is a thick wood, while the area immediately East of it is level and open and affords very suitable sites for Landing Zones (LZs) and Dropping Zones (DZs). There are a number of groups of farm buildings, and the fields are divided by small ditches and three strand wire fences.

Along the Eastern edge of the area runs the River ISSEL. It is not a large river, but it flows between steep banks from 30 to 50 feet apart. It is a tank obstacle, so that it was important to capture and hold the bridges over it as soon as possible.

The unfinished autobahn which also runs along the Eastern edge of the VARSITY area is in most places no more than a large bank of sand. Though not a serious obstacle, it would probably delay wheeled or light tracked vehicles.

The roads running into the area along which enemy counter-attacks might be expected to develop all converge on the village of HAMMINKELN so that this place would also be an important initial objective.

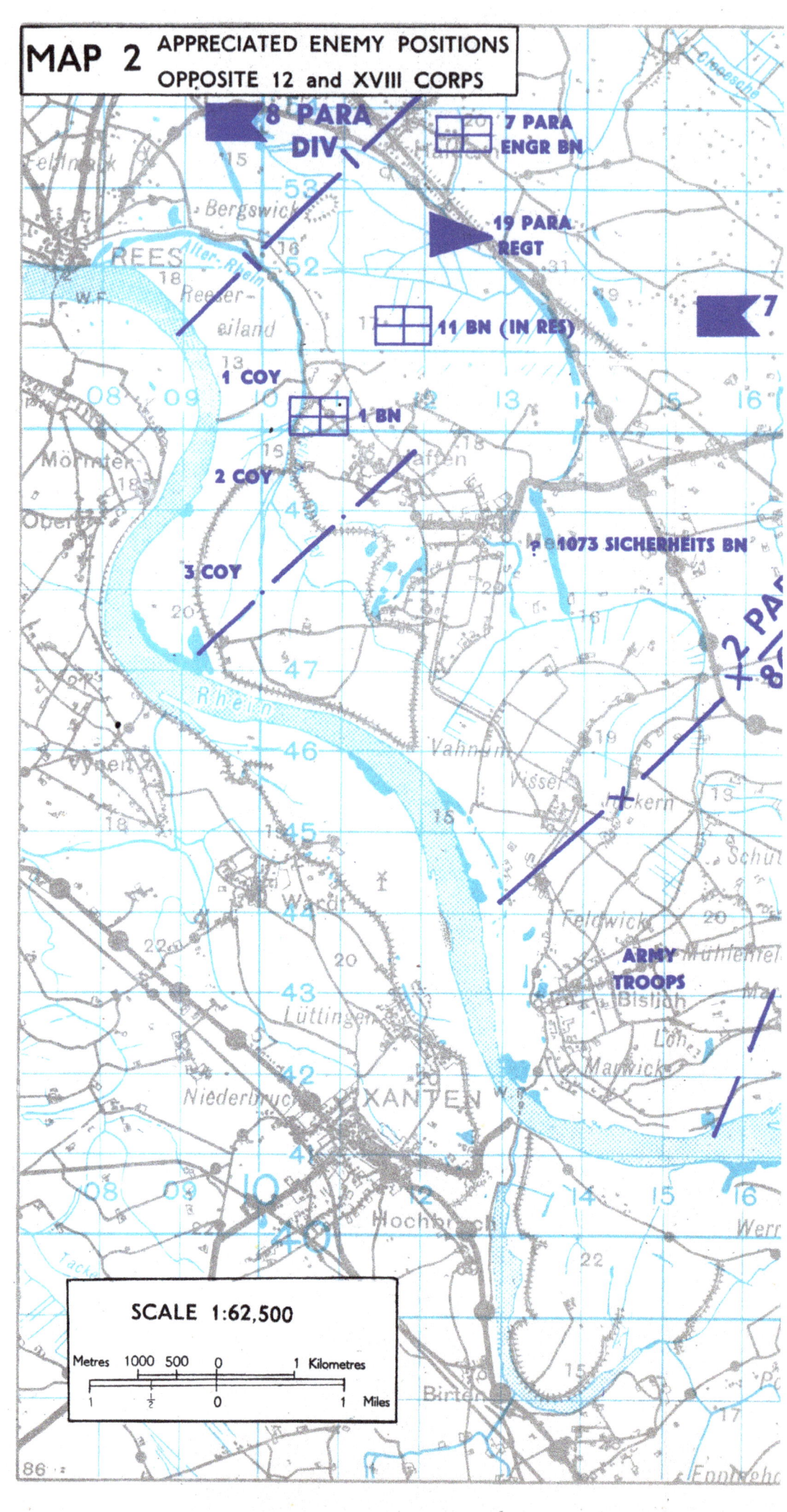

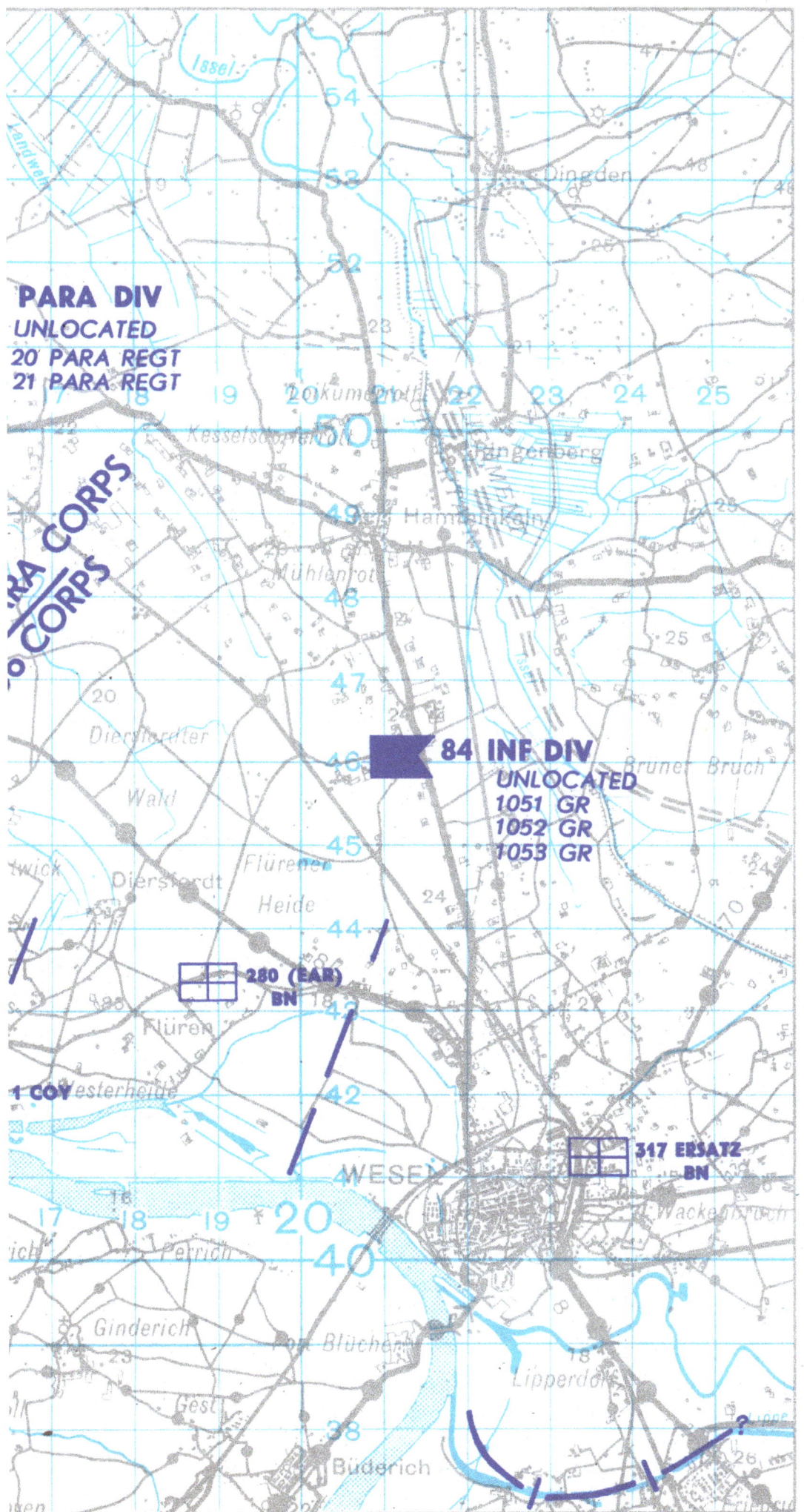

SECTION III

THE ENEMY

A. GENERAL

The enemy opposition in the fighting West of the River RHINE, which came to an end on 9 March, had been intense. His parachutists had fought fanatically and he had more artillery and mortars deployed against 21 Army Group than at any other stage in the campaign.

The German losses, however, had been huge — estimates included about 40,000 men killed or wounded and over 50,000 prisoners. The troops that he was able to withdraw to the East of the river belonged to divisions which had been badly mauled, and apart from their big material losses, their morale left much to be desired.

As a result of the decision to fight West of the river, the acute weapon shortage and the crippling blows their industry and communications were receiving from the Allied Air Forces, the Germans were never able to organise a strong defence to oppose the assault crossings of the RHINE.

B. ENEMY LAYOUT

Field Marshal KESSELRING took over from von RUNDSTEDT as Commander-in-Chief, West, shortly before Operation PLUNDER. The enemy opposite 21 Army Group was mainly under command of Army Group "H" under General BLASKOWITZ.

The defence of the RHINE in the PLUNDER sector was in the hands of First Parachute Army. This Army had three Corps on the line of the river, Right 2 Para Corps, Centre 86 Corps, Left 63 Corps. The dispositions of 2 Para and 86 Corps as appreciated by Second Army are shown on Map 2.

The reserve consisted of 47 Panzer Corps, in an area about 15 miles North East of EMMERICH with 116 Panzer and 15 Panzer Grenadier Divisions under command.

C. ENEMY OPPOSITION TO OPERATION VARSITY.

As will be seen from the map, opposition to the airborne landings was likely to come from 7 Para and 84 Inf Divs.

7 Para Div

This division was believed to be on the Left of 2 Para Corps. There was some evidence to support this belief, and it was in any case unlikely that 8 Para Div could be holding so long a front as to have a common boundary with 84 Div on its Left.

The following table gives the estimated strength of 7 Para Div when it was withdrawn across the RHINE after Operation VERITABLE (operations to clear the RHINELAND, 8 February–11 March).

It should be noted that strengths given for infantry units are fighting strengths and exclude 'B' echelons, while those for divisional supporting groups (artillery, engineers, etc) include all personnel.

Unit	Estimated Strength on 12 March	Remarks
19 Para Regt		Had battalion CRAHS under command — strength 100.
I Bn	100	
II Bn }	250	
III Bn }		
HQ and Regt Coys	75	
20 Para Regt }	500	Combined strength.
21 Para Regt }		
7 Para Recce Coy	Destroyed	
7 Para Arty Regt	500	20 × 10.5 cm (possibly some 7.5 cm) 3 × 15 cm.
7 Para A Tk Bn	100	4 × 7.5 cm Pak
7 Para Engr Bn	350	
7 Para Mortar Bn	350	20 × 12 cm
7 Para Sigs Bn	300	
7 Para Flak Bn	200	4 × 88 mm : 4 × 2 cm AA
7 Para Services	700	

No information had been received about reinforcements since this date, but it reasonable to assume that parachute formations were still at a high priority for receiving them.

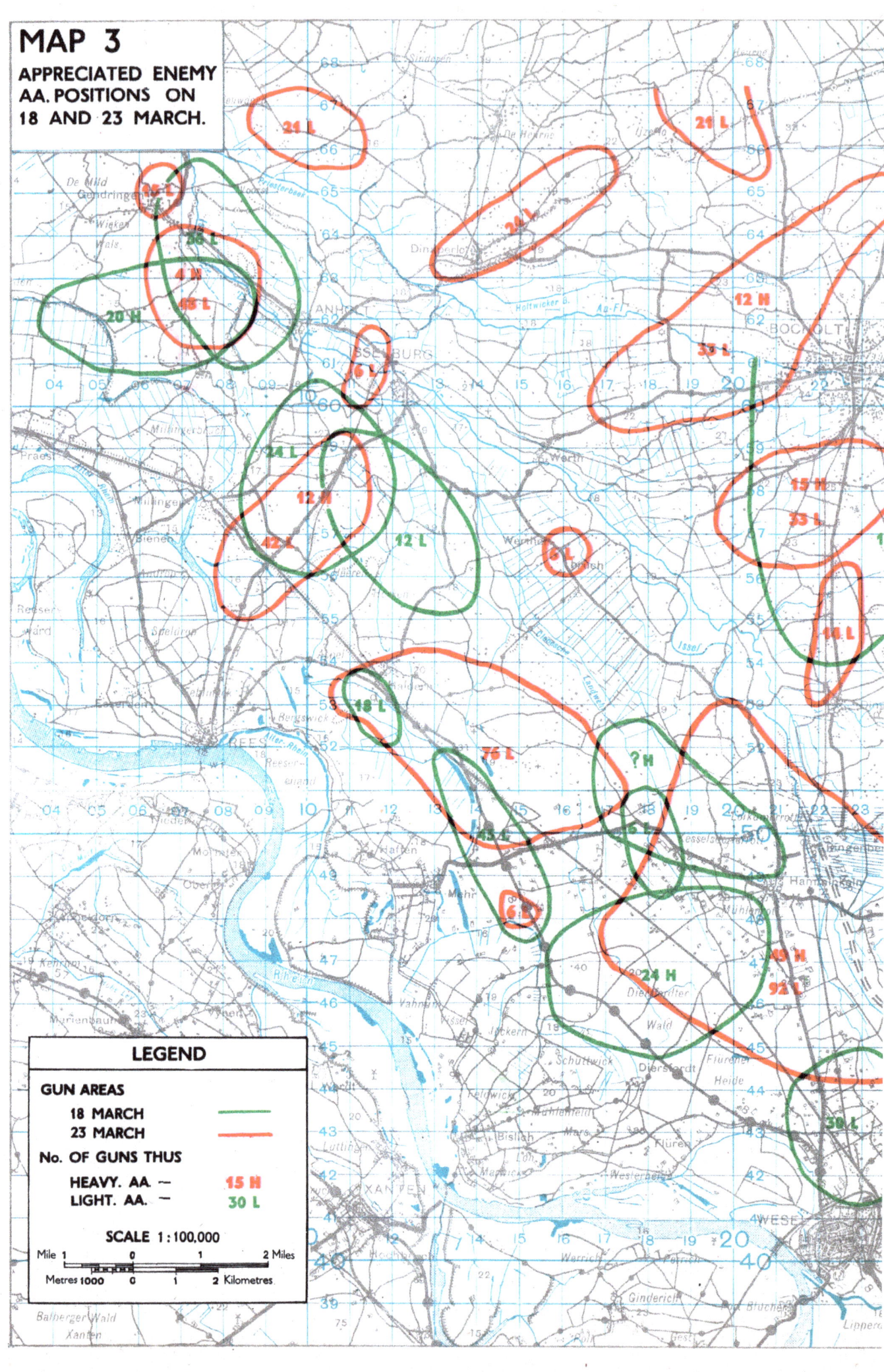

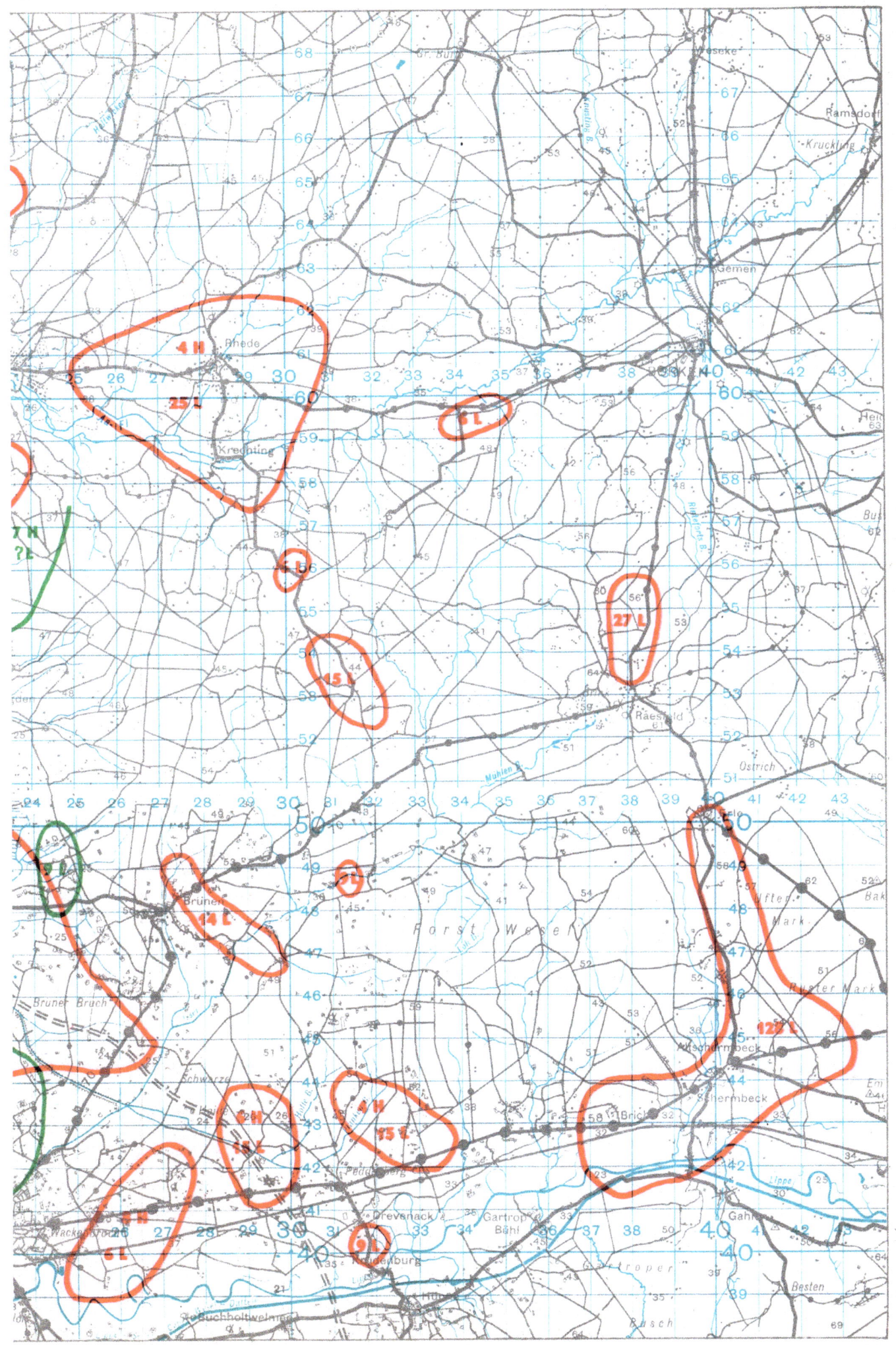

Printed by 14 Field Survey Squadron. R.E. Jan. 1948

84 Inf Div

It was almost certain that 84 Inf Div was on the Right of 86 Corps. This was a luckless formation, having been virtually destroyed at the beginning of Operation VERITABLE in February, and since reformed only to be decimated again, as will be shown, in Operation VARSITY. The estimated strength of 84 Inf Div on 12 March was a follows :—

Unit	Estimated Strength on 12 March	Remarks
1051 GR } 1052 GR } 1062 GR }	500	Mostly newly arrived reinforcements.
184 Arty Regt	300	10 × 10.5 cm guns
184 Engr Coys	150	
84 Fus Bn	Destroyed	
184 A Tk Bn	100	2 × 7.5 cm Pak
184 Sigs Bn	200	
184 Services	300	

Major General FIEBIG, Commander 84 Inf Div, who was captured later, and interrogated by Canadian Historical Officers, made some interesting observations :—

"General FIEBIG claimed that the Germans were not unaware of our preparations for an airborne operation in support of the RHINE crossings and appreciated that no fewer than four allied airborne divisions were available, although he confessed he had been badly surprised by the sudden advent of two complete divisions in this particular area, and throughout the interrogation reiterated the shattering effect of such immensely superior forces on his already badly depleted troops, which did not number more than 4,000 in all.

"General FIEBIG had no exact advance information about landing and dropping zones, or times, although he had fully appreciated the likelihood of a landing somewhere in his area. He rather expected the landing farther from the RHINE, in the area East of the River ISSEL and thought it would take place either at dusk before the land assault or else simultaneously with it."

Other Troops

84 Inf Div was so weak that it was safe to assume that it was being bolstered up by certain other troops which probably included some Volksturm (German "Home Guard") and static Wehrkreis troops. 286 "Ear" Bn, made up entirely of deaf soldiers, was also identified near WESEL.

Type of Defences

The Germans had not been able to prepare a strong defence line on the River RHINE : in fact, they had little more formidable than simple earthworks, and many of those were not by any means strongly held. The defences were mainly concentrated round the possible crossing sites of EMMERICH, REES, XANTEN and WESEL, and civilians were known to be helping in their construction.

Field and Medium Artillery

On the 12 Corps front and in the VARSITY area, 84 Inf Div assisted by GHQ non-divisional resources, was thought to have only about fifty medium or field guns ; these were very difficult to locate as they were mostly sited in very enclosed country.

Anti-Aircraft Artillery

There was no doubt that the enemy was expecting an airborne operation of some kind to be staged in connection with the river crossing.

The estimate of the number of AA guns in the EMMERICH-BOCHOLT-WESEL triangle on 17 March was 153 light and 103 heavy. Less than a week later, just before Operation PLUNDER began, the figures had risen to 712 light and 114 heavy. Map 3 shows how these were distributed.

Armour

The local armoured reserve consisted of 47 Pz Corps with 116 Pz and 15 PG Divisions. Both these divisions had been employed in covering the withdrawal across the RHINE and had suffered badly. However, reliable information pointed to their having been reinforced, and on 22 March 116 Pz Div was credited with up to seventy tanks and 15 PG Div with fifteen tanks and twenty to thirty assault guns. A heavy anti-tank battalion had also possibly arrived in the area.

A figure of between one hundred and one hundred and fifty was given as the total number of AFVs at the disposal of First Para Army.

SECTION IV

PLAN FOR OPERATION PLUNDER

A. TASK OF SECOND BRIT ARMY

Second Army's task was to assault the River RHINE in the area of XANTEN and REES, and establish a bridgehead from exclusive DORSTEN — all inclusive BORKEN—AALTEN—DOETINCHEM—HOCH ELTEN feature; subsequently the advance was to be continued on a three corps front North-Eastwards in the direction of RHEINE.

B. SECOND ARMY OUTLINE PLAN

Commander, Second Army decided to assault with two corps, Right 12 Corps, Left 30 Corps, each with one division up. 8 Corps was to hold securely the West bank of the River RHINE during the concentration period, until the assault corps were ready to assume control, on 20 March, of divisions holding the river line.

XVIII US Corps (Airborne) was to be dropped East of the RHINE after the river assaults had taken place. The principles for its employment were that it should drop within range of artillery sited on the West bank of the river and that the link up with the ground forces should take place on D-Day.

To release HQ XVIII US Corps (Airborne) as soon as possible, HQ 8 Corps was to take over from that corps within seven days.

Second Army would then be correctly positioned to continue the advance into the North German plain with Right 8 Corps, Centre 12 Corps and Left 30 Corps.

2 Cdn Corps was to be passed through the Left of Second Army bridgehead and handed back to First Cdn Army when it was in a position to exercise command.

XVIII US Corps (Airborne) was to drop on the front of 12 Corps. The latter's plan is therefore given in outline in the following sections.

C. 12 CORPS INTENTION

12 Corps, in conjunction with XVIII US Corps (Airborne), was to force a crossing over the River RHINE, establish bridges across the river and operate Eastwards.

D. TROOPS AVAILABLE TO 12 CORPS

12 Corps consisted of :—

        7th Armoured Division (7 Armd Div)
        15th (Scottish) Infantry Division (15 (S) Div)
        52nd (Lowland) Infantry Division (52 (L) Div)
        53rd (Welsh) Infantry Division (53 (W) Div)
        4th Armoured Brigade (4 Armd Bde)
        34th Armoured Brigade (34 Armd Bde)
        1st Commando Brigade (1 Cdo Bde)
        115 Infantry Brigade (115 Inf Bde)

E. FORMATION TASKS

52 (L) Div

This division was to provide the firm base for 12 Corps and assist 15 (S) Div with the movement and parking of stormboats being used for the assault crossing.

1 Cdo Bde (Operation WIDGEON)

At 2200 hours D-1, 1 Cdo Bde was to cross the RHINE North of the village of PERRICH, seize WESEL, and the bridges over the River LIPPE, if possible intact, to the South of it. At 2230 hours, when 1 Cdo Bde would be only 1,500 yards from the target area, two hundred heavy bombers of the RAF were to attack WESEL. Thereafter, the brigade was responsible for holding the Eastern and Southern exits from WESEL and was to be prepared to come under command 17 US Airborne Div when ordered.

15 (S) Div (Operation TORCHLIGHT)

This division was to carry out the initial assault (see paragraph F below).

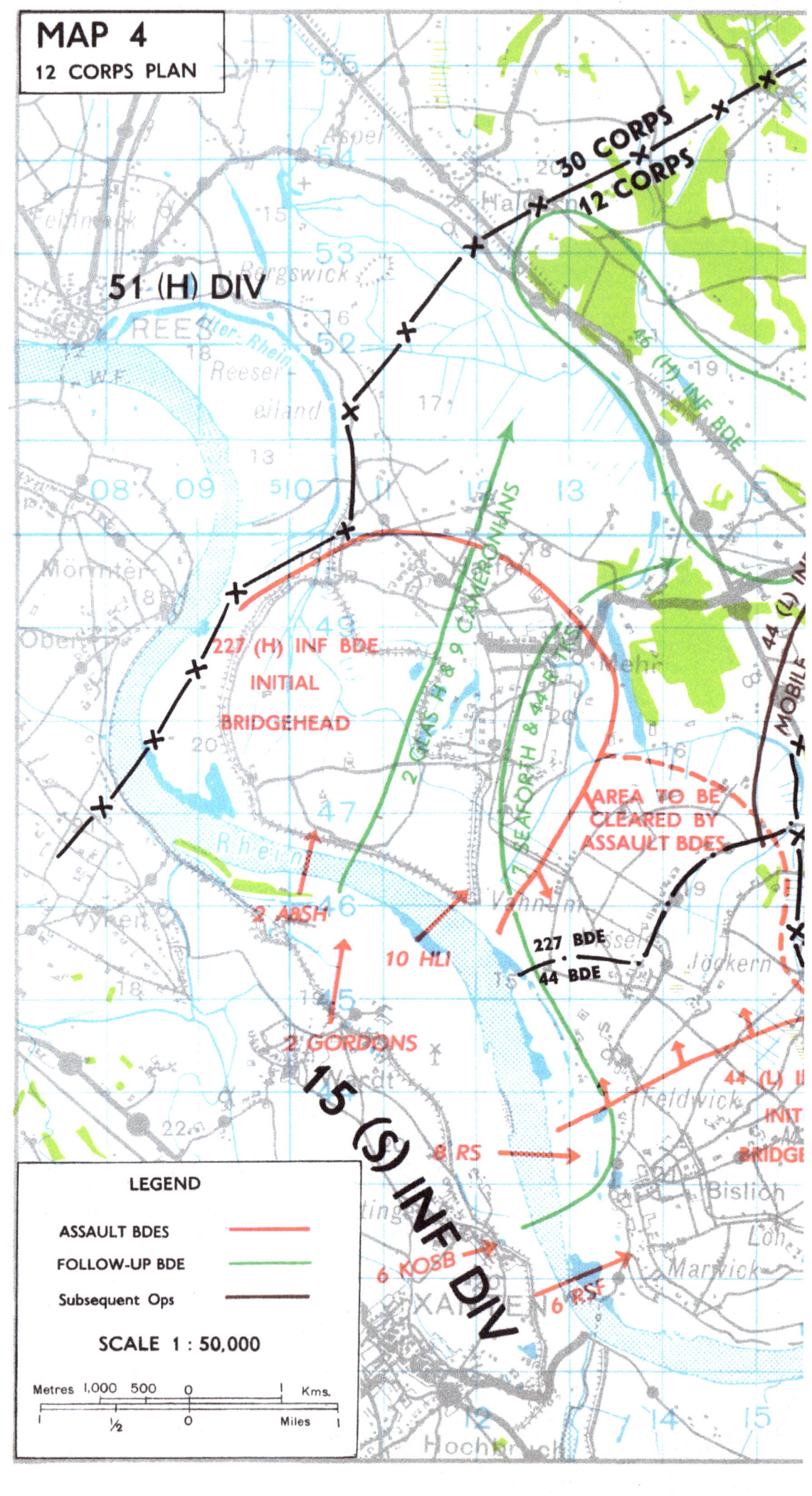

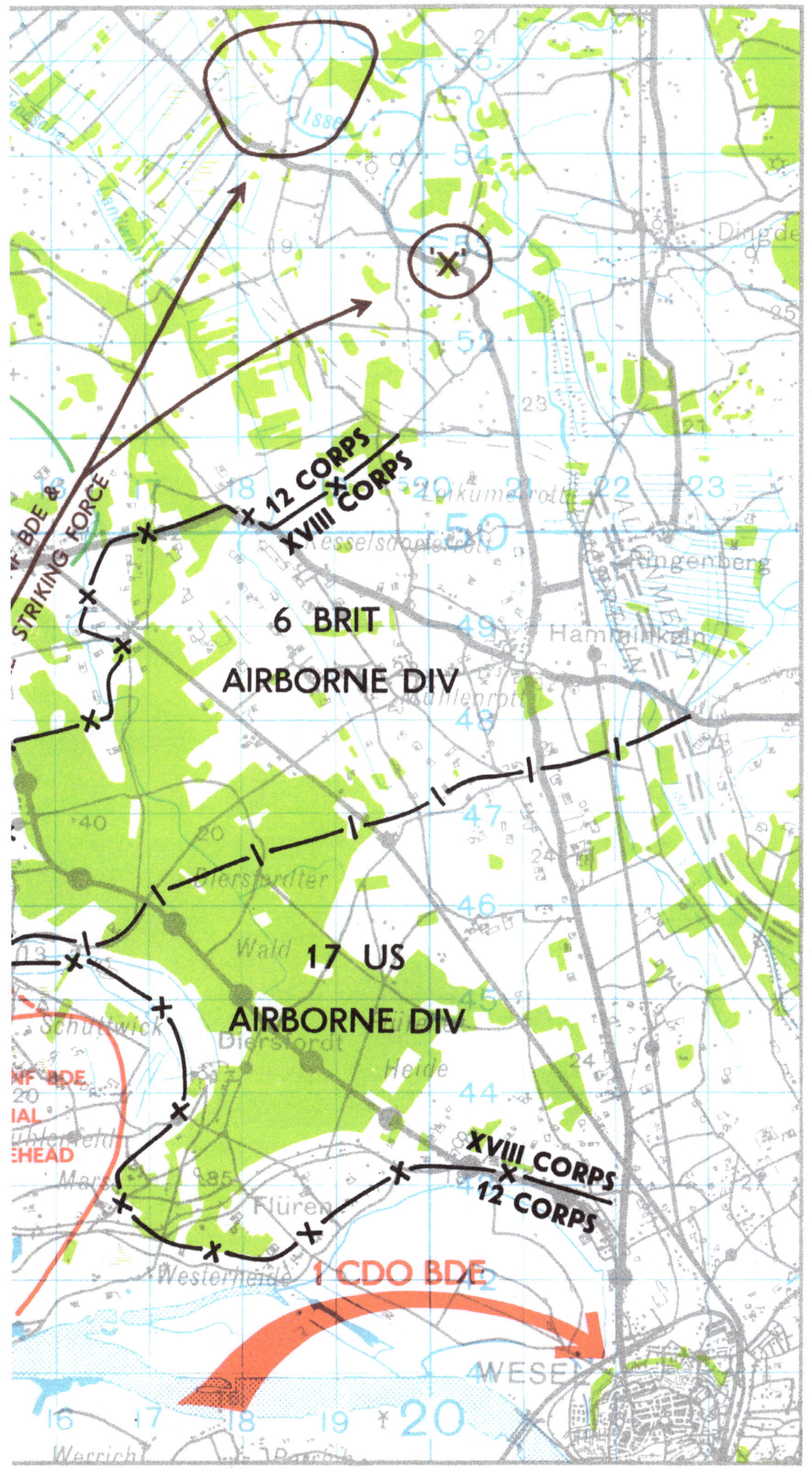

53 (W) Div

One brigade of this division, organised on a jeep and carrier basis, was to be at three hours notice to move across the river from 1200 hours D-Day, with a view to passing through 15 (S) Div and operating towards BOCHOLT.

7 Armd Div

This formation was to be prepared to cross the RHINE by class 40 bridge, probably on D+1, and operate towards BORKEN and STADTLOHN.

F. 15 (S) DIV PLAN

Intention

"15 (S) Inf Div will force the passage of the River RHINE between inclusive BISLICH and VYNEN and capture the area CLASEN HO—MEHRHOO—SCHUTTWICK—LOH—BISLICH —MEHR—HAFFEN, preparatory to securing the area WISSMANN—bridge at GERVERSHOF (marked 'X' on Map 4) and relieving 6 Brit Airborne Div in area HAMMINKELN and bridges over the River ISSEL there."

Additional Troops

The following additional troops were available to 15 (S) Div for the operation (excluding RE) :—

Under Command :
   4 Armd Bde (including 44th Royal Tank Regiment (44 R Tks), trained in DD)
   One battery 86 A Tk Regt.

In Support :
   2nd County of London Yeomanry (Westminster Dragoons) (W DGNS) less one squadron (Flails)
   7th Royal Tank Regiment (7 R Tks) less one squadron (Crocodiles)
   East Riding Yeomanry (E RIDING YEO) (LVsT)
   11th Royal Tank Regiment (11 R Tks) (LVsT)
   One squadron 49th Armoured Personnel Carrier Regiment (49 APC Regt)

Method

The assault was to be made with two brigades up. On the Right, 44 (L) Inf Bde supported by 11 R Tks (LVsT) was to capture and hold the area SCHUTTWICK—LOH—BISLICH. On the Left, 227 (H) Inf Bde, supported by E RIDING YEO (LVsT) was to capture and hold the area HAFFEN—MEHR. Responsibility for clearing the area between these two objectives was divided between the two brigades; the inter-brigade boundary is shown on Map 4.

46 (H) Inf Bde, with 44 R Tks (DD) in support, was in reserve. Its task was to capture and hold the area CLASEN HO—MEHRHOO. It was to establish itself firmly on the high ground South East of HALDERN and ensure that the SONSFELD Woods overlooking HALDERN were cleared.

A mobile striking force was to be formed by 4 Armd Bde, consisting of :—

   One armoured regiment (carrying a motor battalion)
   One SP regiment, RA
   One SP anti-tank battery, RA
   One infantry battalion in APCs
   One assault squadron, RE

This was expected to reach the East bank of the river by 1700 hours D+1, and was to be used to capture WISSMANN and the bridge at GERVERSHOF (marked 'X' on Map 4) in support of 44 (L) Bde.

In due course 227 (H) Inf Bde was to relieve 6 Brit Airborne Div, and 46 (H) Inf Bde and 4 Armd Bde were to come into reserve.

H Hour for the assault by 15 (S) Div was to be 0200 hours on D-Day.

SECTION V

COMMAND AND CO-ORDINATION OF OPERATIONS PLUNDER AND VARSITY

A. GROUND

The details of the ground plan were worked out by Second Brit Army working in close conjunction with First Allied Airborne Army, 21 Army Group having confined its instructions to essentials requiring the decision of the Commander-in-Chief.

Operational command of all airborne forces passed to Commander, Second Army, as soon as the airborne troops landed in the area of the objective.

B. AIR

Air planning was the responsibility of Second Tactical Air Force, in co-operation with Second Army and First Allied Airborne Army.

Second Tactical Air Force (2 TAF) also commanded all air forces taking part in the operation, although 83 Tactical Group, RAF, controlled fighter aircraft in the immediate battle area.

C. AIRBORNE

Airborne planning was supervised by First Allied Airborne Army, and details were worked out by XVIII US Corps (Airborne), IX US Troop Carrier Command and 38 Group, RAF.

Operational command was exercised as follows :—

Commanding General, First Allied Airborne Army	Troop Carrier Forces at all times, and Airborne Forces until landed.
Commanding General, XVIII US Corps (Airborne)	Airborne Forces
Commanding General, IX US Troop Carrier Command.	All Troop Carrier Forces.

AOC, 38 Group RAF, exercised control of troop carrier units operating from ENGLAND.

D. COMBINED COMMAND POST (CCP)

A CCP, controlling all troop carrier and airborne forces operated at HQ First Allied Airborne Army, near PARIS. Present at the CCP were Commanding General, IX US Troop Carrier Command, a deputy of AOC 38 Group, and staff and liaison officers from First Allied Airborne Army, IX US Troop Carrier Command, 38 Group RAF, and XVIII US Corps (Airborne).

A small Tactical HQ, First Allied Airborne Army, was established at HQ 2 TAF. Since HQ 2 TAF was situated close to HQ 21 Army Group and Commanding General First Allied Airborne Army was present at his tactical HQ from 22 to 25 March, joint discussions could easily be held between the three senior commanders concerned for making last minute decisions.

SECTION VI

PLAN FOR OPERATION VARSITY

A. OBJECT

The mission given to XVIII US Corps (Airborne) was "to disrupt the hostile defence of the RHINE in the WESEL sector by the seizure of key terrain, by airborne attack, in order to deepen rapidly the bridgehead to be seized in an assault crossing of the RHINE by British ground forces, and to facilitate the further offensive operations of Second Army."

The airborne troops had to ensure that the enemy was not allowed to seal off the bridgehead before enough troops could be concentrated in it for the advance to continue. At all costs the momentum of the advance must be maintained.

B. DECISIONS AFFECTING XVIII US CORPS (AIRBORNE)

In planning Operation VARSITY care was taken to profit by experience gained in the British airborne operation at ARNHEM the previous autumn. The whole corps was to be flown in in "one lift": this had not been done at ARNHEM, and later lifts had been delayed, with most serious results. Again, this was the first airborne operation of the war in which airborne forces were to be dropped, *following* the ground assault, and for the first time, they were to land actually on the top of their objectives.

In order to take full advantage of Allied air supremacy, and overwhelming superiority in artillery, the operation was to take place in daylight. The time at which the first airborne troops were to land was called P-Hour, and was to be 1000 hours 24 March.

The Commander-in-Chief, 21 Army Group, agreed to defer the assault for up to five days, should it be necessary to do so, in order to obtain suitable weather conditions for the airborne operation.

Commander, Second Army, decided that, if it were not possible to carry out the operations as planned and PLUNDER had to be launched without VARSITY, then he would request that airborne troops be dropped on the first favourable day in the general area of ERLE, thereby deepening the bridgehead. Commander, XVIII US Corps (Airborne) therefore drew up an alternative plan which was not executed.

C. TROOPS AVAILABLE

The corps consisted of 17 US Airborne Div and 6 Brit Airborne Div. In addition, 1 Cdo Bde was to pass to operational command of 17 US Airborne Div after the capture of WESEL, and 6 Gds Armd Bde was available to the corps on call: one battalion of the latter was to be attached to 6 Brit Airborne Div and be phased across the RHINE with the land tails of the division.

D. TASK OF 17 US AIRBORNE DIV

17 US Airborne Div was to drop during daylight on 24 March starting at P-Hour. It was to seize, clear and secure the divisional area with priority to the high ground East of DIERSFORDT (E), and the bridges over the River ISSEL (F) marked on Map 5: to protect the Right (South) flank of the corps: and to establish contact with 1 Cdo Bde, 12 Corps and 6 Brit Airborne Div. Objectives were to be held at all costs.

The DZs and LZs selected for this division are shown on Map 5.

E. TASK OF 6 BRIT AIRBORNE DIV

The task of this formation was to drop during daylight 24 March, beginning at P-Hour. It was to seize, clear and secure the divisional area with priority to the high ground in the North West part of DIERSFORDTER WALD, the town of HAMMINKELN and the bridges over the River ISSEL marked X, Y and Z on Map 5. It was to protect the Left (North) flank of the corps and establish contact with 12 Corps and 17 US Airborne Div. Objectives were to be held at all costs.

F. PLAN OF 6 BRIT AIRBORNE DIV

Broadly, the division was to land with Right (forward) 6 Airlanding Bde Group, Centre 5 Para Bde Group, Left (rear) 3 Para Bde Group. Apart from artillery, which is dealt with in Section VIII, each brigade group included one troop of Royal Engineers and a parachute or airlanding field ambulance (for further details see Appendix 'A'). Divisional reserve included two troops of light tanks from 6 Airborne Armd Recce Regt. Order of landing was to be 3 Para Bde, 5 Para Bde, 6 Airlanding Bde, Div HQ Group, RA Group.

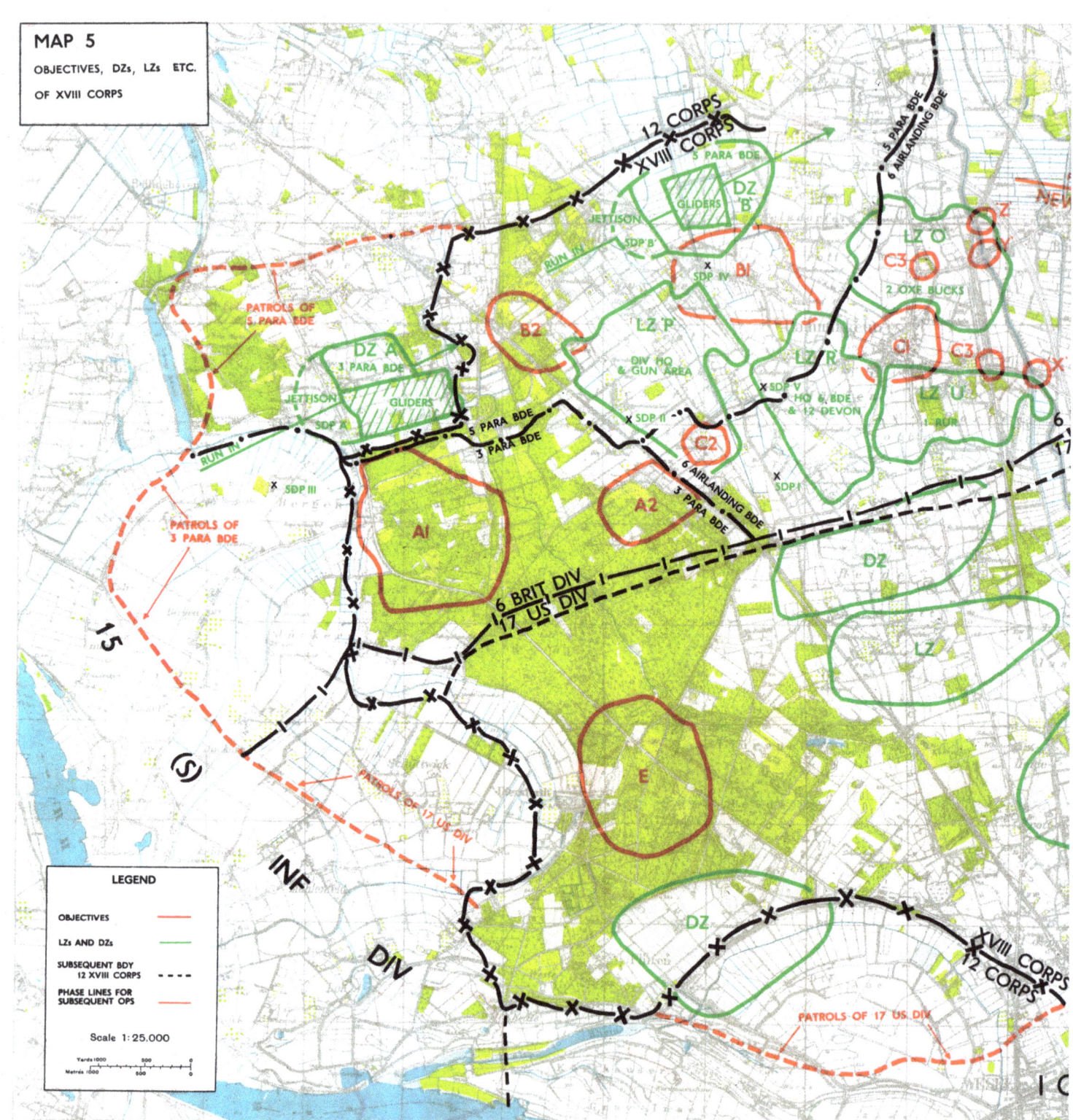

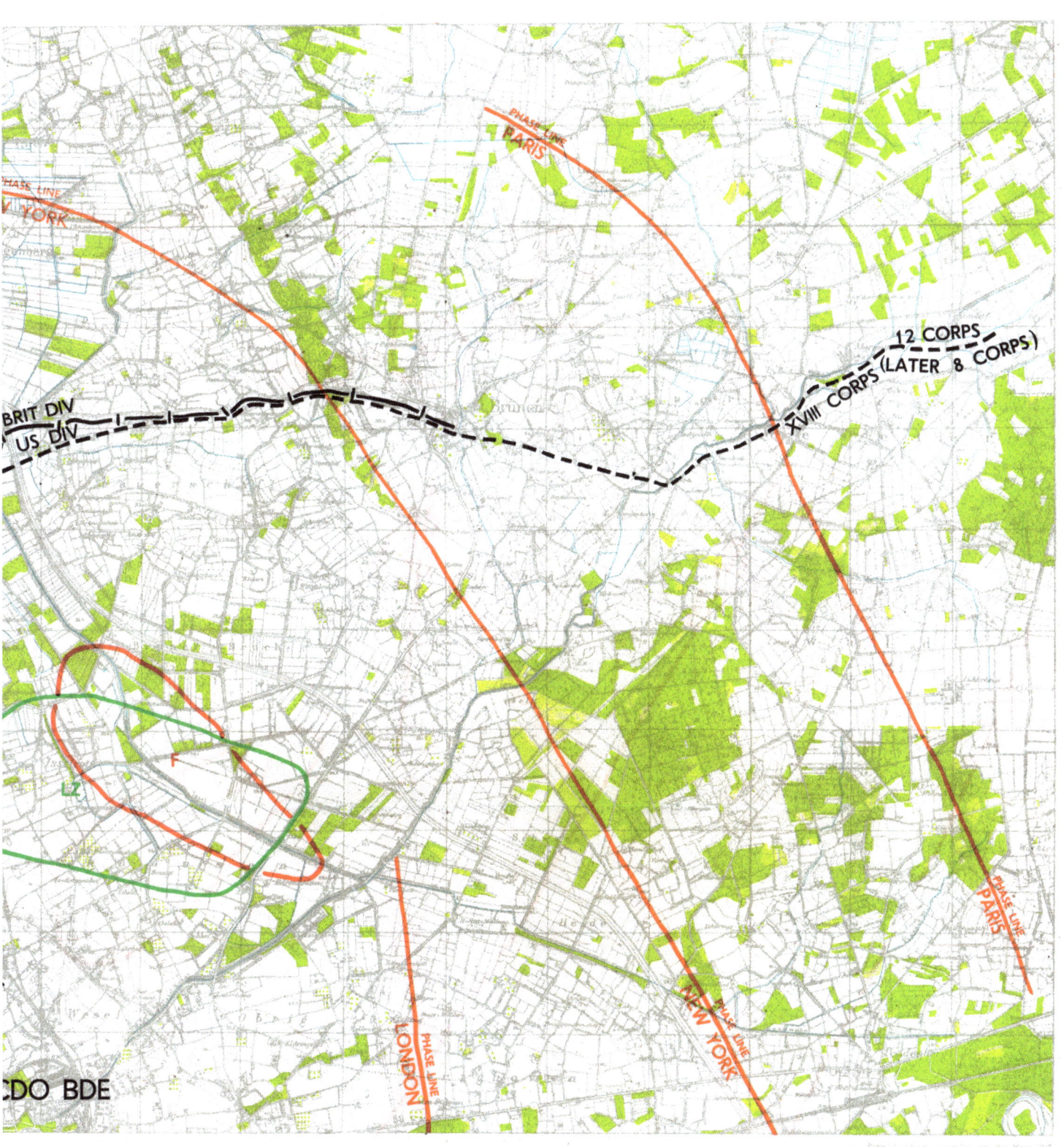

Brigade tasks are given below, with an indication of which battalions were to carry them out. The objectives of the three brigades, their DZs, LZs and boundaries, are shown on Map 5.

3 Para Bde Group

Units were to drop in the following order :—

> 8 Para Bn
> HQ 3 Para Bde
> 1 Cdn Para Bn
> 9 Para Bn
> Troop 3 Para Sqn RE
> 224 Para Fd Amb
> Glider element

8 Para Bn was responsible for clearing the DZ and establishing the Brigade Rallying Point, and tasks were then to be carried out as follows :—

(i) Clear and hold area A1 (North 1 Cdn Para Bn, South 9 Para Bn).

(ii) Patrol out to and be prepared to hold area A2 (8 Para Bn, which was to be in brigade reserve until ordered to carry this out).

5 Para Bde Group

Order of landing in this brigade was to be :—

> 13 Para Bn and HQ 5 Para Bde
> 12 Para Bn
> 225 Para Fd Amb
> Part of 591 Para Sqn RE
> 7 Para Bn
> Remainder of 591 Para Sqn RE

Tasks included the following :—

(i) Clear and hold the area B1 (North East 12 Para Bn, South West 13 Para Bn).

(ii) (a) Prevent enemy from approaching area B1 from North and East until operations of 12 and 13 Para Bns were complete (7 Para Bn).

(b) Protect the DZ (7 Para Bn).

(iii) Establish a patrol of platoon strength at the cross roads in area B2, and, if necessary, be prepared to move the whole battalion to that area, forming the brigade reserve until called upon to carry out this task (7 Para Bn).

6 Airlanding Bde Group

This brigade group was given the following tasks, in order of priority :—

(i) Seize and hold certain bridges over the River ISSEL (1st Battalion The Royal Ulster Rifles (1 RUR) 'X', 2nd Battalion The Oxfordshire and Buckinghamshire Light Infantry (2 OXF BUCKS) 'Y' and 'Z')

(ii) Clear the area C2 required for Div HQ (12th Battalion The Devonshire Regiment (12 DEVON))

(iii) Seize and hold road junction C3 (2 OXF BUCKS) and road and railway crossing C3 (1 RUR)

(iv) Seize and hold the village of HAMMINKELN (C1) (12 DEVON, which was afterwards to come into brigade reserve)

The CRE was to co-ordinate the laying of anti-tank minefields as soon as possible after landing, including one designed to block the approaches to the DIERSFORDTER WALD from the North and East. This was to follow approximately the line of the 3 Para Bde/5 Para Bde and 3 Para Bde/6 Airlanding Bde boundaries. No anti-personnel mines were to be laid.

Bridges over the River ISSEL were to be prepared for demolition, but were not to be blown unless their capture by the enemy appeared certain. The decision whether or not the bridges were to be blown rested with Commander 6 Airlanding Bde.

G. ROLE OF 6 GDS ARMD BDE

The task of 6 Gds Armd Bde was to supply an early reinforcement to the airborne formations starting with a crossing by Left Flank Squadron 3rd Tank Battalion Scots Guards (3 Tk SG) to join up with 6 Brit Airborne Div on D+1. The remainder of 3 Tk SG and the other two battalions in the brigade (4th Tank Battalion Grenadier Guards (4 Tk GREN GDS) and 4th Tank Battalion Coldstream Guards (4 Tk COLDM GDS)) were to cross later, at a time and place to be dictated by the development of the battle. The two latter were to be in support of 17 US Airborne Div.

The Commanding Officer and Squadron Leaders of 3 Tk SG had flown to ENGLAND to meet officers of 6 Brit Airborne Div during March and officers of the other battalions had met 17 US Airborne Div.

H. PLAN FOR SEABORNE TAIL OF 6 BRIT AIRBORNE DIV

(NOTE: When 6 Brit Airborne Div returned from HOLLAND to ENGLAND at the end of February 1945, certain small detachments (mostly transport) were left in BLA. These were known as the "land element". All that part of the division which returned to ENGLAND in February, but which was not taken on Operation VARSITY by air, was called the "seaborne tail").

The detailed composition of the seaborne tail is given in Appendix 'A'. Vehicles were to be passed across the river under arrangements made by 15 (S) Div. The first instalment of some 400 vehicles was to move into 15 (S) Div Marshalling Areas on the West bank of the RHINE on the morning of D-Day. From there, 15 (S) Div would call them forward and receive them into its Forward Assembly Areas on the East bank. It was to be prepared to have them parked there until the roads leading to XVIII US Corps (Airborne) area were open, and an area was to be allotted in case this situation arose.

J. SUBSEQUENT OPERATIONS OF XVIII US CORPS (AIRBORNE)

The plan for operations of XVIII US Corps (Airborne) once the initial objectives had been captured, was as given below (Phase Lines are marked on Map 5):—

(i) 17 US Airborne Div to advance to Phase Line LONDON by 0700 hours D+1.

(ii) 6 Brit Airborne Div and 17 US Airborne Div (with 1 Cdo Bde under command) to advance to Phase Line NEW YORK by 1700 hours D+1)

(iii) Elements of 6 Brit Airborne Div North of the proposed inter-corps boundary to be relieved by troops of 12 Corps during the night D+1/D+2.

(iv) Advance to Phase Line PARIS on D+2.

(v) Continue the advance as ordered by Commander, Second Army.

DIAGRAM 1

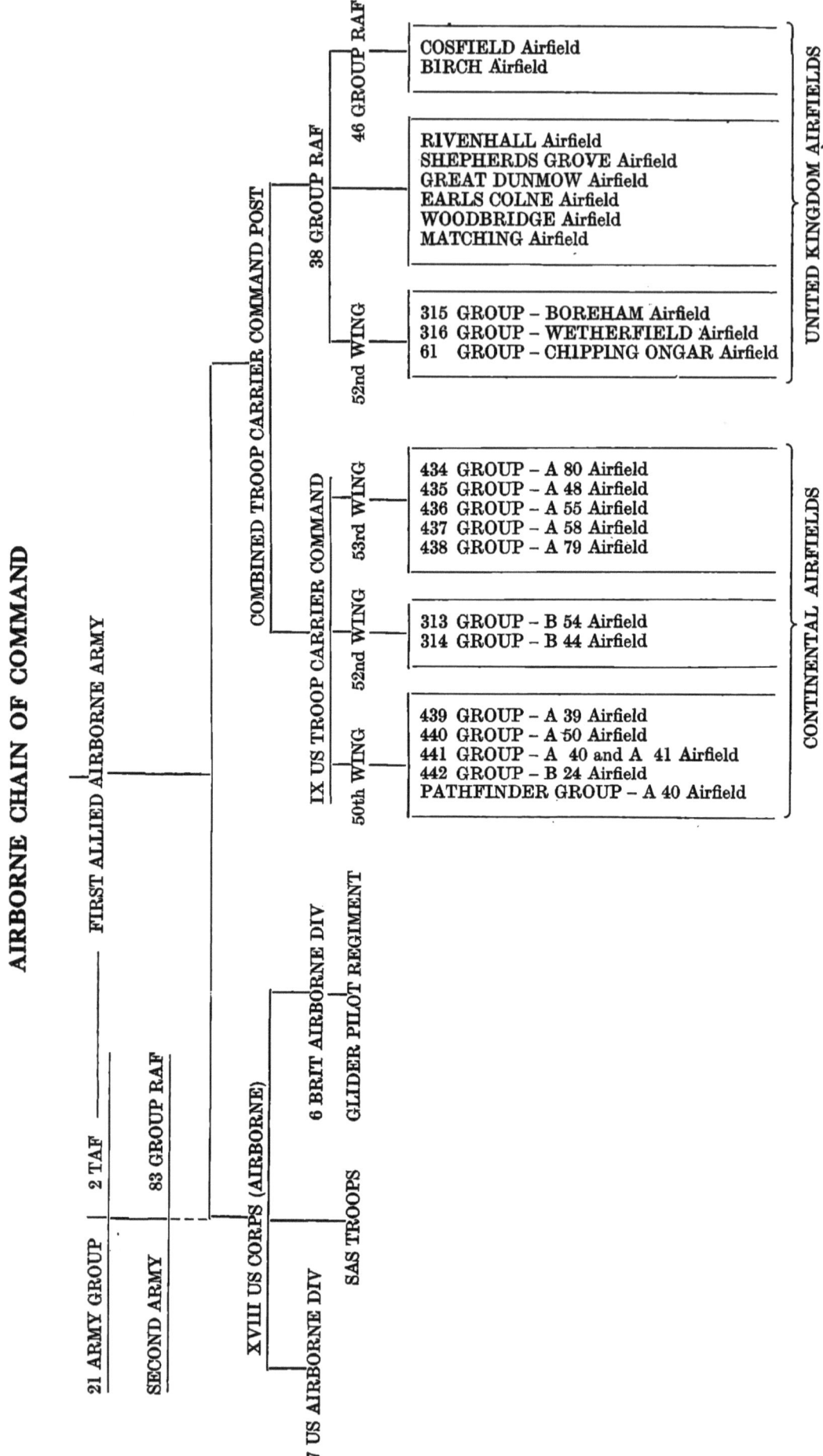

SECTION VII

PLANNING BY AIR FORCES

A. INTRODUCTION

Air Forces Available

The Deputy Supreme Commander indicated that the airborne operations would have overriding priority over all other air force operations and that all elements of the theatre air forces would be made available to support the operation.

Air Forces under control of the Supreme Commander which could be called on to support Operation VARSITY were :—

        RAF Second Tactical Air Force (2 TAF)
        IX United States Army Air Force (IX USAAF)
        RAF Fighter Command

In addition the Supreme Commander could call on VIII USAAF, RAF Bomber Command and RAF Coastal Command if required.

Command (See Diagram 1)

Prior to reaching the actual assault area all airborne troops and their transport aircraft were under the overall command of Commanding General, HQ First Allied Airborne Army, PARIS. The troop carrier aircraft were provided as follows :—

        IX US Troop Carrier Command : 1112
        38 Group, RAF : 320
        46 Group, RAF : 120

Commanding General, First Allied Airborne Army appointed Commanding General IX USTCC as Commander Transport Forces, and he delegated all planning for the transport aircraft based in UK to AOC, 38 Group.

The Deputy Supreme Commander appointed Air Marshal Commanding 2 TAF as Air Commander for Operation VARSITY since it was in his Tactical area that the operation was to take place. AOC-in-C in turn delegated the planning of detailed operations in the Assault area to AOC, 83 Group, the RAF Group associated with Second Army.

Responsibility for Planning

There were then four formations interested in planning the major air operation in connection with VARSITY :—

        HQ 2 TAF, BRUSSELS
        HQ 83 Group RAF, EINDHOVEN
        HQ IX USTCC, PARIS
        HQ 38 Group RAF, EARLS COLNE, ESSEX

SHAEF was also concerned since, firstly, the Deputy Supreme Allied Commander was responsible to the Supreme Commander for all air operations in the SHAEF area and secondly, it was on this level that the requests were made to the agents of the Combined Chiefs of Staff (Chief of the Air Staff and Commanding General, USAAF) to divert the strategic bombers from their normal role.

As already stated, Air Marshal Commanding 2 TAF, as the Air Commander, was the Commander responsible for the co-ordination of all air operations in support of VARSITY. These included escort of the troop transport aircraft and gliders from bases in ENGLAND and FRANCE en route to 2 TAF area by RAF Fighter Command and IX USAAF (Fighter), Air/Sea Rescue and diversion attack by RAF Coastal Command, and attacks and re-supply missions by heavy bombers of VIII USAAF. All these operations had to be co-ordinated with the large scale pre-arranged support planned by the Tactical Air Forces themselves.

AOC, 83 Group, RAF, was responsible for all tactical air operations in the assault area.

Commanding General, IX USTCC, was responsible for the production of the airborne plan as a whole.

AOC, 38 Group, RAF, was responsible for that part of the airborne plan for units operating from the UK. This amounted to the lift of 6 Brit Airborne Div so that in effect nearly half the total effort was the responsibility of 38 Group, RAF.

It will be seen from the above that major planning for this operation was going on in four different places, RHEIMS, PARIS, BRUSSELS and EARLS COLNE. That this dispersion did not lead to any serious breakdown can be attributed to the diligence of the individuals concerned, and to the good flying weather that allowed planners to move rapidly from place to place.

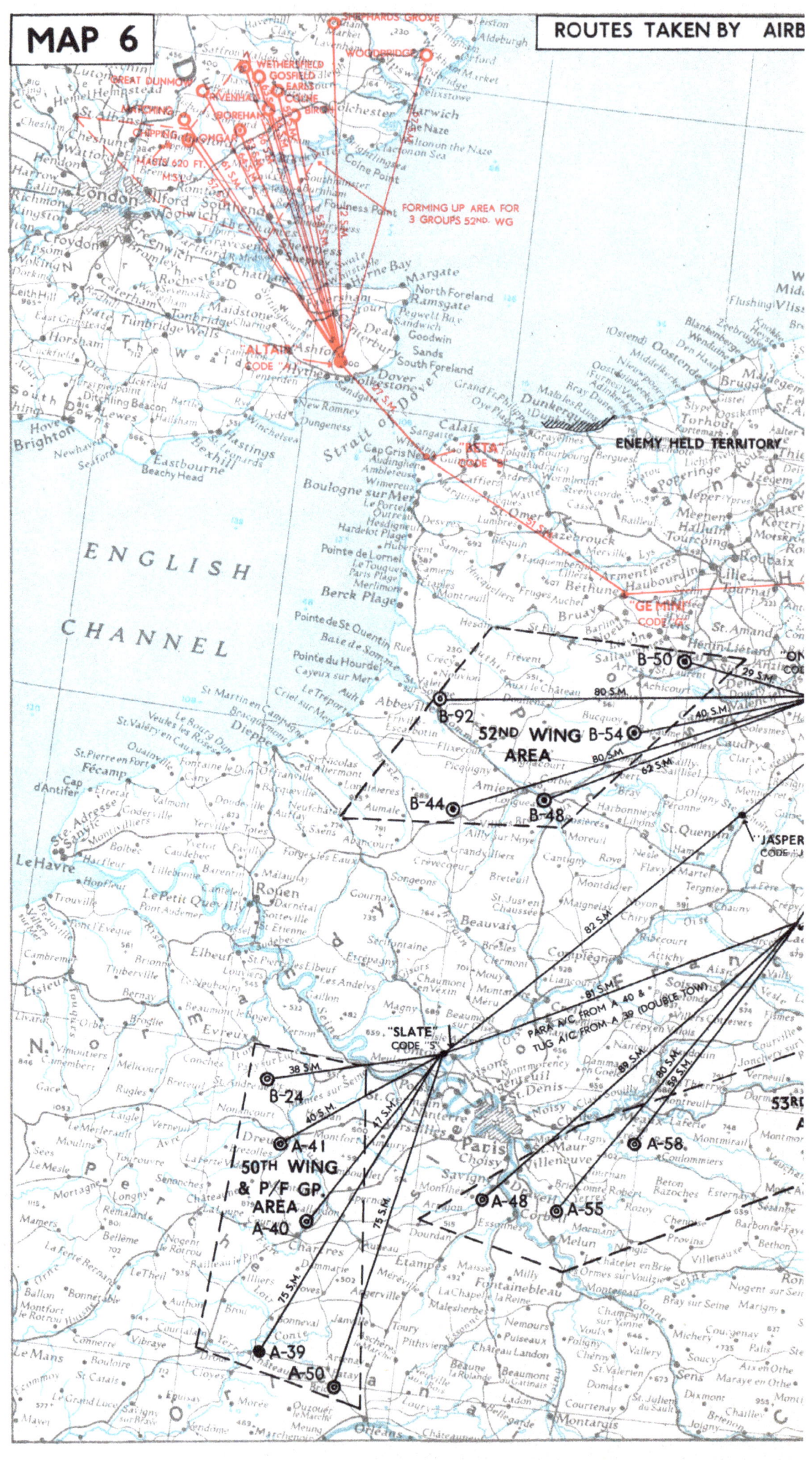

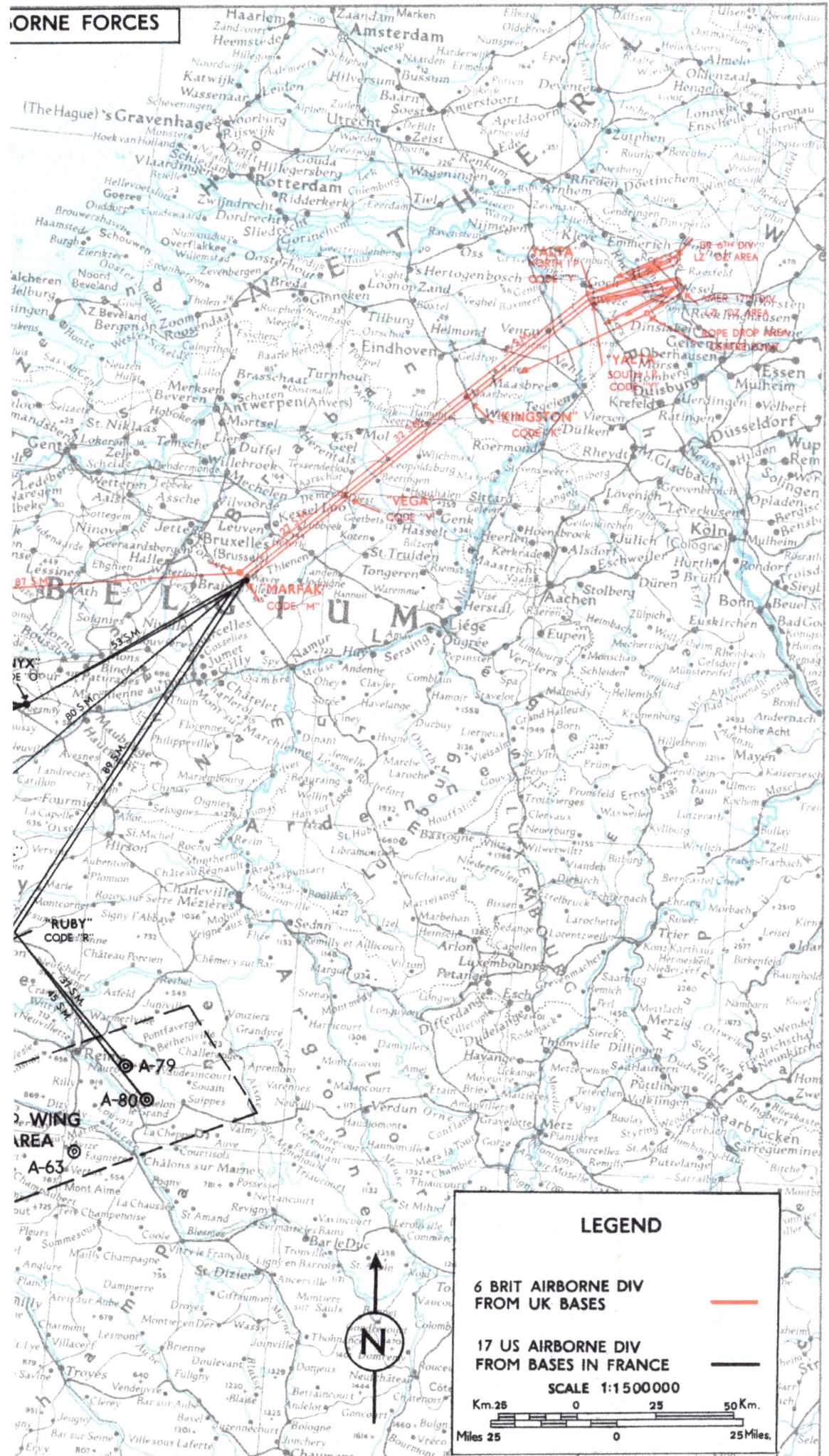

Planning began on 10 February 1945, with a probable D-Day in mid-March. During and prior to this period interdiction operations had been in progress to isolate the RUHR and later to isolate the battle area. Extensive and continuous visual and photographic reconnaissance of the areas likely to be used for the airborne assault was also started at this time.

B. AIRBORNE PLAN

(NOTE : This plan though mainly concerned with the British airborne effort will from time to time make reference to the plans for operations in other sectors, where they affected the British area).

Responsibility for Air Lift

The reponsibility for lifting 6 Brit Airborne Div from the UK was allotted as follows : —

(a) 38 and 46 Groups, RAF, would undertake all glider towing.

(b) Three Groups of 52 Wing IX USTCC would undertake all parachute drops.

The lifting of 17 US Airborne Div from the continent was allotted to IX USTCC.

The main military tasks were clearly interdependent as were the air tasks : therefore a joint flight plan was necessary to ensure complete co-ordination, whilst by combining the UK and continental based Air Forces into one for the greater part of the flight, fighter escort and ground aids could be shared.

Tactical Groups

Two lessons that had been learnt at ARNHEM (operations of 1 Brit Airborne Div, September 1944) governed the selection of LZs and DZs, and methods of landing, for this operation :

- (i) That it was preferable to land smaller forces of gliders, providing they contained *tactical groups* on or adjacent to the objectives, rather than to make massed glider landings some distance away.
- (ii) That if the greatest advantage was to be taken of the initial surprise, the division must be landed complete in one operation.

The conception of landing by tactical groups, that is, with gliders landing in groups to conform with army requirements, was quite new. Previously it had been the aim to land the gliders 'en masse' in the smallest possible space so that the division was concentrated on arrival. It was realised that the landing would have to be made in the face of enemy fire from the ground. The new tactical method of landing had the additional advantage of dispersing groups of gliders over a greater area, which would increase the enemy's difficulty in defending it.

The other major problem, that of landing the division in one operation was overcome by increasing the number of aircraft in 38 Group squadrons by nearly a third from twenty-four to thirty-four aircraft. This could only be done by great efforts on the part of the maintenance organisation and by intensive training of new crews in the weeks before the operation. Both these expedients were successful and 38 Group's strength was raised from two hundred and twenty to three hundred and twenty aircraft.

Troop Carrier Tasks

The airborne movement was to be one main lift in daylight, followed by re-supply operations by 2nd Bombardment Division, VIII USAAF. Additional re-supply operations were planned for D+1 unless cancelled by Commander, Second Army, who would be in a position to decide whether the RHINE bridging operations and the link up between 15 (S) Div and 6 Brit Airborne Div had been successful, and so enable supplies to be transported overland.

38 and 46 Groups total lift of four hundred and forty aircraft was insufficient to lift 6 Brit Airborne Div in one operation. The group was therefore reinforced with two hundred and forty-three aircraft of 52 Wing, IX USTCC. These aircraft were to provide the lift for the parachute element of the division with 38 and 46 Groups towing the gliders.

Lift of 6 Brit Airborne Div

(a) *Paratroop Lift (D-Day)*
  (i) **DZ 'A'** One hundred and twenty-two aircraft of 52 Wing IX USTCC, to drop the main body of 3 Para Bde at 1000 hours.
  (ii) **DZ 'B'** One hundred and twenty-one aircraft of 52 Wing, IX USTCC, to drop the main body 5 Para Bde at 1011 hours.

(b) *Glider Lift (D-Day)*
  (i) **LZ 'O'** Eight aircraft of 46 Group to tow eight Horsa gliders, to release at 1021 hours, carrying elements of 2 OXF BUCKS. These troops to form a coup-de-main party on the road bridge 'Y' (See Map 5).

  Fifty-eight aircraft of 46 Group to tow fifty-eight Horsa gliders, to release at 1023 hours, carrying elements of 6 Airlanding Bde Group.
  (ii) **LZ 'U'** Seven aircraft of 46 Group to tow seven Horsa gliders, to release at 1022 hours, carrying elements of 1 RUR. These troops to form a coup-de-main party on the road bridge 'X' (See Map 5).

Forty-eight aircraft of 46 Group and eleven aircraft of 38 Group, to tow fifty-nine Horsa gliders, to release at 1028 hours, carrying elements of 6 Airlanding Bde Group.

(iii) **LZ 'R'** Ninety-four aircraft of 38 Group, to tow eighty-eight Horsa and six Hamilcar gliders, to release at 1034 hours, carrying elements of 6 Airlanding Bde Group.

(iv) **LZ 'P'** One hundred and forty-four aircraft of 38 Group to tow one hundred and sixteen Horsa and twenty-eight Hamilcar gliders, to release at 1035 hours, carrying elements of HQ 6 Brit Airborne Div and 6 Airlanding Bde Group.

(v) **DZ 'A'** Twenty-four aircraft of 38 Group, to tow twenty-one Horsa and three Hamilcar gliders, to release at 1057 hours, carrying elements of 3 Para Bde Group and 6 Airlanding Bde Group.

(vi) **DZ 'B'** Forty-six aircraft of 38 Group, to tow thirty-five Horsa and eleven Hamilcar gliders, to release at 1057 hours, carrying elements of 5 Para Bde Group and 6 Airlanding Bde Group.

(c) *Total Lift : D-Day*

243 Parachute aircraft
440 Tug aircraft
440 Glider aircraft

1123 Total aircraft

Re-supply Tasks

(i) *2nd Bombardment Division, VIII USAAF*

2nd Bombardment Division, VIII USAAF, was to undertake an automatic re-supply mission approximately fifteen minutes after the last glider landing, using two hundred and forty Liberators.

(ii) *38 Group, RAF*

On return to base, six Halifax aircraft of 38 Group were to load six jeeps and six six-pounder guns, and all other serviceable aircraft in the Group were to load containers and stand by at 1¾ hours call from 0700 hours on D+1.

(iii) *46 Group, RAF*

Three squadrons of aircraft from 46 Group RAF, were to land back at NIVELLES, and load panniers. These aircraft were to stand by to re-supply in emergency only, and were to be at two hours call from dawn on D+1.

Navigational Aids

In addition to normal aids, Eureka Beacons and Compass Beacons were to be set up at the various turning points. Midway on the leg between WAVRE and the target area additional Eureka Beacons and coloured panels, etc, were to be set up. Immediately prior to crossing the RHINE, Eureka Beacons and coloured strips with distinctive letter panels were to be set up for the guidance of all streams. No ground markings were to be put on the DZs and it was not anticipated that aircrews would have any difficulty in finding the correct drop or release points, having regard to the close proximity of the RHINE crossing to the DZs and LZs.

The Flight Plan (See Maps 6 and 7)

The combined flight plan was drawn up by the joint planning staff of 38 Group, RAF, and IX USTCC at HQ IX USTCC, PARIS. The Base airfields for the complete operation formed two distinct groups — a Northern group of eight British and three US airfields in the UK, and a Southern group of fifteen US airfields on the continent. Aircraft from the Northern group were to form up over HAWKINGE and those from the Southern group over PONTOISE, LE QUESNOY and LAON. From these assembly points streams were to proceed to a Command assembly point at WAVRE, and thence in double stream to the target area. Details of the routes and run-in to the target area are shown on Maps 6 and 7.

Aircraft operating from the UK carrying 6 Brit Airborne Div were to fly one mile to the Left of the route markers, and aircraft based on the continent were to fly one mile to the Right of the route markers, maintaining a space of two miles between columns to the target RV (Indicator Point). From this point columns were to diverge on their respective DZs and LZs and turn Left and Right respectively after their release or drop. (See Map 7)

Routes and timings of aircraft of 2nd Bombardment Division VIII USAAF, were co-ordinated so as not to interfere with aircraft carrying the airborne forces.

C. AIR SUPPORT

Neutralisation of Enemy Air Forces

The task of neutralisation of enemy air forces was given to AOC-in-C 2 TAF, who had the complete resources of the Allied Tactical Air Forces in the Western European theatre at his disposal. Several days previous to the operation, enemy airfields were to receive attention from our bomber forces. Whilst the troop carrier forces were airborne, in addition to escorting fighters, offensive patrols were to be maintained over the enemy fighter airfields. It was anticipated that as the result of these and previous operations, the enemy air forces would be incapable of operating an appreciable air effort against the troop carrier streams.

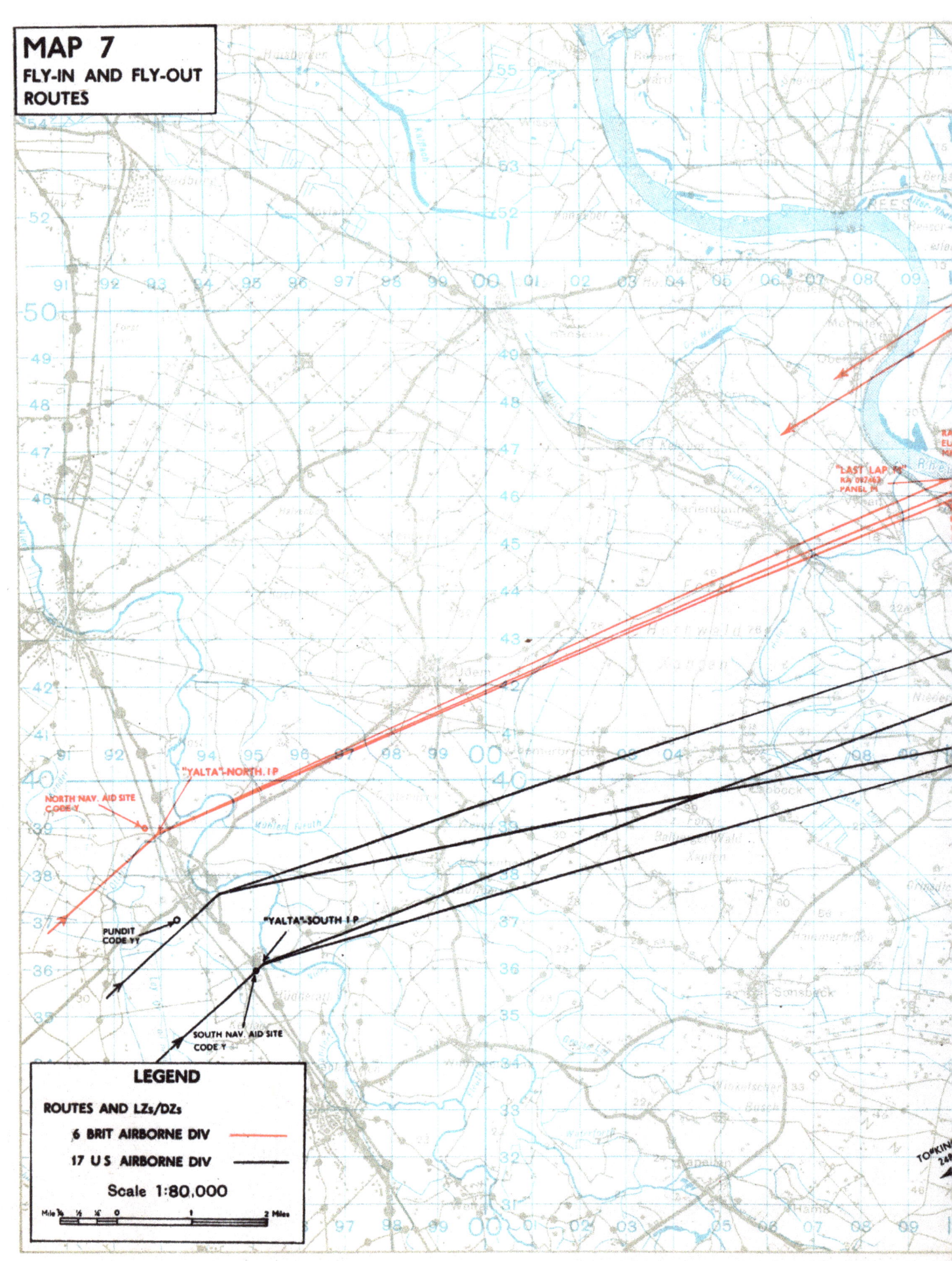

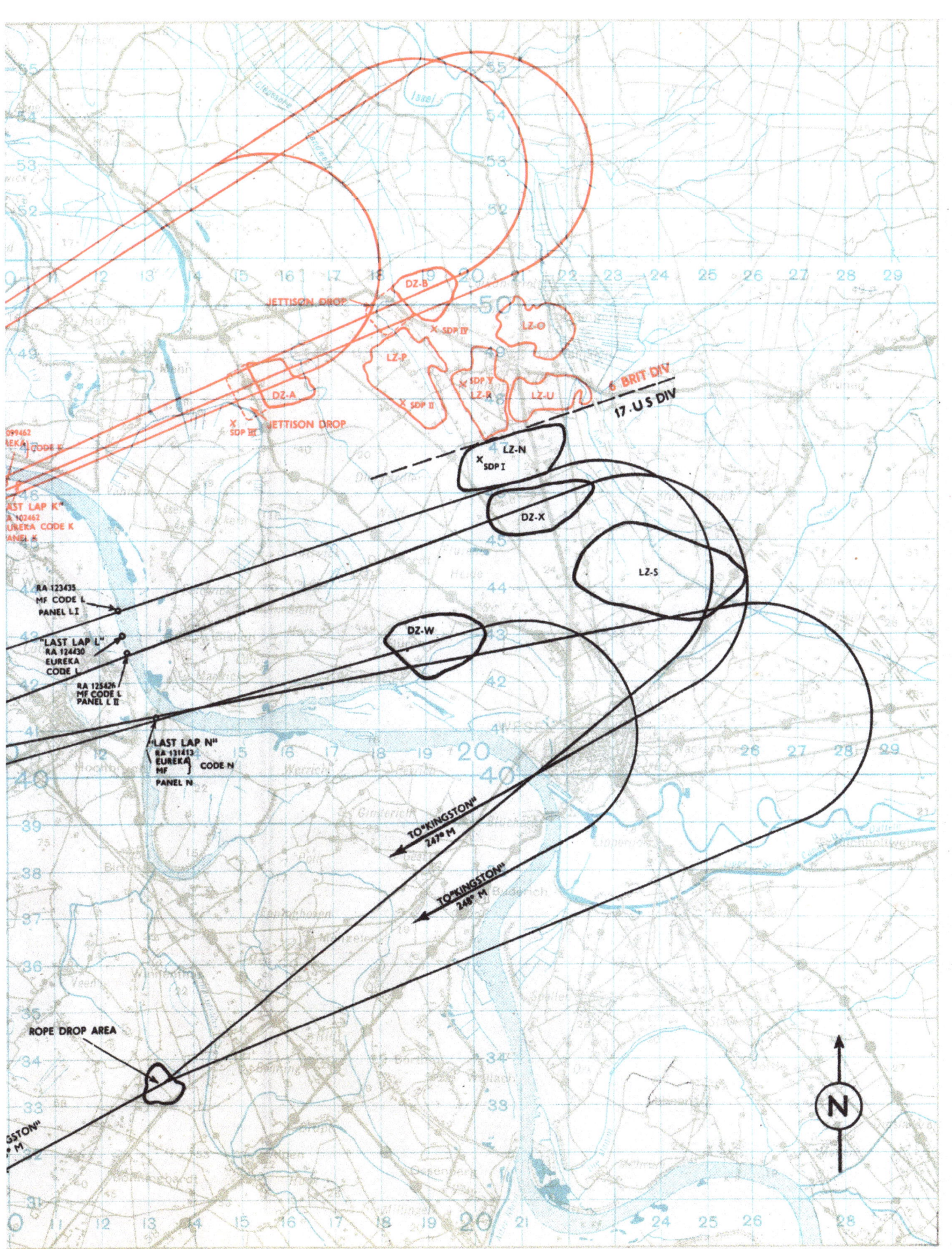

Neutralisation of Enemy Flak

The neutralisation of enemy flak was the joint responsibility of AOC, 83 Group RAF and Commander, Second Army. A special anti-flak committee was set up to study all flak problems, and collect all up-to-date information about the area.

Artillery fire against flak positions was to be continued until the leading aircraft of the troop carrier stream crossed the RHINE. At the same time, fighter bombers and fighters were to attack all flak positions which were known to us. During the landings, a continuous patrol of anti-flak fighters was to be maintained in the area to deal with any flak position which might open up against the troop carrier aircraft.

Tasks of Air Forces in support of VARSITY

The tasks allotted for D-Day to the various Air Forces in support of VARSITY were:—

Air Force	*Task*
VIII USAAF	Patrol and attack enemy fighter airfields East of the RHINE. Cover for XV USAAF attacking BERLIN in a diversionary attack. Re-supply mission by heavy bombers within two hours of the airborne landings being completed.
RAF Fighter Command	Escort Northern column from UK.
IX USAAF	Escort Southern column from bases on the continent.
2 TAF	Cover of target area, anti-flak direct support
RAF Coastal Command	Diversionary attack on BORKUM; Air/Sea Rescue.
XV USAAF	Diversionary attack on BERLIN (from bases in ITALY).

Lift of Forward Visual Control Posts (FVCPs)

Arrangments were made for three FVCPs to be flown into 6 Brit Airborne Div landing zone to control direct support aircraft, and provide communications with re-supply aircraft and the Group Control Centre (GCC). The allocation of these FVCPs was one to 6 Brit Airborne Div, one to 17 US Airborne Div and one spare. The unit destined for 17 US Airborne Div was to proceed under orders of Commander 6 Brit Airborne Div to 17 US Airborne Div as soon as the ground situation permitted. Details of air support communications are given in Section IX, paragraph D.

D. FINAL PREPARATION AND TIMINGS

Briefing

RAF Station and Squadron Commanders were briefed at Headquarters 38 Group, on 19 March 1945, and aircrew briefing commenced on 21 March 1945. Airborne formations were ready to take off as from 24 March 1945.

Command

The Commanding General First Allied Airborne Army moved to the Tac HQ set up in BRUSSELS adjacent to HQ 21 Army Group/2 TAF, and, as the result of meteorological conferences held at BRUSSELS by AOC-in-C 2nd Tactical Air Force and Commanding General First Allied Airborne Army, and in PARIS by Commanding General IX USTCC, Commander-in-Chief 21 Army Group was informed that from an air point of view there was no reason why Operation VARSITY should not take place as planned on 24 March.

The Commander-in-Chief 21 Army Group accepted this recommendation and issued the executive signal to the land forces before 1700 hours on 23 March.

SECTION VIII

FIRE PLAN

A. CHAIN OF COMMAND AND PLANNING

The combined fire plan for 12 Corps in Operation PLUNDER and XVIII US Corps (Airborne) in Operation VARSITY was made by CCRA 12 Corps in co-operation with the Artillery Commander of XVIII US Corps (Airborne) and the CsRA of the airborne divisions.

The Artillery Commander XVIII US Corps (Airborne) established his tactical HQ near the HQ of CCRA 12 Corps before the battle started. This very much simplified communications.

The following timetable gives the main events in the planning by CRA 6 Brit Airborne Div :—

Date	Event
End of February 1945	Warning that an airborne operation would take place about the end of March (later advanced one week).
1 March	Outline plan received.
3 March	CRA visited CCRA 12 Corps. General allotment of artillery agreed.
3–11 March	Divisional planning.
12 March	CRA visited CCRA 12 Corps again. Following points were agreed :— (i) General lines of the plan. (ii) Detailed allotment of artillery. (iii) Control and communications. (iv) Emergency arrangements.
20 March	BM RA visited HQ RA 12 Corps. Final details settled.
22 March	6 Brit Airborne Div fire plan traces received in British Liberation Army (BLA) (delayed in transit).
23 March	BM RA returned from BLA.
24 March (early morning)	Take off for Operation VARSITY.

It will be seen from this timetable that there was very little time for planning, and, in any case, planning between headquarters situated in different countries some 300 miles apart does not make for flexibility. It was very lucky that the weather was good throughout the planning period, and officers were able to fly to and fro without being delayed. Even so, RA 12 Corps had to cope with some aspects of the planning which under more favourable circumstances would have been covered by the CsRA of the airborne divisions.

B. ALLOTMENT OF ARTILLERY FOR OPERATION VARSITY

(i) *Artillery of 17 US Airborne Div*

17 US Airborne Div flew in two Parachute Field Artillery battalions, two Glider Field Artillery battalions and one anti-aircraft battalion.

(ii) *Artillery of 6 Brit Airborne Div*

53 (Worcestershire Yeomanry) Airlanding Light Regiment RA, organised for this operation into two batteries each of 12 × 75 mm guns, was flown in with the division. 2 Airlanding A Tk Regt less one battery was also flown in, and the third battery crossed the RHINE with the land tail.

The divisional artillery was allotted as follows :—

3 Para Bde

Under command	One 6-pounder troop 3 Airlanding A Tk Bty RA

5 Para Bde

Under command	4 Airlanding A Tk Bty RA (8 × 17-pounders, 8 × 6-pounders)
In support	One battery 53 (WY) Airlanding Lt Regt RA (12 × 75 mm)

6 Airlanding Bde

Under command	3 Airlanding A Tk Bty RA less two 6-pounder troops and one 17-pounder section (total : 6 × 17-pounders)
In support	One battery 53 (WY) Airlanding Lt Regt RA (12 × 75 mm).

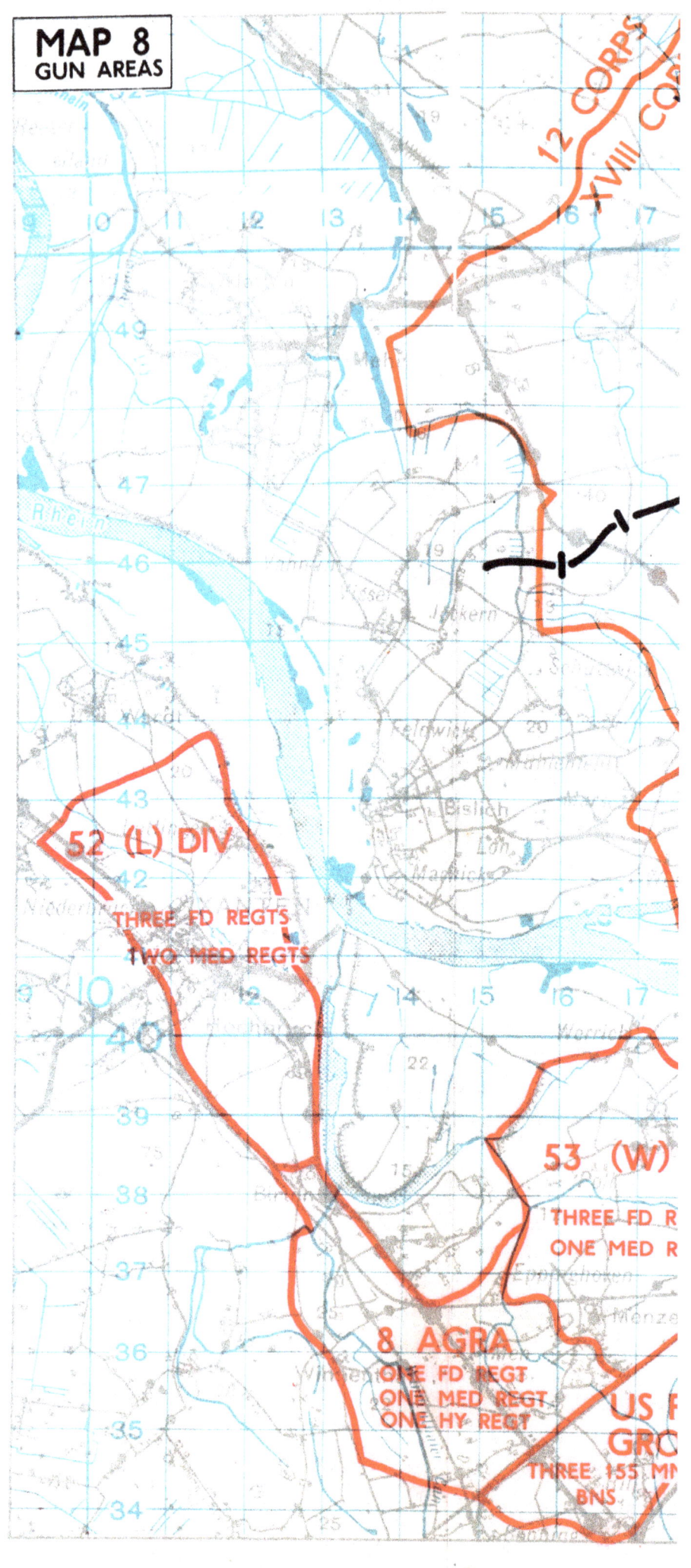

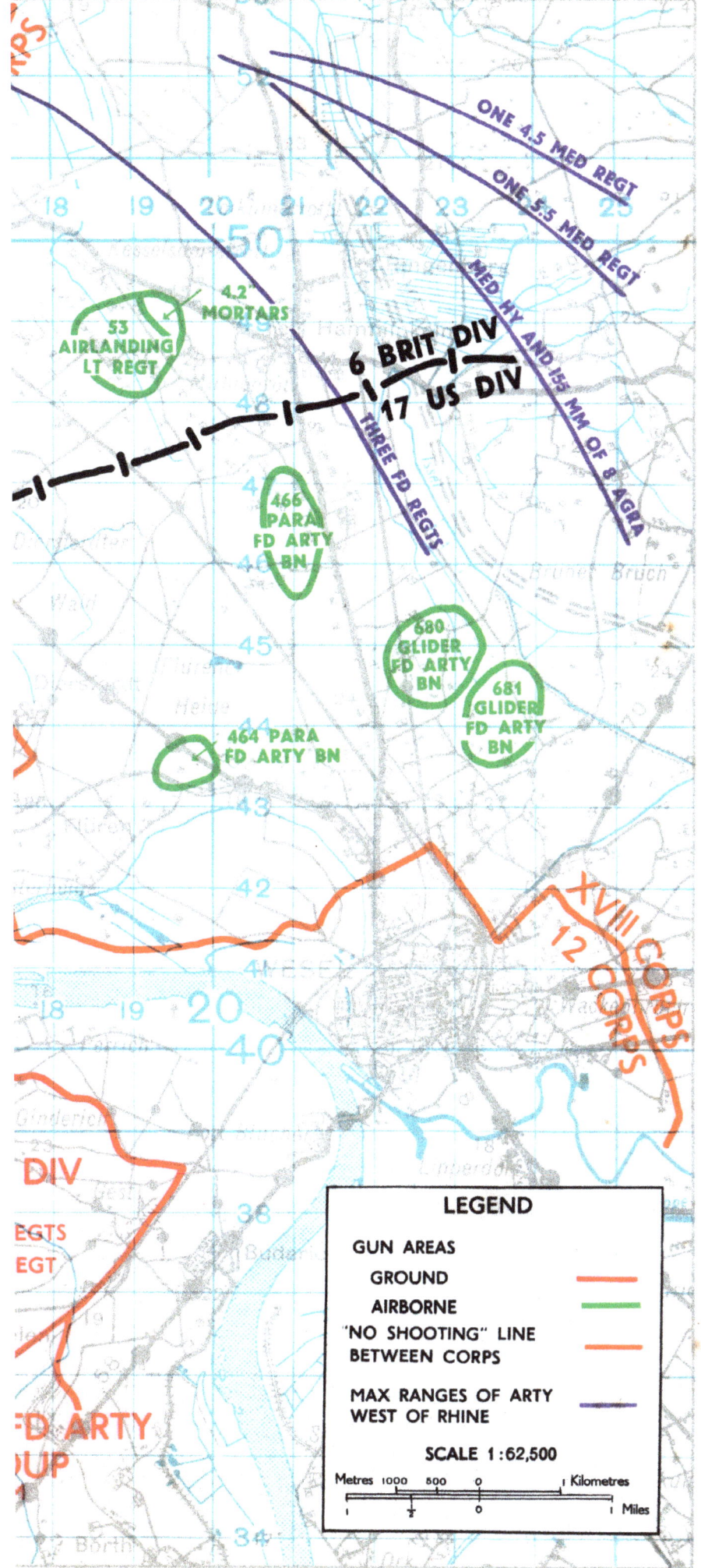

Divisional Reserve

Airborne — One 6-pounder troop and one 17-pounder section from 3 Airlanding A Tk Bty RA

Plus, *after* link up with land tail — 6 Airlanding A Tk Bty RA (4 × 17-pounders : 12 × 6-pounders) 146 SP A Tk Bty RA (12 × SP 17-pounders) – under command from 8 Corps.

(iii) *Artillery allotted by CCRA 12 Corps*

At P-Hour the following were to pass under operational command of XVIII US Corps (Airborne) :—

RA 52 (L) Div Group – in direct support of 6 Brit Airborne Div. Sub-allotted in support of brigades in the initial phase as follows :—

    3 Para Bde — three field regiments
    5 Para Bde — one medium regiment
    6 Airlanding Bde — one medium regiment

5 Para and 6 Airlanding Bdes were not within range of 25-pounders : medium regiments were shooting at about 16,000 yards and therefore might not be expected to be very accurate. Where the fire of medium guns had to be called for on targets within 300–400 yards of our own troops, the risk of casualties being caused by inaccuracy at so long a range was accepted, and arrangements were made for calls for fire to be answered.

RA 53 (W) Div Group — in direct support of 17 US Airborne Div : included three field regiments and one medium regiment.

8 AGRA Group — in general support: included one field regiment, one medium regiment, one heavy regiment, three battalions 155 mm guns from Ninth US Army.

All these guns were in position West of the RHINE as far forward as possible. Fire from the divisional artillery groups in direct support of the airborne divisions could be called for by the CRA of the airborne division concerned as soon as his communications had been established after landing (see paragraph E below). Until that time, the fire of the divisional artillery groups would be controlled by their own CsRA, with the proviso that FOOs with the airborne brigades could themselves call for the fire of their own direct support regiment(s). One field regiment from 15 (S) Div was to be available as additional support later in the battle, the exact time to be dependent on the arrival of 17 US Airborne Div artillery moving with the land tail.

4 RHA was to have an early priority to cross the RHINE on class 50/60 rafts, under command CRA 15 (S) Div probably on D+1. This regiment although primarily in support of the mobile striking force of 4 Armd Bde would be the first field regiment to come within supporting distance of the whole of 6 Brit Airborne Div.

C. TASKS AND TIMINGS

Pre-arranged fire support laid on by CCRA 12 Corps in support of Operation VARSITY included the following :—

(i) Counter Battery bombardment covering 12 Corps and XVIII US Corps (Airborne) areas (BLOTTER)
(ii) Softening bombardment for Operation VARSITY (CLIMAX)
(iii) Anti-flak bombardment for Operation VARSITY (CARPET)

The following table gives particulars of each of these tasks :—

Task and Code name	Day	Time	Regiments	Remarks
CB Bombardment BLOTTER	D–1	To start 1800 hours and last 2 hours	Eleven medium regiments Two heavy regiments One super-heavy regiment One HAA regiment Three US 155 mm battalions	Programme arranged by Commander 9 AGRA, to cover all located hostile batteries. Shooting started on orders of CCRA 12 Corps.
Softening Bombardment CLIMAX	D	P–100 minutes to P–40 minutes (0820—0920)	Nine field regiments Eleven medium regiments One heavy regiment Four heavy batteries One HAA regiment One super-heavy battery Three US 155 mm battalions	Targets supplied by XVIII US Corps (Airborne) from information obtained from air photographs by CsRA 6 Brit and 17 US Airborne Divs. Programme arranged by CCRA 12 Corps. VT Fuzes used to avoid cratering on DZs and LZs.
Anti-flak bombardment CARPET	D	P–½ to P–Hour	Eleven field regiments Eleven medium regiments Two heavy regiments One super-heavy regiment One HAA regiment Three US 155 mm battalions	Target information supplied by RA Second Army and 83 Group RAF. Programme arranged by CCRA 12 Corps. Engagement of targets depended to some extent on progress made by 15 (S) Div and 1 Cdo Bde.

The artillery of 17 US Airborne Div was given tasks by its own Artillery Commander of a similar type to those given to 6 Brit Airborne Div.

The 75 mm guns of 53 (WY) Airlanding Lt Regt could be used for any of the following tasks :—

(i) Close defensive fire (these guns fired accurately at ranges from 1—5,000 yards: their maximum range was 9,000 yards).

(ii) Counter-mortar shooting.

(iii) Close support of infantry in battalion, company and platoon actions.

The divisional anti-tank reserve amounted to one troop of 6-pounders and one section of 17-pounders : they were to be used for the protection of Div HQ and the gun area from the West and South West.

The 4.2" Mortar troop of 6 Airborne Armd Recce Regt which was to go into action in the area shown on Map 8, could be called upon through any FOO, via the RA representatives at HQ 5 Para or 6 Airlanding Bdes.

The division had one Air OP Flight in direct support, working on a regimental net as decided by CRA 52 (L) Div Artillery Group.

D. SAFETY PRECAUTIONS AND THEIR EFFECT

"The overriding principle is that NO GUN MUST FIRE ALONG OR ACROSS THE ROUTE TAKEN BY ANY AIRCRAFT during the fly-in and fly-out."

The ultimate responsibility for ensuring that this instruction by RA 12 Corps was obeyed lay with Gun Position Officers (GPOs). They were to stop the fire of their guns if they considered that any aircraft was flying into their line of fire, and a look-out was to be posted on every troop position.

The anti-flak bombardment (CARPET) was timed to finish just before the leading aircraft passed over the general line of the gun areas, but GPOs were to be prepared to stop it early if necessary. Once they had been stopped all guns were to remain silent until CCRA 12 Corps authorised them to start shooting again.

As an additional precaution an observer on the CCRA's net was stationed 10 miles behind the gun areas to give advance warning of the arrival of the aircraft, and another observer on the same net was posted in an observation tower in XANTEN woods. In practice, the leading aircraft did arrive eight minutes early, and the latter observer gave the order "Stop" to all the corps artillery.

A "NO FIRE" line was laid down between 12 Corps and XVIII US Corps (Airborne) to be observed from the time that the airborne troops had landed.

The complete ban on firing while aircraft were overhead which was imposed by Second Army meant that :—

(i) There could be no fire support at time of landing.

(ii) There could be no major bombardment during fly-in.

(iii) The anti-flak bombardment was only effective for the leading waves of aircraft, and thereafter the enemy could shoot undisturbed : and, in the event, this bombardment had to be stopped before it had been completed.

(iv) The 12 Corps artillery, where the trajectory crossed the fly-in or fly-out routes, had to stop firing altogether for 2—3 hours. (The North fly-in route was expected to be clear by P+70 minutes and the South by P+210 minutes).

No AA fire was allowed under any circumstances between P-1 and P+4 hours.

E. LIAISON AND COMMUNICATIONS

It had been found from previous experience that the FOOs with the airborne formations and units, when calling for fire, must speak to some one on the gun position whom they knew and with whom they had trained. It was not satisfactory for them to come down from the sky and begin talking to complete strangers on the wireless.

6 Brit Airborne Div therefore had a Forward Observer Unit, which provided both parachute FOOs and liaison parties on the gun positions and at the various RA Headquarters West of the RHINE, to receive and interpret requests for fire support passed back by the airborne troops. The liaison parties joined their regiments on D-4.

17 US Airborne Div made up a similar organisation for this operation, and their liaison parties were trained to interpret American fire orders for the British gunners.

Good communications were essential for proper support. The layout is shown in Diagram 2. In practice, the system worked very well, and FOOs were able to call for fire from the other side of the RHINE within a few minutes of landing. It will be seen from the diagram that, in the early stages, FOOs at brigade and battalion headquarters were able to call for fire direct to the regiments West of the RHINE, pending the setting up of HQ RA and the normal, and more flexible, airborne support net.

The rear link from CRA 6 Brit Airborne Div was to Artillery Commander XVIII US Corps (Airborne), and CCRA 12 Corps had a set on this net also. In view of this and of the fact that HQ RA 12 Corps and the HQ of Artillery Commander XVIII Corps were sited very close together, the CCRA was able to keep fully in touch with what was happening in the Airborne Corps. 17 US Airborne Div also had a set on the same net, which could be used for obtaining medium and heavy fire support, in addition to that already allotted to the airborne divisions, and also for the passing of information.

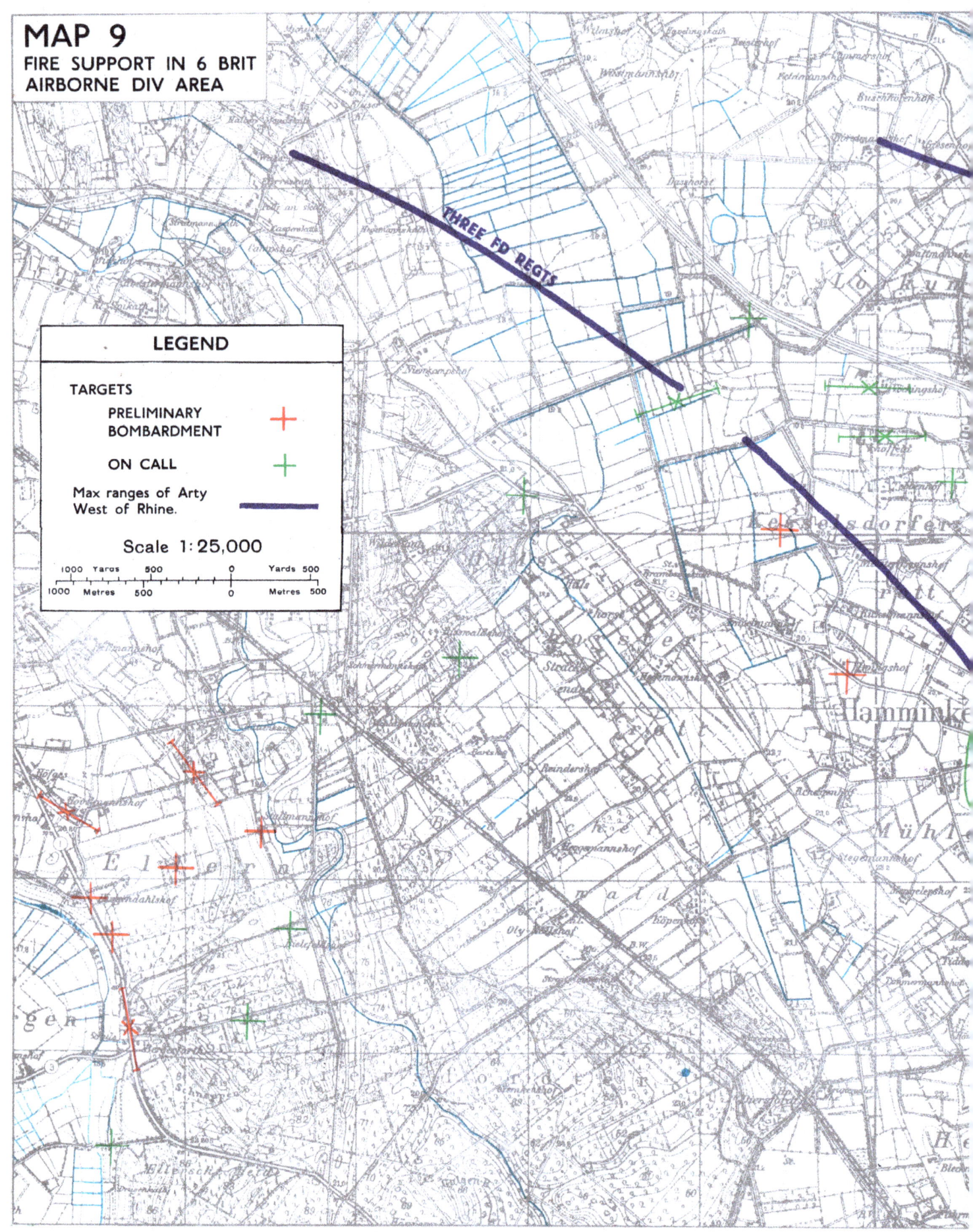

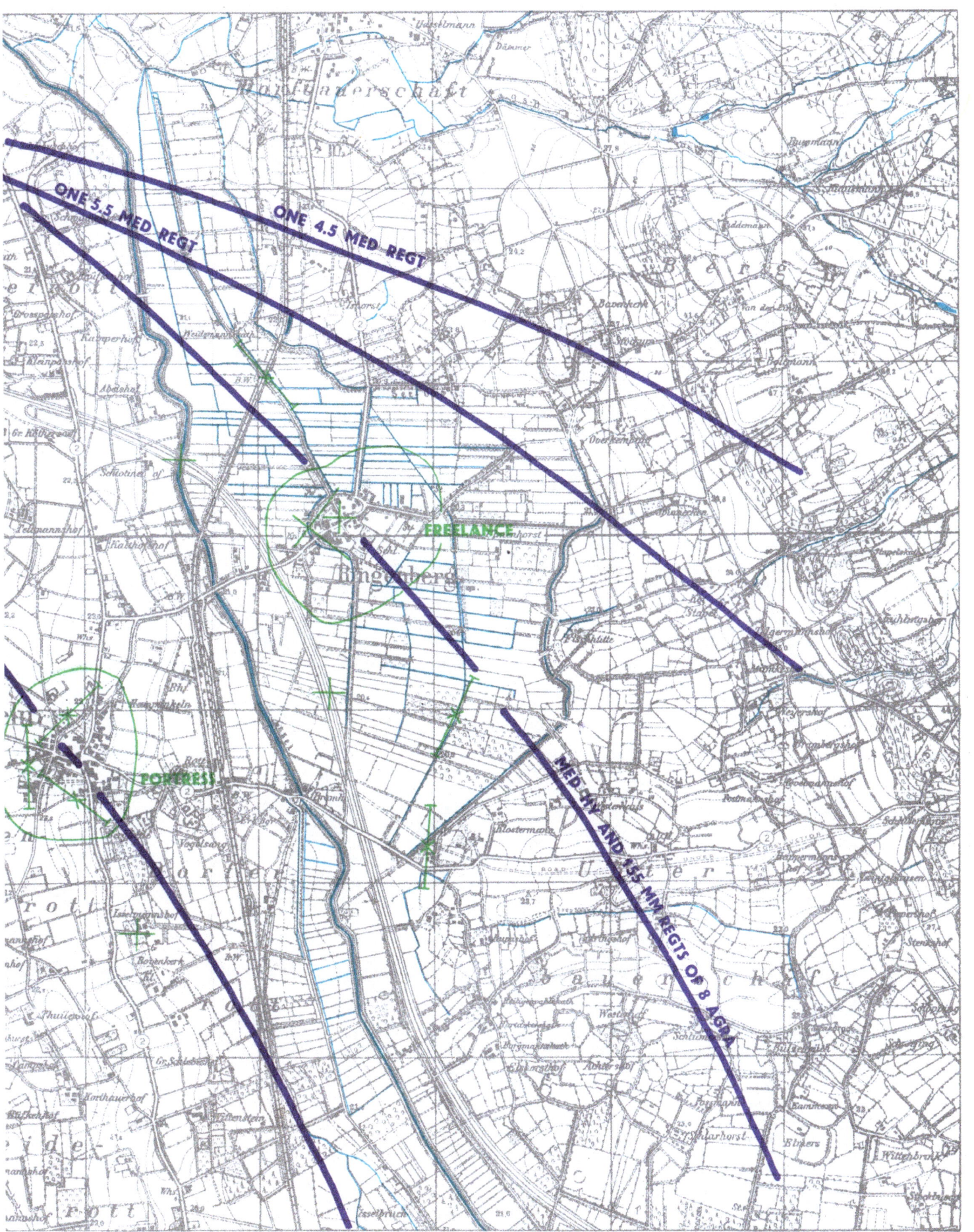

SECTION IX

COMMUNICATIONS

A. GENERAL

Any airborne operation, both in planning and execution, is dependent on good communications. In Operation VARSITY, the provision of them was a particularly complicated task owing to the number of different headquarters involved, the very large distances which separated them, and the short time available. Signal planning was, however, assisted by the fact that CR Signals, 6 Brit Airborne Div was in a position to have much preliminary discussion with Chief Signal Officer, Second Army, whilst the division was in HOLLAND, and that a draft signal plan had been prepared previously with Signal Officer XVIII US Corps (Airborne) for a similar operation. Final details were settled at a conference held by CSO, Second Army, attended by all CSOs and signal officers concerned. In addition much administrative preparation was undertaken by CSO 1 Brit Airborne Corps and Base Details 6 Brit Airborne Div Sigs before the division returned to ENGLAND.

In the event, excellent communications were provided and they did much to ensure the success of the operation.

B. COMMUNICATIONS FOR PLANNING AND LAUNCHING

All the principal headquarters involved in the planning were linked both by wireless and line : in each case there were several alternative routes by line. Security precluded the use of special planning wireless links below corps level, whilst a wireless deception plan was, in addition, put into operation.

Commanders and staff officers were able to visit other headquarters as necessary, since, fortunately, the weather was suitable for flying. An extensive line and SDS system, based on previous experience, was required during the last days before the operation, when 6 Brit Airborne Div was dispersed to its airfield transit camps. This was provided under orders of CSO, 1 Brit Airborne Corps and manned by base section 6 Brit Airborne Div Sigs, supplemented from corps resources. Such a comprehensive system is vital to the smooth launching of a division on an airborne operation.

C. OPERATIONAL COMMUNICATIONS

Line communications are not considered in detail here. All headquarters to the West of the RHINE were linked by a comprehensive line layout, and arrangements were made for cables to be laid across the river as soon as the situation permitted. 6 Brit Airborne Div flew in line detachments at both divisional and brigade level for use as early as the tactical situation permitted. A considerable line build-up was included in the first echelon of the seaborne tail.

The wireless communications of XVIII US Corps (Airborne) with higher, flanking and lower formations are shown on Diagram 3. It will be noticed that the principle of not mixing American and British operators on the same net was observed. American operators flew in with HQ 6 Brit Airborne Div whilst British operators flew in with 17 US Airborne Div, and were attached to HQ XVIII US Corps (Airborne).

Wireless links from HQ 6 Brit Airborne Div are shown on Diagram 4.

RA communications have already been dealt with in Section VIII, paragraph E.

Wireless sets were flown in for the working of fourteen links at Div HQ, plus a reserve of about 60%. Sets at brigades and battalions were in all cases duplicated, and sometimes triplicated. 100% duplication of equipment and sets would however, have been no over-insurance, as casualties to signals equipment on landing were about 50%. VARSITY was the first operation for which a British airborne division was equipped with an adequate three-man pack set, the Wireless Set No 62, for use by parachute brigades and RA FOOs ; this set could be dropped with the man in a kit-bag. An adequate divisional rear-link set, the No 52, was also used for the first time. Both these sets proved their worth beyond question.

Certain vital frequencies, such as the Airborne Base wave, and the RA Airborne Support net were "cleared" throughout the theatre. Crystal control was used wherever possible : where this was not possible, sets were netted by pre-checked crystal wavemeters, and the dials locked and sealed before loading. As an aid to recognition and linking up, the "common recognition wave" was kept by all formations concerned down to battalion level.

All airborne sets were to open up as soon as they landed : sets with ground formations opened up before the landing started at times laid down by the CSOs concerned.

Each operator was fully briefed and was issued with codesigns and other information for D-Day only, to enable him to work on any link on which his set was capable of working, and for which it might be required in an emergency. The necessary documents were rolled up and carried inside one of the hollow aerial rods.

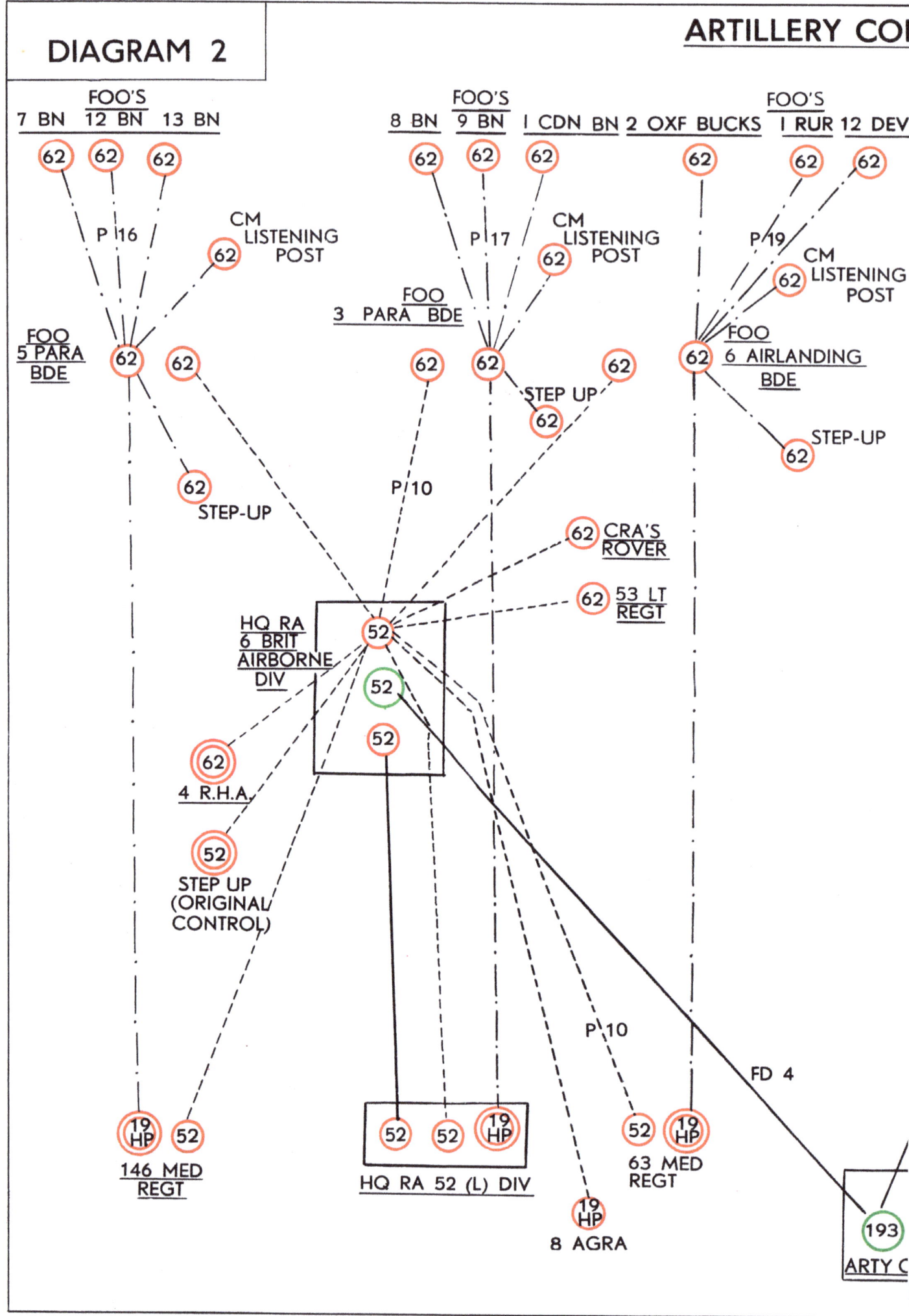

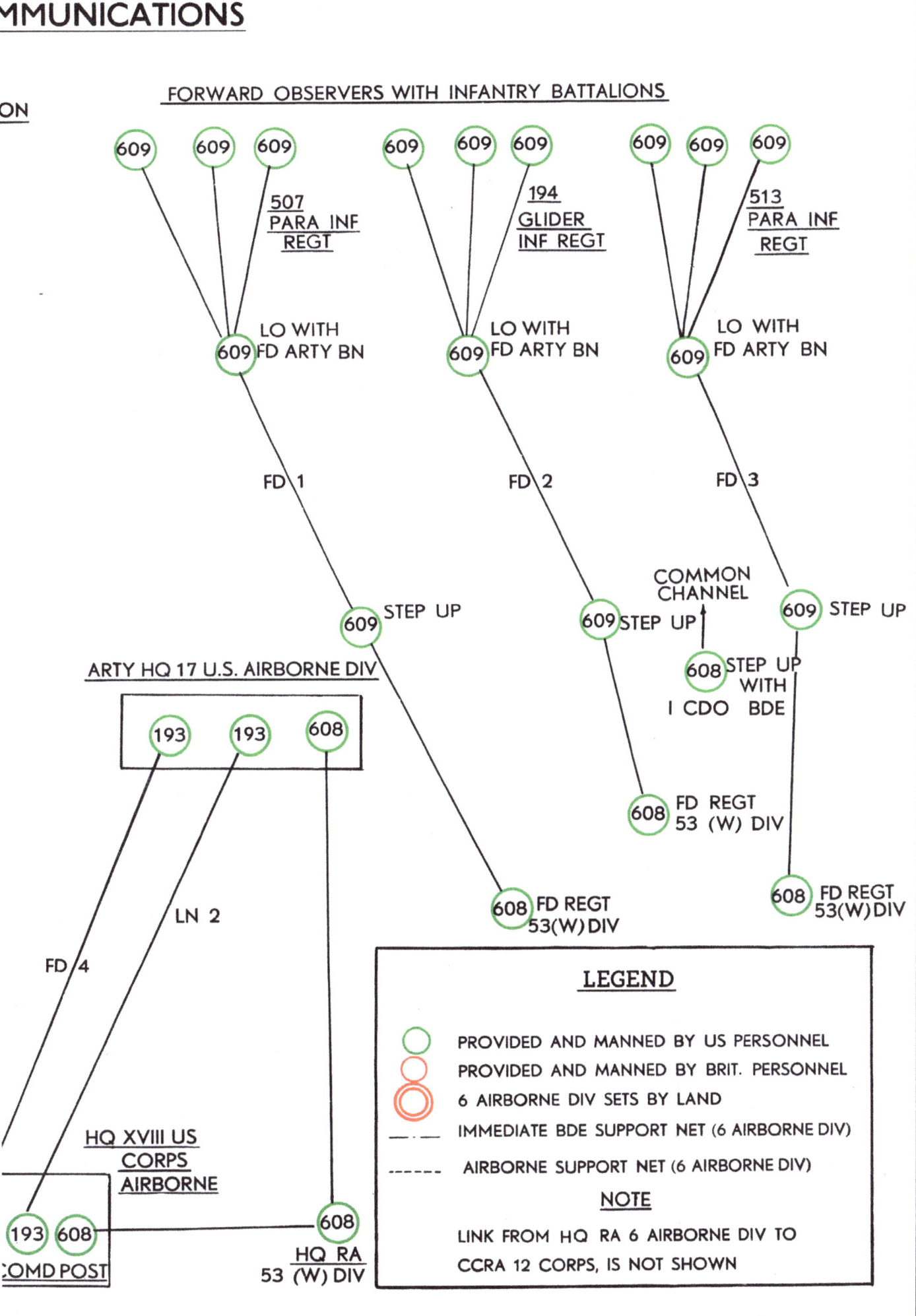

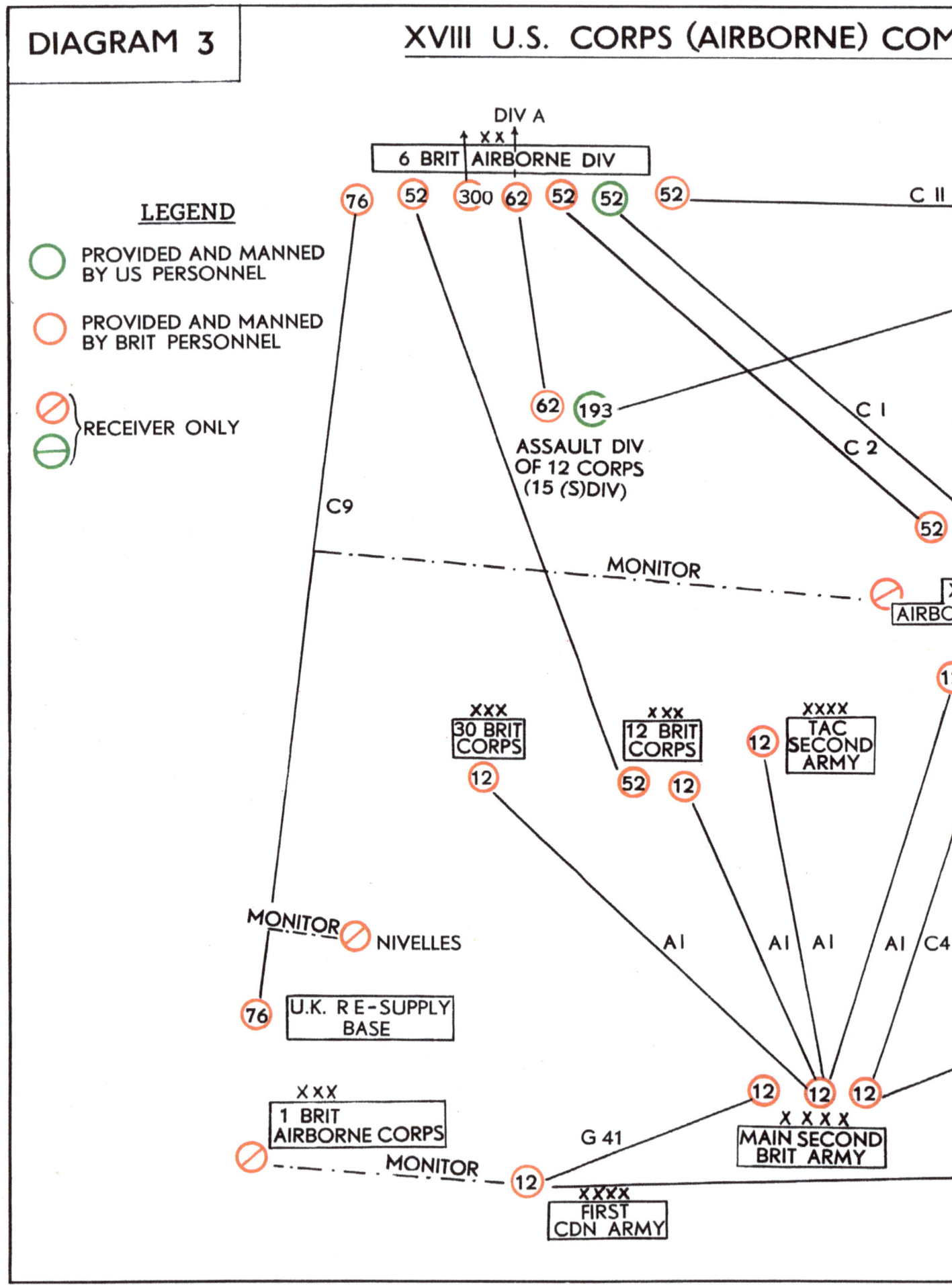

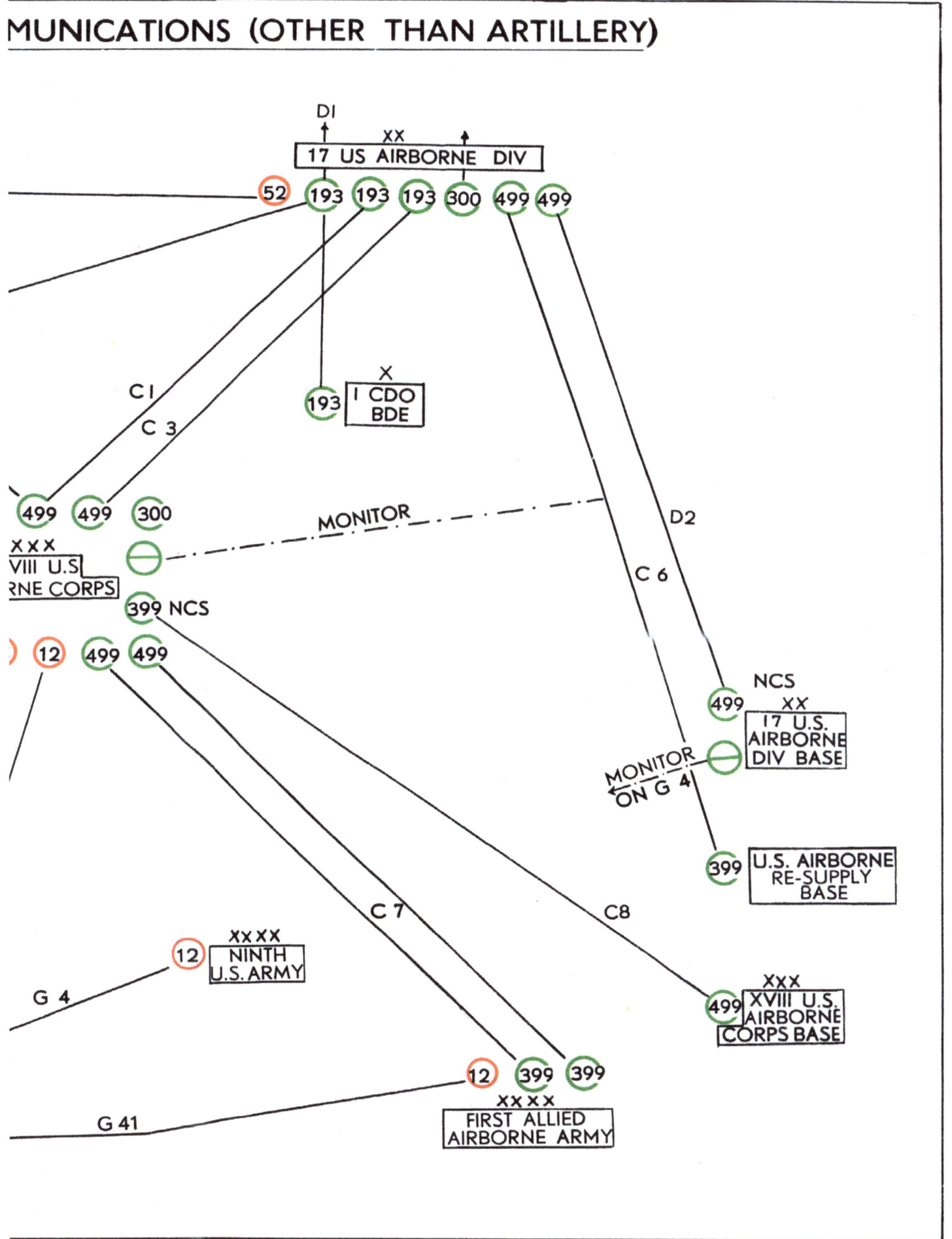

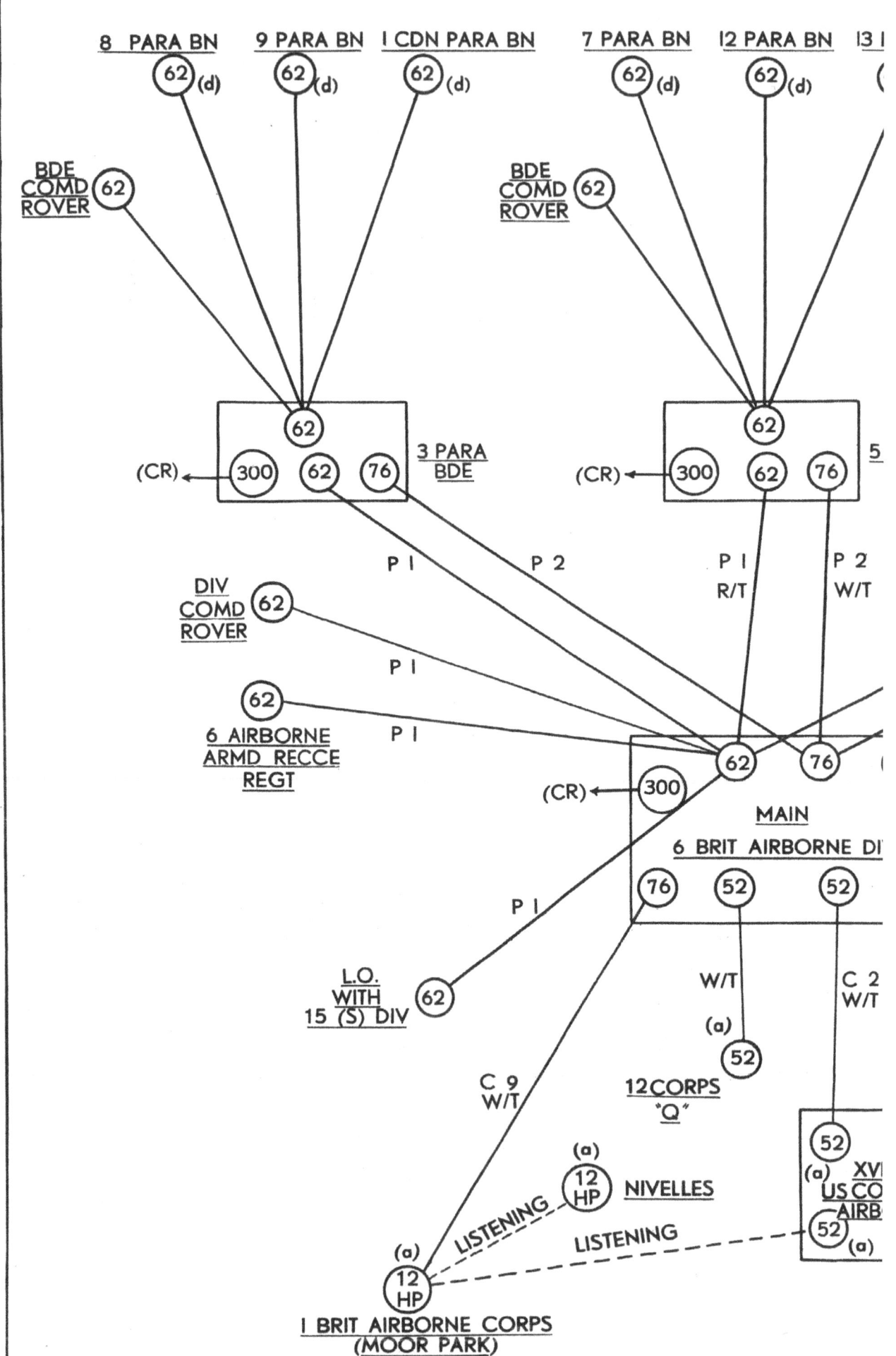

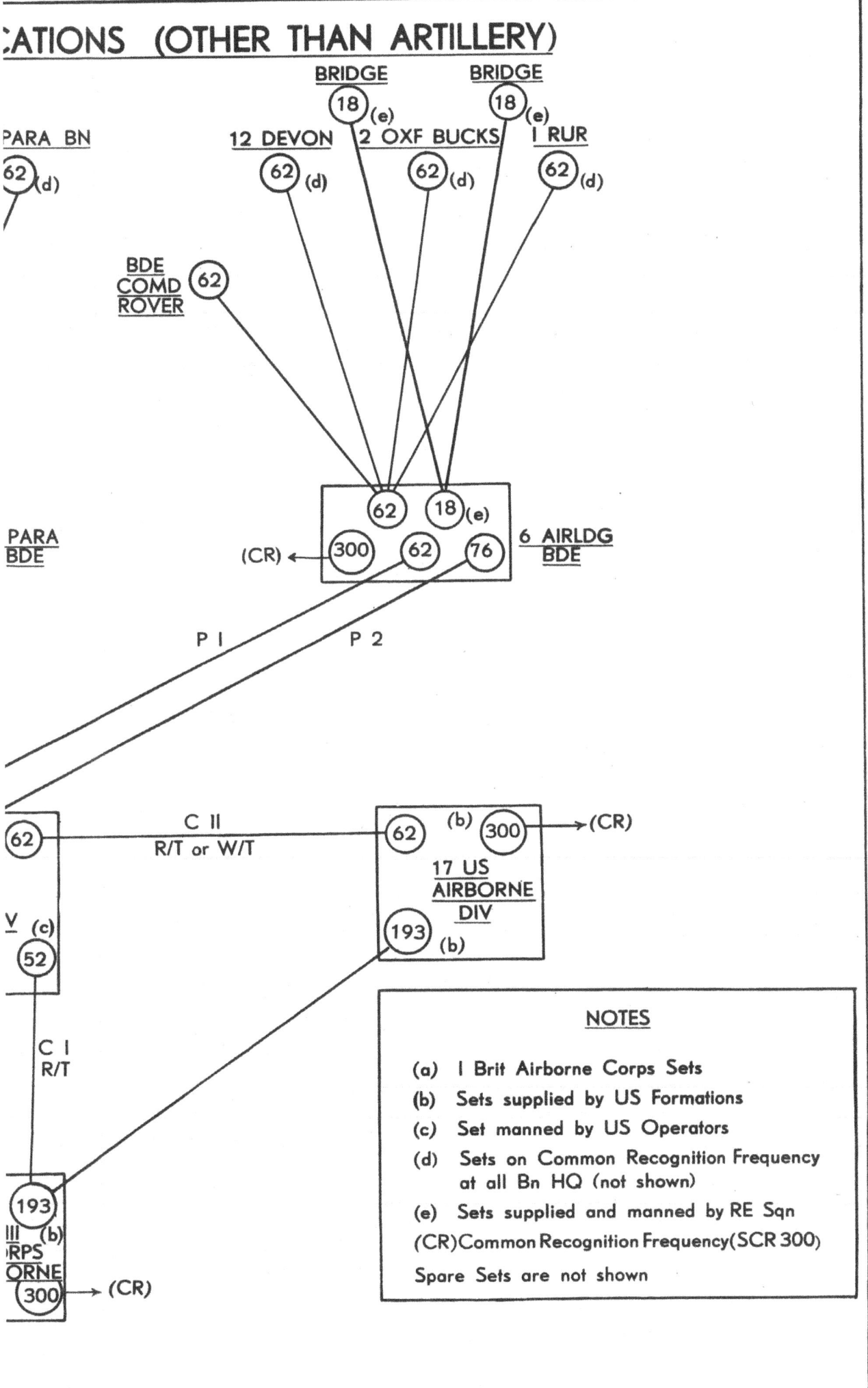

DIAGRAM 5

AIR SUPPORT CO[N]

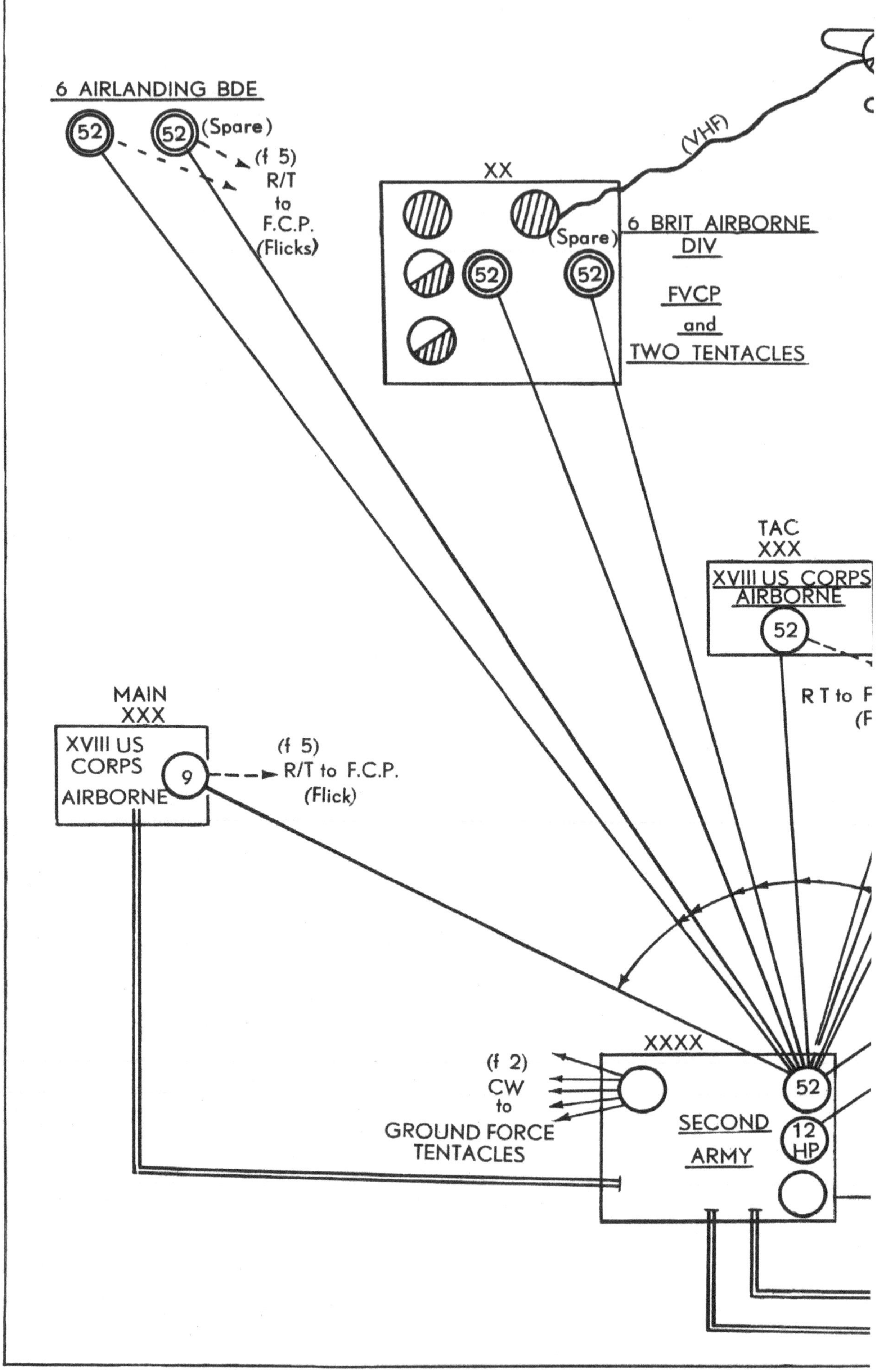

6 AIRLANDING BDE

(52) (52) (Spare)

(f 5) R/T to F.C.P. (Flicks)

XX

(Spare)

6 BRIT AIRBORNE DIV

FVCP and TWO TENTACLES

(VHF)

TAC XXX

XVIII US CORPS AIRBORNE

(52)

R T to F (F

MAIN XXX

XVIII US CORPS AIRBORNE

(9) → (f 5) R/T to F.C.P. (Flick)

XXXX

(f 2) CW to GROUND FORCE TENTACLES

(52)

(12 HP)

SECOND ARMY

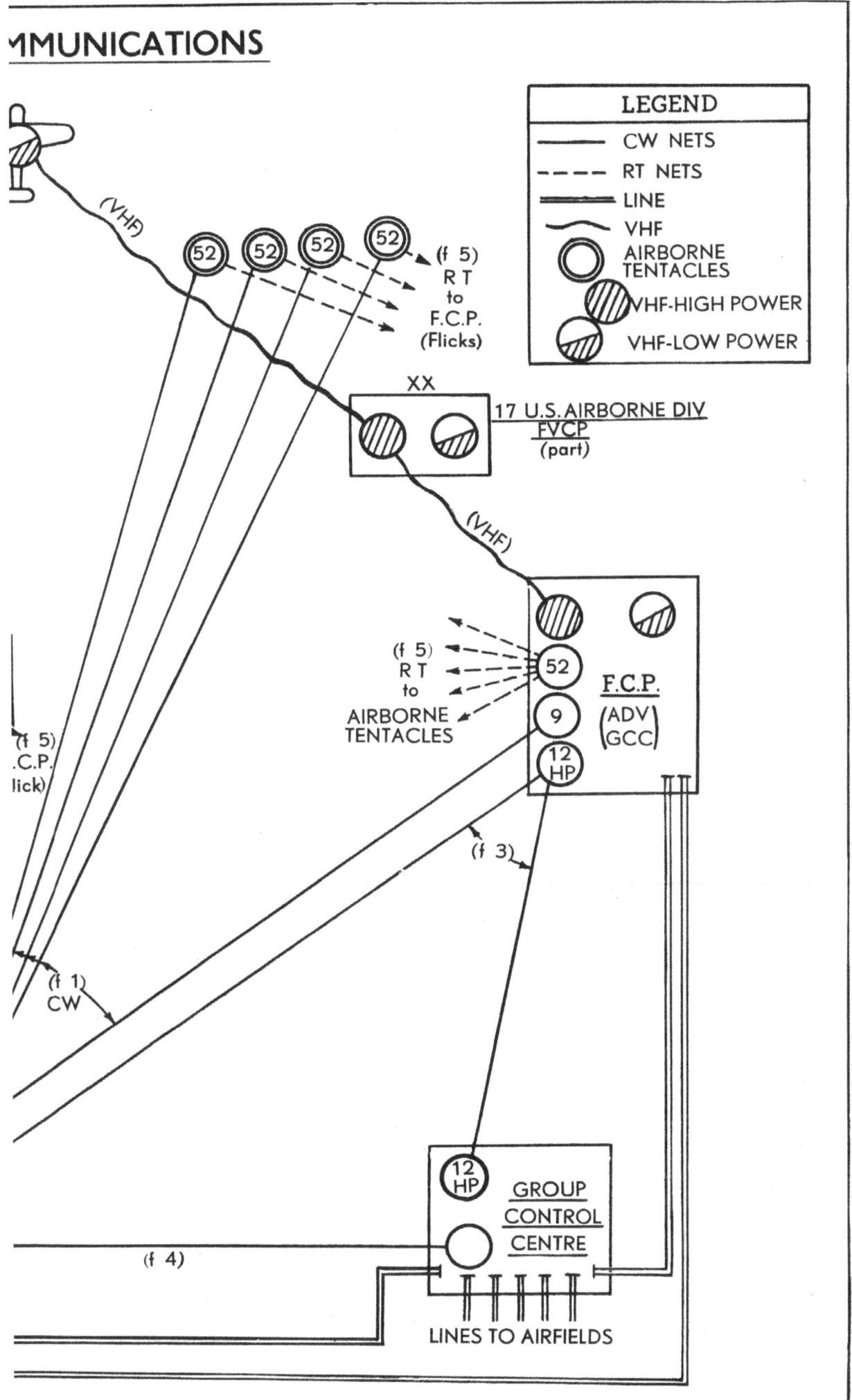

The necessary codes for D-Day to D+2 were carried by air in special "instant destructor tubes" by certain officers only. Further codes, including the code signs and frequencies of ground formations were carried enciphered by two Royal Signals officers at Div HQ only. These were to be deciphered on landing. The airborne codes were held by all the ground formations concerned, while the supporting ground artillery was to use the airborne RA code keys until a firm link-up had been established. This was to ensure that in an emergency an FOO could communicate on any supporting artillery net.

To prevent compromise of normal ciphers, only special ciphers were carried by air. No ciphers were carried by 6 Brit Airborne Div below Bde HQ, and the use of ciphers below Div HQ was considered most unlikely.

A DR service was to be established as soon as possible after landing, subject to the condition that no DR was to be dispatched from any HQ until the route to his destination was confirmed as clear of enemy. Pigeons were not considered necessary, and no provision was made for their use.

D. AIR SUPPORT COMMUNICATIONS

Three Forward Visual Control Posts (FVCPs) were flown in as already mentioned, one for 6 Brit Airborne Div, one for 17 US Airborne Div and one spare. There were also four Air Support Signals Unit (ASSU) jeep and trailer tentacles with 6 Brit Airborne Div of which the crews and equipment were supplied by 1 Brit Airborne Corps signals. 2 ASSU, which supported Second Army, assisted with the training of the crews. Two tentacles were allotted to Div HQ and two to HQ 6 Airlanding Bde, one at each headquarters being a spare.

Diagram 5 shows the layout of air support communications.

SECTION X

ADMINISTRATIVE PLANNING

(This section deals with 6 Brit Airborne Div only. The responsibility for the administration of 17 US Airborne Div lay with First Allied Airborne Army for maintenance by air and Ninth US Army for maintenance by land).

A. GENERAL

The administrative organisation for Operation VARSITY differed in two important respects from previous operations. Firstly, immediately contact with the ground forces had been made, the responsibility for administration devolved on 12 Corps, and was to be carried out in the normal way. Secondly, it was not intended that the Airborne division should be withdrawn after the airborne operation was over. In previous operations it had been intended to withdraw the airborne force after a few days, and the second and third line administrative organisation had not been set up. It had, however, frequently proved operationally impossible to withdraw the airborne force, and this had entailed improvised and unplanned arrangements, which were unsatisfactory to the force itself and imposed an unnecessary burden on the administrative resources available.

A factor which assisted the administrative planning was that 6 Brit Airborne Div had been used as a normal ground division during the German ARDENNES offensive (December 1944/January 1945), and therefore the administrative staff and services had acquired considerable experience both of normal supply arrangements and in estimating their requirements. It was therefore possible to consider the administrative aspect of this operation as a normal commitment, and not merely as a temporary arrangement to maintain a force having specialised requirements for a short period.

The administrative planning, although under discussion and planned in broad outline during February, did not begin to take definite detailed shape until the second week in March. The fact that D-Day was, owing to the success of preliminary operations, brought forward from 30 March to 24 March at short notice, and the necessity for moving some parts of the airborne base in ENGLAND from the NETHERAVON (WILTSHIRE) area to the Eastern Counties, made urgent adjustments in the planning and packing programme necessary: this adjustment was effected without detriment to the final administrative situation.

The necessity for despatching before the operation the seaborne tail which contains principally administrative units, and the fact that Div HQ was in ENGLAND, made delays in transmitting detailed requirements to the various HQ in BLA inevitable. This was partly overcome by the provision of two liaison officers, provided by 1 Brit Airborne Corps, one to 12 Corps and one to XVIII US Corps (Airborne), and by many visits between representatives of HQ 1 Brit Airborne Corps and Div HQ to BLA. The divisional administrative staff could not have provided the liaison personnel required without considerable help from 1 Brit Airborne Corps.

B. SEABORNE TAIL

One of the main difficulties in planning this operation was the necessity to send off the seaborne tail (consisting of all personnel and vehicles not to be flown in to BLA) in time to deploy themselves and to build up the necessary stores, before the operation. This left the division immobile in ENGLAND, and without the services of many much needed officers and units.

The seaborne tail under the command of an officer from Div HQ, moved from ENGLAND in three parties on 15, 19 and 24 March, and passed to command HQ 12 Corps on arrival on the continent. A careful schedule was made of the order in which these units and vehicles were to join up with the division and of the loads they were to carry.

C. MAINTENANCE BY AIR

Maintenance by air was organised as set out below, but it was intended that the ground forces should join up at the latest on D+1. Previous experience in North West Europe had shown that continued maintenance by air of an airborne force was almost impossible owing to

(i) the uncertainty of the weather, even in the summer months
(ii) the difficulty of collecting and distributing stores dropped, in the vehicles available.

Moreover, the cost in the number of aircraft employed entails a heavy burden on the air forces concerned.

Each formation flown in carried with it supplies of ammunition and rations for about two days.

In addition, there were the "hidden" reserves carried both on the man and in the vehicles flown in, which cannot be taken into account in planning but are nevertheless of great value.

Re-supply missions were planned as follows :—

(i) Automatic re-supply by VIII USAAF from Liberators at P+2¾ hours : 145 tons.

(ii) Automatic re-supply by 38 Group, RAF, from Stirlings and Halifaxes during the morning of D+1 subject to cancellation by Second Army : 536 tons.

(iii) Automatic medium level re-supply from 7,000 feet by 38 Group if (ii) proved to be a requirement but was not possible owing to the amount of flak opposition : 154 tons.

(iv) One day's re-supply by 38 Group at call from D+2 : 260 tons.

(v) Automatic emergency re-supply by 46 Group, RAF, from Dakotas based on B75 (NIVELLES) if weather conditions forbade any re-supply missions being flown from the United Kingdom : 170 tons.

In addition, four jettison containers were carried on each parachute aircraft not carrying unit containers, and twelve Hamilcar gliders allotted to RASC for flying in carriers were packed with one hundred and sixty-two panniers of stores.

In order to collect, control and issue the airborne supplies, a detachment of 716 Light Composite Company RASC, commanded by the Company Commander, and composed of eighty all ranks, flew in by Hamilcar with twelve carriers and trailers. Although this was not really a large enough force to deal with the quantity of airborne supplies expected, it was all that the available air lift allowed. The detachment was to be assisted by the loan of forty jeeps and trailers from 6 Airlanding Bde and RA, from P+6 hours until arrival of a jeep and trailer platoon, which was being phased over the river on a high priority.

D. MAINTENANCE BY GROUND RESOURCES

As has been already stated, once the airborne and ground forces had joined up, responsibility for maintaining 6 Brit Airborne Div passed to 12 Corps.

A dump was formed on the West side of the RHINE adjacent to the Corps Forward Maintenance Centre (FMC). This dump contained two days' normal supply and other items likely to be required by the division immediately, and before normal supply could be started. CRASC 6 Brit Airborne Div was responsible for arranging the details with 12 Corps and 15 (S) Div.

Sixty-nine DUKWs were allotted to the division and were loaded with one day's requirements. These were to be phased across the river under the orders of the Bank Group and a dump formed as soon as possible on the East side of the river under CRASC's direction.

Planning was based on the assumption that normal second and third line maintenance would be started as soon as the administrative resources of the division could be reorganised.

E. ADMINISTRATIVE COMMUNICATIONS

There were to be two administrative wireless links from HQ 6 Brit Airborne Div. One was to the Airborne Base (HQ 1 Brit Airborne Corps) in ENGLAND : HQ XVIII US Corps (Airborne) and NIVELLES Airfield had listening sets on this net. The other was a link to 'Q' 12 Corps. Both these nets worked on CW only. There was no link direct to the seaborne tail, which was to be contacted through 'Q' 12 Corps. There was no forward administrative net in 6 Brit Airborne Div.

F. ADMINISTRATIVE SERVICES

The AQ staff and Heads of Services of the division disposed themselves and their staffs between the airborne force and the seaborne tail in accordance with their own particular functions. In general, the Heads of Services remained with the seaborne tail where they could be of most use in getting forward supplies to units in the first critical period. Thereafter, they were to join Rear Div HQ.

Two Ordnance personnel were flown in, and were to be employed to assist 716 Lt Composite Coy RASC with the establishment of the air re-supply dumps, and in the recognition of ordnance stores.

Detachments of LADs glided or parachuted with their brigades, and one 'Z' trailer was flown in in a RASC Hamilcar. An Advanced Workshops Detachment of eight jeeps and trailers was given a high priority to cross the RHINE.

G. REINFORCEMENTS

It was arranged that 6 Brit Airborne Div should be reinforced through the same channels as the formations on the ground. This meant that it did not receive airborne trained reinforcements. The only airborne trained reinforcements that there were, were left in ENGLAND, and would not join the division until it was withdrawn from the battle to prepare for a possible future airborne operation.

PART II

Account of the Battle

SECTION I

INTRODUCTION

The final decision that Operation PLUNDER was to take place was made by Commander-in-Chief 21 Army Group at 1700 hours 23 March. The weather forecast was reported by the experts to be favourable for the launching of Operation VARSITY, and no amendments were made to the timings originally planned for the various parts of Operation PLUNDER: they are given below:—

D-Day — 24 March 1945.

Operation	Codename	H-Hour
Assault crossing by 30 Corps (51 (H) Div) on Left of 12 Corps	TURNSCREW	2100 hours D—1
Assault crossing by 1 Cdo Bde (12 Corps)	WIDGEON	2200 hours D—1
Attack by RAF Heavy Bombers on WESEL		2230 hours D—1
Assault crossing by 15 (S) Div (12 Corps)	TORCHLIGHT	0200 hours D-Day
Assault crossing by Ninth US Army on Right of 12 Corps	FLASHPOINT	0200 hours D-Day
XVIII US Corps (Airborne) begins landing	VARSITY	1000 hours D-Day (P-Hour)

The following is the Commander-in-Chief's personal message which was read out to all troops on the eve of the battle:—

1. *On the 7th February I told you we were going into the ring for the final and last round: there would be no time limit: we would continue until our opponent was knocked out. The last round is going very well on both sides of the ring—and overhead.*

2. *In the West, the enemy has lost the Rhineland, and with it the flower of at least four armies —the Parachute Army, Fifth Panzer Army, Fifteenth Army, and Seventh Army. The First Army, further to the South is now being added to the list. In the Rhineland battles, the enemy has lost about 150,000 prisoners, and there are many more to come: his total casualties amount to about 250,000 since 8th February.*

3. *In the East, the enemy has lost all POMERANIA east of the ODER, an area as large as the Rhineland: and three more German armies have been routed. The Russian armies are within about 35 miles of BERLIN.*

4. *Overhead, the Allied Air Forces are pounding GERMANY day and night. It will be interesting to see how much longer the Germans can stand it.*

5. *The enemy has in fact been driven into a corner, and he cannot escape. Events are moving rapidly.*
    The complete and decisive defeat of the Germans is certain: there is no possibility of doubt on this matter.

6. *21 ARMY GROUP WILL NOW CROSS THE RHINE.*
    The enemy possibly thinks he is safe behind this great river obstacle. We all agree that it is a great obstacle: but we will show the enemy that he is far from safe behind it. This great Allied fighting machine, composed of integrated land and air forces, will deal with the problem in no uncertain manner.

7. *And having crossed the RHINE, we will crack about in the plains of Northern Germany, chasing the enemy from pillar to post. The swifter and the more energetic our action the sooner the war will be over, and that is what we all desire: to get on with the job and finish off the German war as soon as possible.*

8. *Over the RHINE, then, let us go. And good hunting to you all on the other side.*

9. *May "the Lord mighty in battle" give us the victory in this our latest undertaking, as He has done in all our battles since we landed in Normandy on D-Day.*

Germany
March 1945.

(Signed) B. L. MONTGOMERY
Field Marshal,
C-in-C,
21 Army Group.

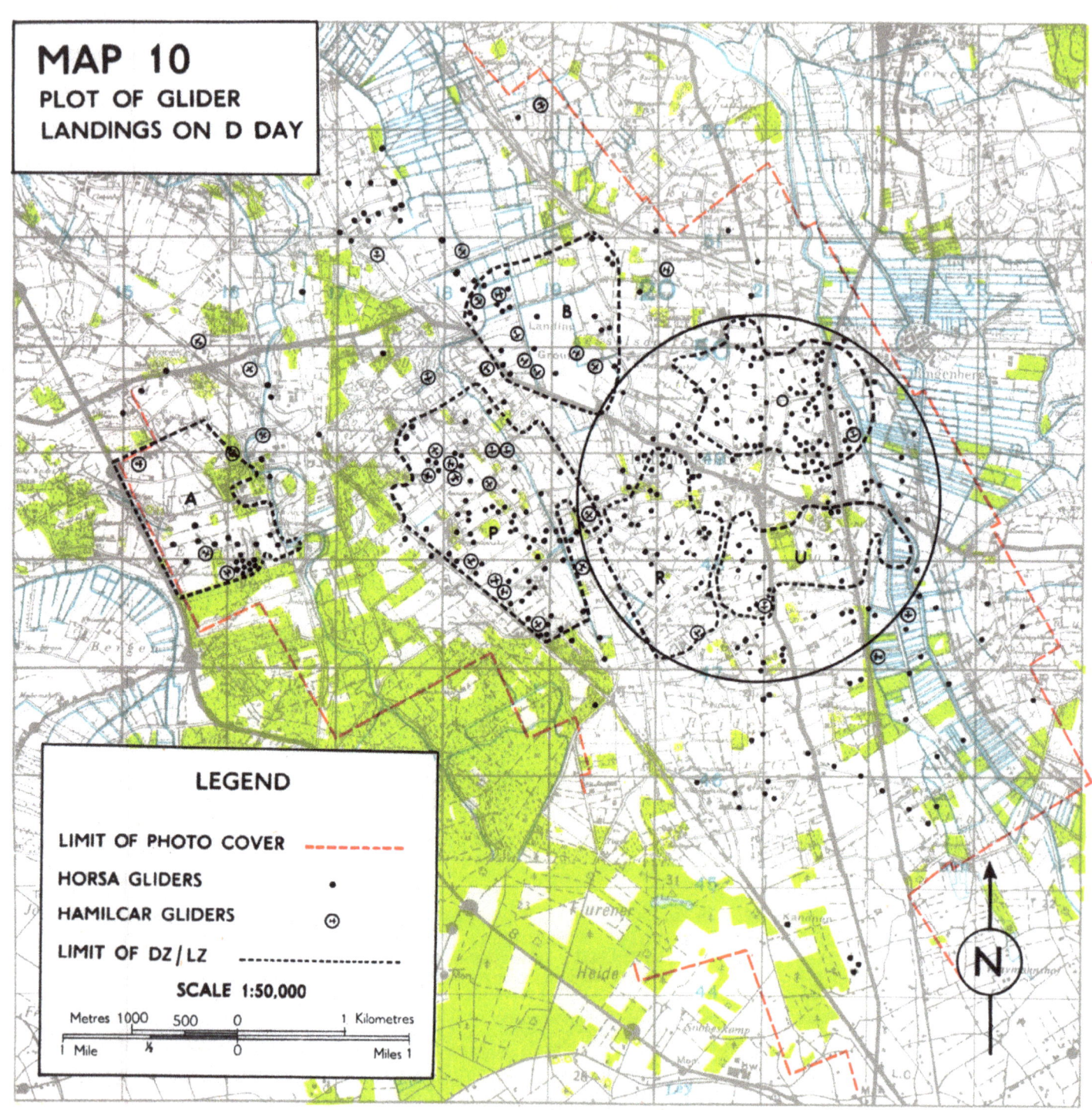

SECTION II

OPERATIONS 24 MARCH

A. FLIGHT OF 6 BRIT AIRBORNE DIV TO THE OBJECTIVE

Final Preparations

While final preparations were being made in GERMANY for the ground assault, 6 Brit Airborne Div was getting ready in ENGLAND. On 19 and 20 March the division moved to the airfield transit camps, and on 21 March briefing began. Visits were paid to units by various senior officers and on 22 March, the Divisional Commander visited the camps and addressed all troops taking part in the operation. During this period also, parachute aircraft and gliders had to be stowed with vehicles, equipment and rations, and parachutes had to be fitted.

Weather

The morning of 24 March was fine. There was no early morning mist or fog, and weather at all bases was fit for take off. Visibility was good even at 0600 hours, and soon improved to 10–12 miles. There was no cloud and the flight to the target was made in perfect flying conditions.

The emplaning and take off of 6 Airlanding Bde was watched by the Secretary of State for Air, and the Deputy Supreme Commander, AEF.

Parachute Lift

(DZs and LZs are shown on Map 5 in Part I, *facing page* 11).

61, 315 and 316 Groups of 52 Wing, IX USTCC, carried the main bodies of 3 and 5 Para Bdes, together with a jettison re-supply drop. Two hundred and forty-two C.47 and C.53 aircraft were used.

The paratroop landings commenced at 1000 hours, and successful drops were made on to DZ 'A' (3 Para Bde) and DZ 'B' (5 Para Bde). Some of the aircraft afterwards landed at bases on the Continent. Reports show that eighteen aircraft were destroyed or missing, and one hundred and fifteen damaged by flak.

Study of the photo cover showed that very accurate drops were made on both DZs, and that the jettison container drop was made as planned. Reports from the Army stated that most of the containers were readily available and were retrieved without undue inconvenience.

Glider Lift

38 and 46 Groups, RAF, despatched four hundred and forty Tug and Glider combinations. The first glider of the main lift was airborne at 0600 hours. Of the four hundred and forty aircraft only one failed to take off, the undercarriage of the tug collapsing before it became airborne.

Thirty-five gliders failed to reach the target area due to causes other than enemy action: of these sixteen were prematurely released owing to slipstream trouble, nine due to broken tow ropes, eight due to technical failure, one was late taking off and one failed to take off.

Air/Sea Rescue

Two gliders ditched in the Channel, and Air/Sea Rescue launches which had kept a constant patrol between FOLKESTONE and CAP GRIS NEZ picked up the crews safely.

Route

The fighter escort arranged by RAF Fighter Command and IX USAAF was satisfactory. No enemy fighters were met by the Airborne formations containing 6 Brit Airborne Div.

Target Area

Over the target area there was no cloud, but visibility was poor due to smoke and dust from the artillery anti-flak barrage, fires on the ground and general "fog of war". The weather, generally, was as forecast.

Glider pilots had difficulty in locating their exact landing positions after release, and the tendency was for the gliders to overshoot towards the South onto the 17 US Airborne Div area. For the most part, however, accurate landings were made in the correct areas.

During the landings, the whole area was subjected to enemy fire. Accurate SP gun and 88 mm gun fire was experienced, and it can be said that this was the first time that an airborne landing had been made on a heavily defended area. Light anti-aircraft fire was also experienced. Of the four hundred and thirty-nine aircraft despatched from 38 and 46 Groups RAF, four were known to be shot down and three were missing. Thirty-two aircraft were damaged by flak.

Dropping and Landing Zones

DZ 'A'—Of the twenty-four aircraft detailed, twenty-two reported successful releases.

DZ 'B'—Of the forty-six aircraft detailed, thirty-eight reported successful releases. This DZ appeared to experience heavier flak than the others, one aircraft was known to be shot down, one aircraft was missing, and five were damaged by flak.

LZ 'O'—All the eight aircraft detailed to tow the gliders carrying the coup-de-main party for the bridge over the River ISSEL and the road RINGENBERG–HAMMINKELN reported successful releases, and the photo covers show that the landings were accurately made.

Of the fifty-eight other aircraft detailed, fifty-three reported successful releases.

LZ 'U'—All the seven aircraft detailed to tow the gliders carrying the coup-de-main party for the bridge over the River ISSEL which was one of the objectives of 1 RUR, reported successful releases, and the photo cover shows that the landings were accurately made.

Of the fifty-nine other aircraft detailed, all reported successful releases.

LZ 'R'—Of the ninety-four aircraft detailed, ninety-three were airborne, and eighty-three reported successful releases.

LZ 'P'—Of the one hundred and forty-four aircraft detailed, one hundred and thirty-two reported successful releases.

Air Support for Fly-in

Escort over the battle area was provided by 83 Group RAF. One thousand two hundred and twenty-seven Thunderbolts and Mustangs of VIII USAAF carried out supporting sweeps ahead of the main force. Heavy bombers of VIII USAAF had made strong attacks on airfields in North West Germany on the previous days and on D-Day before P-Hour. As the result of these counter measures, the enemy was reduced to a state of impotence in the air, and no enemy air reaction was reported by the Air Forces lifting the British division.

Enemy Flak

The danger from flak had been considerably reduced by air and artillery attacks before the operation. The heaviest concentration against the 6 Brit Airborne Div landings was the light flak to the North of the DZs and LZs, and there was some scattered light flak on the run-in from the RHINE. All losses were due to flak, slight to moderate. Several aircrew were seen to bale out from aircraft shot down.

Diversionary Attacks

XV USAAF (150 heavy bombers) flew one of its longest missions from FOGGIA in ITALY to bomb BERLIN. This was done in an effort to draw enemy fighters to the East away from the invasion area.

Coastal Command aircraft carried out an attack on BORKUM.

First Tactical Air Command USAAF carried out a diversionary attack in the South.

Summary of Results: Glider Lift

Since the routes and conditions were similar for all LZs and the landings simultaneous, the LZs are not considered separately in this brief summary.

(a) *Coup-de-main (LZs 'O' 'U')*

Aircraft despatched	15
Aircraft reporting successful releases	15 (100%)
Aircraft damaged by flak	—
Aircraft unaccounted for	—

(b) *Tug Aircraft and Gliders (LZs 'O' 'U' 'P' 'R' and DZs 'A' 'B')*

Aircraft despatched	424
Aircraft reporting successful releases	387 (92%)
Aircraft damaged by flak	32 (7.5%)
Aircraft unaccounted for	7 (1.6%)
Unsuccessful sorties	35 (8.2%)

The above completes the outline results for the main 6 Brit Airborne Div glider lift on D-Day. A Plot of the Glider landings on D-Day has been made from the photo cover taken at 1115 hours on that day, and is given at Map 10.

B. ACTION OF 6 BRIT AIRBORNE DIV AFTER LANDING

3 Para Bde

The brigade had taken off at 0700 hours and three hours later, almost exactly according to plan, the leading battalion was flying in over the River RHINE. The order of landing was 8 Para Bn, Bde HQ, 1 Cdn Para Bn, 9 Para Bn, one troop 3 Para Sqn RE, 224 Para Fd Amb, followed later by the Glider element. Enemy anti-aircraft fire was moderate when the leading aircraft arrived, but became more intense for successive waves, as the enemy began to recover from the anti-flak bombardment, and the gun positions had not yet been overrun.

Units reached their RV without much difficulty.

The first task of 8 Para Bn was to clear the DZ. The battalion landed against slight anti-aircraft fire, and by 1100 hours most of the companies were present, with the bulk of their weapons, and the brigade DZ was more or less clear. The glider element arrived about the same time, and work on unloading them began. One glider landed in the wood, killing the Intelligence Officer and injuring the CO. Leaving C Coy to complete the clearing of the DZ, at 1500 hours the battalion was ordered into reserve in the area due East of the SCHNEPPENBERG feature.

1 Cdn Para Bn had captured its objective by 1130 hours. Its link up with the leading elements of 8th Battalion The Royal Scots (The Royal Regiment) (8 RS) (15 (S) Div) was effected about 1500 hours at the bridge marked on Map 11. At 1545 hours, Commander 44 (L) Inf Bde and Commander 8 RS arrived at HQ 3 Para Bde, and (according to 44 (L) Inf Bde's War Diary) "were given a rousing reception by the parachutists."

9 Para Bn collected about 85% of its original strength and moved off to capture the SCHNEPPENBERG feature at 1100 hours, with A Coy leading. An hour later, the Northern part of the feature had been cleared without opposition and twenty-two prisoners had been taken. The Southern part of the objective was clear by 1445 hours : one SP gun had been knocked out and the battalion had taken some two hundred and thirty prisoners. At 1700 hours a patrol was sent out to contact 513 Para Inf Regt (17 US Airborne Div).

At 1830 hours, 8 Para Bn was ordered to clear the area immediately West of Div HQ. It completed this task about an hour before midnight, and took up positions in the area shown on Map 11. Patrols were sent out to contact troops of 17 US Airborne Div to the South, and 6 Airlanding Bde to the East. The battalion spent the night cut off from the rest of 3 Para Bde. Casualties in the battalion for the day amounted to :—

        Killed :   4 officers and 12 other ranks.
        Wounded : 3 officers and 43 other ranks.
        Missing :   50 other ranks.

It was reckoned that on 24 March 3 Para Bde killed about 200 enemy and captured 700 more, while their own casualties totalled some 270.

At 1900 hours the first part of the land tail joined up with the brigade.

5 Para Bde

5 Para Bde began to land according to schedule at 1015 hours. Its drop was not so accurate as that of 3 Para Bde, and was made in fairly heavy anti-aircraft fire, airburst shelling and mortaring of the DZ. These factors, combined with the bad visibility, made it more difficult for the troops to get their bearings, and imposed some delay on the reorganising of battalions. The order of landing was 13 Para Bn, Bde HQ, 12 Para Bn, 7 Para Bn.

7 Para Bn supported by one troop of 6-pounders from the airlanding anti-tank battery, was soon in position covering the DZ from the North and East, having suffered about 30% casualties. At 1200 hours a reconnaissance patrol reported "FORTNUM" cross roads (see Map 11) clear of enemy and a standing patrol of platoon strength was sent there. At 1500 hours the battalion was ordered to move into reserve in the area South West of 13 Para Bn's position. The standing patrol at "FORTNUM" reported enemy in their area during the evening and at 2100 hours, had to withdraw slightly.

12 Para Bn landed slightly North West of its correct DZ, and was subjected to considerable 88 mm gun fire, while trying to reorganise : both its gliders became casualties, one being hit in the air, and the other "brewed up" as soon as it landed. 13 Para Bn landed slightly East of the true DZ, and there was therefore some delay in forming up. One of the battalion gliders, containing a mortar section, failed to arrive.

Although the farm buildings in 5 Para Bde area were mostly held by the enemy, 12 and 13 Para Bns attacked with great speed and vigour and the whole brigade objective was clear by 1530 hours. The two battalions captured over 500 prisoners during the day.

In the late afternoon a counter-attack against 13 Para Bn position from the North was beaten off, and thirty-five of the enemy were killed.

Contact with 12 DEVON (6 Airlanding Bde) was made just West of HAMMINKELN by a patrol of 13 Para Bn.

6 Airlanding Bde

6 Airlanding Bde landed about 1030 hours. Accurate tactical landings were not possible owing to the bad visibility. This was due to dust clouds caused by bombing and shelling, smoke from crashed and blazing aircraft, and smoke put down by the enemy. Parts of 17 US Airborne Div were landed in error in the same area, and gave considerable help in clearing the fairly strong opposition on the LZs during the first hour or so after landing.

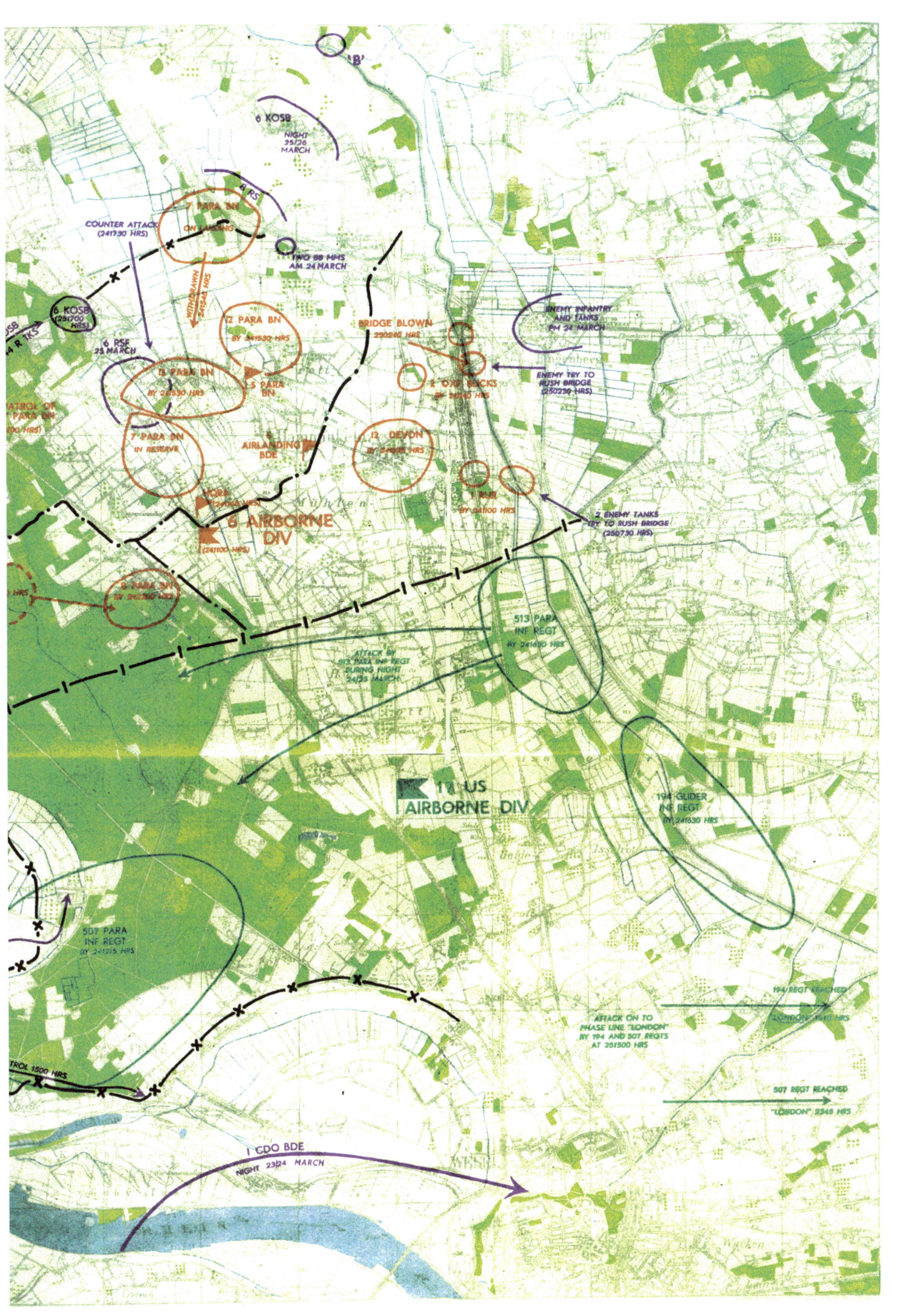

At 1045 hours, 1 RUR reported that battalion HQ and two companies had been collected and were pushing on to the objective. About one hundred prisoners were captured, and two armoured cars of 116 Pz Recce Bn (116 Pz Div) were found on the LZ and knocked out by 6-pounder fire. Although the CO was seriously injured when his glider crashed, and the Second-in-Command did not arrive with the battalion until 1540 hours, 1 RUR reported their objectives gained by 1100 hours.

2 OXF BUCKS sustained heavy casualties in the landing and were short of mortars, 6-pounders and jeeps, which had been lost in landing, or could not be got out of the gliders which were under enemy fire and observation. Nevertheless, by 1140 hours, the battalion was able to report to Bde HQ that all its objectives had been captured. By 1530 hours, everything was quiet except for spasmodic Spandau machine-gun fire. The strengths of companies by the evening was extremely reduced :—

	Officers	Other Ranks
A Coy	4	56
B Coy	2	45
C Coy	4	52
D Coy	5	58

12 DEVON was also troubled by bad visibility at the time of the landing which led to a number of glider crashes, and tactical landings could not be made as had been planned. Despite these difficulties, however, the battalion's main task, the capture of HAMMINKELN, was completed by 1300 hours, and the rest of the day was spent in strengthening the defensive position there. One company of 12 DEVON had been given the task of clearing the Div HQ area—a job which had to be done with only two platoons, as one platoon had landed in the wrong place. At 1800 hours 12 DEVON established an OP in the church tower of HAMMINKELN. The total number of killed, wounded and missing in the battalion on D-Day was 16 officers and 124 other ranks.

The only cohesive enemy force in the area was reported in RINGENBERG during the late afternoon and evening, and included a small number of tanks. 2 OXF BUCKS was too reduced in numbers to be able to deal with it, but medium artillery and RAF Typhoons attacked it, and it caused no further trouble.

The Glider Pilots were employed in the guarding and disposal of prisoners, of which some 650 were taken during the day.

Div HQ and RA Group

Main Div HQ was established at KOPENHOF by 1100 hours and thereafter had little trouble. Rear Div HQ which was about half a mile away was, however, sniped and mortared, and in the afternoon was ordered to join up with Main HQ as there were not enough troops for the protection of both areas.

As equipment became available so communications were established according to the following time table :—

Time	Link
1110 hours	Through to 3 and 5 Para Bdes on 'A' Command Net.
1128 hours	Through to 6 Airlanding Bde on 'A' Command Net.
1200 hours	Divisional Commander's Rover set arrived.
1335 hours	Rear link through to XVIII US Corps (Airborne).
1345 hours	'Q' Base set through (contact lost at 1515 hours and re-established at 0500 hours 25 March).
1600 hours	Ground re-supply link established. Lateral communication established to 17 US Airborne Div.
2100 hours	Line communication established to 5 Para and 6 Airlanding Bdes (to 3 Para Bde at 1700 hours 25 March).

It will be noted that there was no divisional administrative net and the 'B' Command net (CW) was not opened until 27 March.

HQ RA was established in the general area North of Div HQ by 1145 hours : the communications worked well, and the airborne support net was working within one hour after the start of the landing. By the afternoon, 53 (WY) Airlanding Lt Regt had eleven guns in action.

It will be remembered that, for safety reasons, guns West of the RHINE were not to be allowed to fire while the fly-in and fly-out was still going on. In the event, this restriction was relaxed slightly after 1130 hours, in cases where it could be firmly established that firing by a particular gun or troop of guns would not endanger any aircraft.

6 Airborne Armd Recce Regt

Out of a total of eight tanks flown in, four reached the rendezvous successfully, only two of them being completely fit for action. Of the others, one was missing, another overturned on landing, a third was "brewed up" and the fourth put out of action. The enemy was engaged by the serviceable tanks during the day, and with the support of a platoon of 12 DEVON and Glider Pilots, formed a strong point on the edge of the woods West of Div HQ. Attempts were made during darkness to link up with 8 Para Bn but these were not successful until daylight on D+1.

The 4.2" Mortar troop was under command the CRA and landed with 53 (WY) Airlanding Lt Regt.

C. 6 BRIT AIRBORNE DIV ADMINISTRATION

General

Considerable losses of vehicles and equipment and damage to RASC Hamilcar gliders was caused during the initial landing. Details are given in Appendix E. The figures in the Appendix are based on the final count, so that the figures do not show the 20 or 30% more items which were missing during the first few critical hours.

Due to the fact that contact was made with the airborne forces on D+1 and the great efforts by those elements which did land safely, the Commander's plan was not affected by administrative problems.

Casualties to personnel on 24 March were moderately heavy—figures are given in Appendix E. Most of the missing were subsequently accounted for. However, the casualties to AQ staff officers on divisional and brigade HQ (including the AA & QMG and DAAG at Div HQ) made administrative organisation somewhat difficult.

Maintenance by Air

Supplies jettisoned from parachute aircraft remained, to a large extent, an untapped source of supply. This was chiefly owing to the lack of transport and, in the case of 5 Para Bde, to the fact that the area covered by the jettison drop remained for some time under enemy fire. 3 Para Bde managed to gather in approximately 15 to 20% of its drop with the assistance of the Light RASC Platoon which crossed the river on the afternoon of 24 March, and was waiting to get through to the area of the supply-by-air dump. As events turned out, however, very little of this was actually required.

The Liberator re-supply arrived as planned at 1300 hours. It was carried out by two hundred and thirty-nine Liberators of VIII USAAF; fourteen Liberators were reported missing and one hundred and four were damaged by flak. The drop was moderately successful and the pattern on the ground, although rather wide by reason of the formation adopted by the aircraft, was, under the circumstances, fairly good. The planes flew in rather on the low side and some damage was done to stores through delays in parachute developments. 22 Independent Parachute Company had managed to mark the Supply Dropping Points in time, but, out of the eighty RASC personnel and twelve carriers which had left the United Kingdom, only a handful of men and two carriers were available to start work. This had increased to approximately thirty men, six carriers and three trailers by late afternoon and a plea to the depleted Airlanding brigade and RA only produced ten jeeps and trailers, and most of these were not available until just before dusk. There was a short period during the afternoon of 24 March when ammunition demands from 5 and 6 Para Bdes could not be met, but this position was rectified during the evening and a small stock was built up. It is estimated that ultimately 20% of the drop passed through the dump, but as both 5 and 6 Para Bdes were authorised to pick-up anything they could, it is probable that approximately 35% was actually recovered by the division.

During the night a signal was sent to the United Kingdom to adjust the position of the Supply Dropping Point slightly in order that subsequent supplies should fall on the best collecting ground. This adjustment proved unnecessary as, during the early hours of 25 March, a complete link-up was achieved, and Second Army cancelled all further re-supply by air.

Ground Maintenance and Link-up of Land Tail

Although ground maintenance was not in full swing until 25 March, it is most conveniently covered here. During 24 March, a dump and a report centre were established East of the RHINE, and the land elements began to cross the river under the direction of the APM. During the morning of 25 March the APM and RASC representatives contacted Div HQ to obtain locations and orders, the priority land elements began to move forward to join units, and by the late afternoon it was possible to switch 3 Para Bde to the DUKW dump for all maintenance, and the remainder of the division for supplies and petrol, oil and lubricants. The Light Transport Platoon of 716 Coy which arrived early in the afternoon was allotted out to the three brigades, as clearance of the air re-supply was no longer an urgent requirement, and brigades were feeling the acute shortage of light transport.

Medical

All field ambulances established main dressing stations according to plan. 224 Para Fd Amb began evacuation on the afternoon of 24 March, and the other two field ambulances on the following day. From 26 March, the medical situation was well under control, and evacuation was going smoothly.

Ordnance

Of the ordnance stores dropped by Hamilcar and re-supply missions, 19% of the total was actually collected into the dump. It is possible that a further 5% was used by units direct. Issues were made on the authority of Div HQ from the evening of 24 March onwards, and all demands for weapons were met. There was, however, a difficulty with wireless stations and batteries, as, except for seven 38 sets and a quantity of 38 set batteries, nothing was collected. Wireless replacements were brought forward from the DUKW dump on the evening of 25 March, but the situation during the night 24/25 March was fairly critical. Ordnance maintenance continued either from the air re-supply or the DUKW dump according to availability until 27 March when the Ordnance Field Park crossed the RHINE.

REME

Owing to the tactical situation, no recovery work could be carried out in the early stages. The 'Z' trailer landed safely and the Light Advanced Workshops detachment crossed the RHINE on the afternoon of 25 March and was joined the following day by the main workshops.

D. 17 US AIRBORNE DIV

The division was led by 507 Para Inf Regt, which began to land at 0950 hours. Two battalions landed on the proper DZ and one landed some distance to the North West of it. The main task of this regiment was to capture DIERSFORDT and the attack was launched at 1100 hours.

In spite of enemy small arms and light artillery fire on the DZ, the whole regimental group was established in its pre-selected positions shortly after midday. By the end of the day, 507 Para Inf Regt had established firm contact with 6 Brit Airborne Div to the North and 1 Cdo Bde at WESEL. It had taken about 1,000 prisoners, destroyed five tanks and destroyed or captured several batteries of artillery.

513 Para Inf Regt landed after 507 Para Inf Regt, starting at 1010 hours. Most of the regiment landed some 2,500 yards North and North East of the correct DZ, in the same area as 6 Brit Airlanding Bde around HAMMINKELN. The First Battalion lost contact with its commander, adjutant and other important officers and was not in a position to move South East to its allotted area in regimental reserve, before 1330 hours. The Second Battalion, though it took only about thirty minutes to reorganise, met considerable resistance in fighting its way to its objective. On arrival there, it was discovered that the First Battalion had already cleared it. Most of the Third Battalion landed among heavy opposition and arrived at the assembly area in three groups between 1300 and 1530 hours. It had taken its objective by 1630 hours and contacted 194 Glider Inf Regt on its Right and 6 Brit Airborne Div on its Left by 1700 hours.

The artillery battalion with 513 Para Inf Regt landed on the correct DZ. As it was alone there, considerable opposition was encountered. However, some of its guns had been assembled after half an hour, and opportunity targets near the DZ were engaged. By 1200 hours, the battalion, in spite of heavy casualties, was supporting 513 Para Inf Regt from its allotted positions, and by 1500 hours it had thirteen guns in action. During the day, the regiment captured over 1,100 prisoners and destroyed two tanks, one SP gun and two batteries of 88 mm guns.

194 Glider Inf Regt began landing on its correct LZ at 1030 hours. The First Battalion made a successful landing and had captured its objectives by 1400 hours. A few gliders of the Second Battalion landed East of the ISSEL, but the battalion captured its objectives without undue difficulty. The Third Battalion landed against heavy anti-aircraft and small arms fire, and it was some time before the LZ was clear. Objectives had been reached by 1600 hours. During the day 194 Glider Inf Regt captured 1,150 prisoners and destroyed or captured nearly fifty guns and ten tanks. 681 Glider Fd Arty Bn supporting 194 Glider Inf Regt landed on the correct LZ and fought its way to firing positions. By 1600 hours ten guns were in action out of twelve originally landed. Wireless communication was quickly established with artillery West of the RHINE, and supporting fire was being given by 1300 hours.

680 Glider Fd Arty Bn (105 mm guns) landed at 1140 hours. In spite of suffering a number of casualties on the LZ, some guns went into action at once, and by the afternoon, nine guns were in action and 900 rounds of ammunition had been assembled.

E. 12 CORPS

1 Cdo Bde

The attack by 1 Cdo Bde on WESEL (Operation WIDGEON) was launched at 2200 hours 23 March, and at 2230 hours the attack by RAF heavy bombers was put in as planned. The assault was conducted with the greatest energy and enemy resistance was not great. By first light 24 March, the whole brigade, except 1st Battalion The Cheshire Regiment (1 CHESHIRE), was in the town, although much mopping up remained to be done. By midnight, 1 Cdo Bde reported that the town was clear (a report which later proved to be somewhat premature), and that work was in progress on the clearing of a route through the debris of the town. Engineers of Ninth US Army had not however started bridging owing to enemy shelling.

15 (S) Div

15 (S) Div began Operation TORCHLIGHT at 0200 hours on 24 March. 44 (L) Inf Bde attacking on the Right, passed 8 RS and 6th Battalion The Royal Scots Fusiliers (6 RSF) across the river without encountering serious opposition. The reserve battalion, 6th Battalion The King's Own Scottish Borderers (6 KOSB) however, attracted some attention in crossing and suffered casualties from artillery fire, but it landed without difficulty and quickly captured BISLICH.

On the Left, 227 (H) Inf Bde crossed against greater opposition, and was delayed by mud on the East bank. Two battalions were, however, across by first light on 24 March but 10th Battalion The Highland Light Infantry (City of Glasgow Regiment) (10 HLI) reported enemy resistance just South of OVERKAMP and 2nd Battalion The Argyll and Sutherland Highlanders (Princess Louise's) (2 A & SH) reported a counter-attack from the direction of HAFFEN. This attack was later broken up by artillery fire.

46 (H) Inf Bde started to cross the river early in the morning, supported by 44 R Tks, the DD regiment under command of 15 (S) Div.

By midday on 24 March, 44 (L) Inf Bde had cleared the villages around BISLICH. 6 RSF captured LOH and 8 RS captured VISSEL. On the Left, resistance to 227 (H) Inf Bde was stiffer. 7th Battalion The Seaforth Highlanders (Ross-shire Buffs, The Duke of Albany's) (7 SEAFORTH) with a squadron of 44 R Tks, prepared to pass through 10 HLI and attack, first HAGENSHOF, and then MEHR. A small counter-attack from the North East was beaten off without difficulty.

During the afternoon of 24 March, 12 Corps made several contacts with XVIII US Corps (Airborne). 6 RSF established contact with 507 Para Inf Regt of 17 US Airborne Div North East of LOH. 6 KOSB occupied SCHUTTWICK and sent out a patrol which met 507 Para Inf Regt in DIERSFORDT. In the North of the 44 (L) Inf Bde sector, 8 RS made contact with 3 Para Bde of 6 Brit Airborne Div at the bridge indicated on Map 11. 46 (H) Inf Bde employed 7 SEAFORTH and a squadron of 44 R Tks to clear MEHR and on the Left 2nd Battalion The Gordon Highlanders (2 GORDONS) attacked HAFFEN.

By midnight 24 March, 15 (S) Div had made firm contact with both airborne divisions and cleared the area between 44 (L) Inf Bde and the airborne divisional objectives.

Enemy artillery fire on the river banks was not so heavy in the corps sector as further North. Ferries worked well throughout the day, class 9 rafts starting at 0630 hours on the Right and at 1215 hours on the Left. Class 50/60 rafts started at 2030 hours and the DUKW ferry at 1500 hours. By 2300 hours the first bridge, a class 9 folding boat, was completed. It was closed between 0200 and 1500 hours on 25 March to repair damage.

F. ENEMY

12 Corps summed up the enemy position at the end of D-Day in the following words:—

There were no surprises in the enemy layout opposing us. As expected 84 Inf Div proved to be in control from the LIPPE river to the area of VISSEL with from Left to Right the WESEL Garrison, 1052 GR, 1062 (Mtn) Regt and 1051 GR. Moreover, if the PW figures are to be trusted, the division seems to be well in the running for a second destruction within a period of six weeks. Our own total must be well over a thousand, while the airborne forces claim 3,500 and a high proportion of both totals must come from the luckless 84 Inf Div. Incidentally, to round off what must have been a black day for the division, its HQ was bombed this morning.

By comparison, 7 Para Div, whose Right extends on to our Left-hand neighbour's front (30 Corps), has not fared too badly. Both 19 and 21 Para Regts have been identified, but so far 20 Para Regt does not appear to have been involved.

The enemy layout as it was found to be in the VARSITY area is shown on Map 12.

G. AIR SUPPORT

Forward Visual Control Posts (FVCP)

Three Horsa gliders carried three FVCPs with jeeps into the 6 Brit Airborne Div landing zone to control direct support aircraft and provide communications with the re-supply aircraft and the 83 Group Control Centre.

All three gliders made good landings close to their appointed rendezvous and the unloading of the FVCPs for 6 and 17 Airborne Divisions was completed successfully. The spare set was burnt out after being hit by enemy gun fire.

Both FVCPs performed satisfactorily, though the value of that allotted to 17 US Airborne Div was reduced as it was not in position until the morning of D+1.

ASSU Tentacles and Communications

The first tentacle arrived by glider shortly after HQ 6 Brit Airborne Div and quickly established communication. It was sited with the FVCP. They had one exchange telephone line and a "two-to-one" line to G (Ops) and HQ RA. They had a remote control on the divisional 'A' Command Net, and, in addition, when one particular brigade was likely to require air support, a set was netted on that brigade FOO net, so that immediate "cab rank" support could be made available to a battalion if necessary. A Communication Diagram is given at Diagram 6. The GSO II (Air) at Div HQ acted as Air Liaison Officer to the FVCP.

Generally speaking air support communications were very satisfactory.

H. SUMMARY

Operations on 24 March had been thoroughly successful. XVIII US Corps (Airborne) had captured almost all its objectives. Contact had been made with 15 (S) Div and 1 Cdo Bde. Casualties generally, had been no heavier than had been anticipated. The enemy had been overwhelmed and was not in a position to take effective action against any part of the bridgehead, or to reduce the momentum of Second Army's advance.

In his report, the Commanding General of the Airborne Corps said:—

The airborne drop was of such depth that all enemy artillery and rear defensive positions were included and destroyed, reducing in one day a position that might have taken many days to reduce by ground attack only.

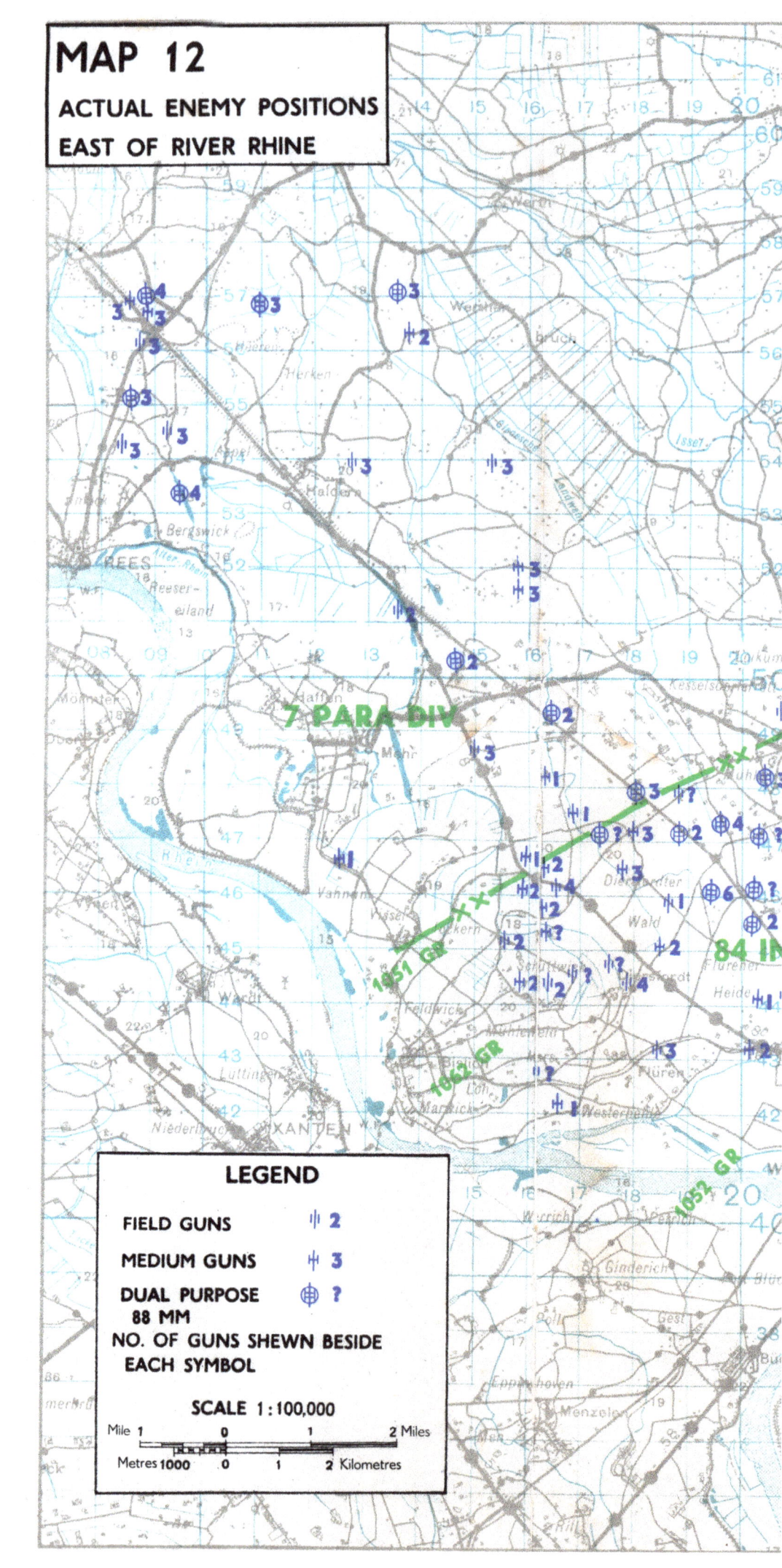

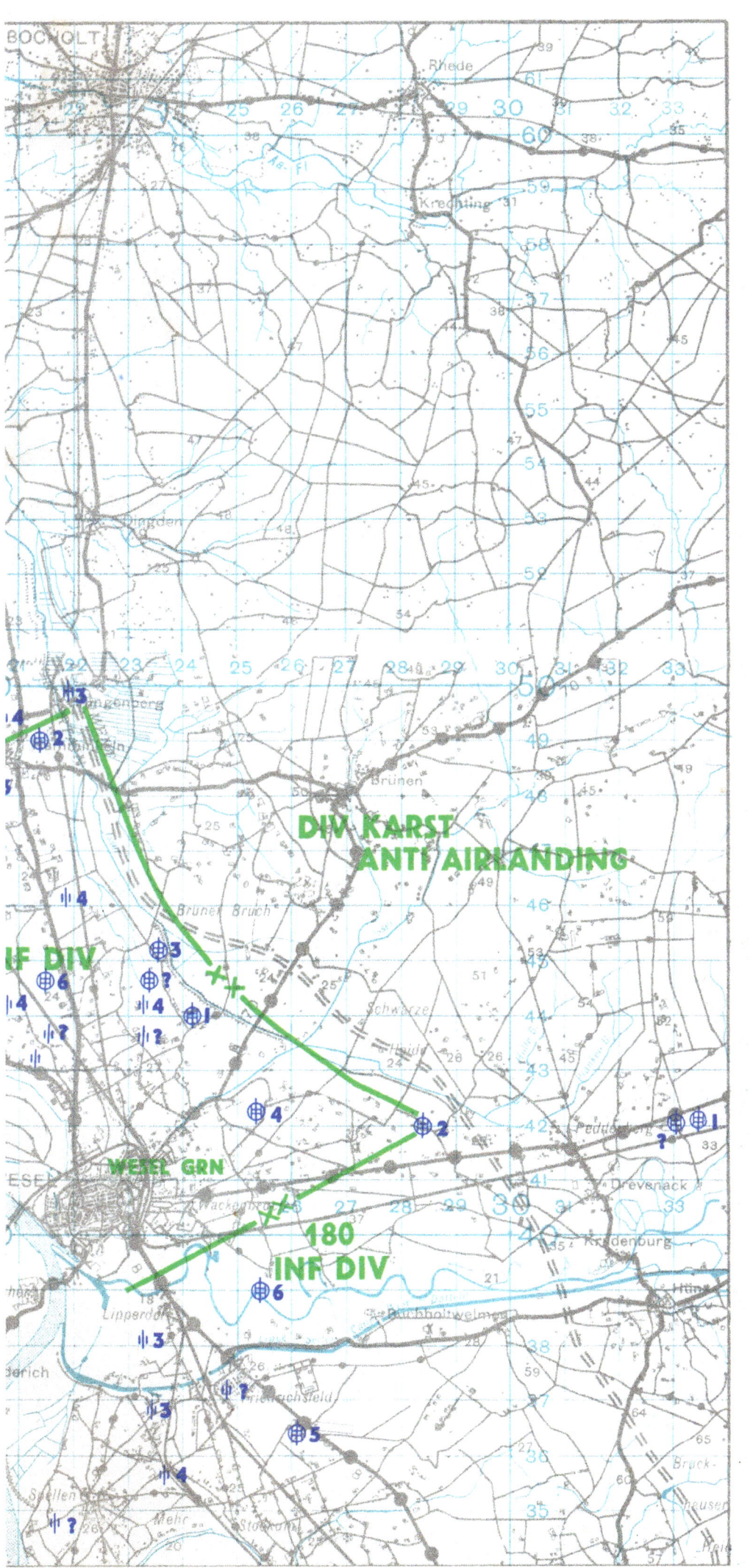

DIAGRAM 6

LAYOUT OF FVCP AND ASSU
at
HQ 6 BRIT AIRBORNE DIV

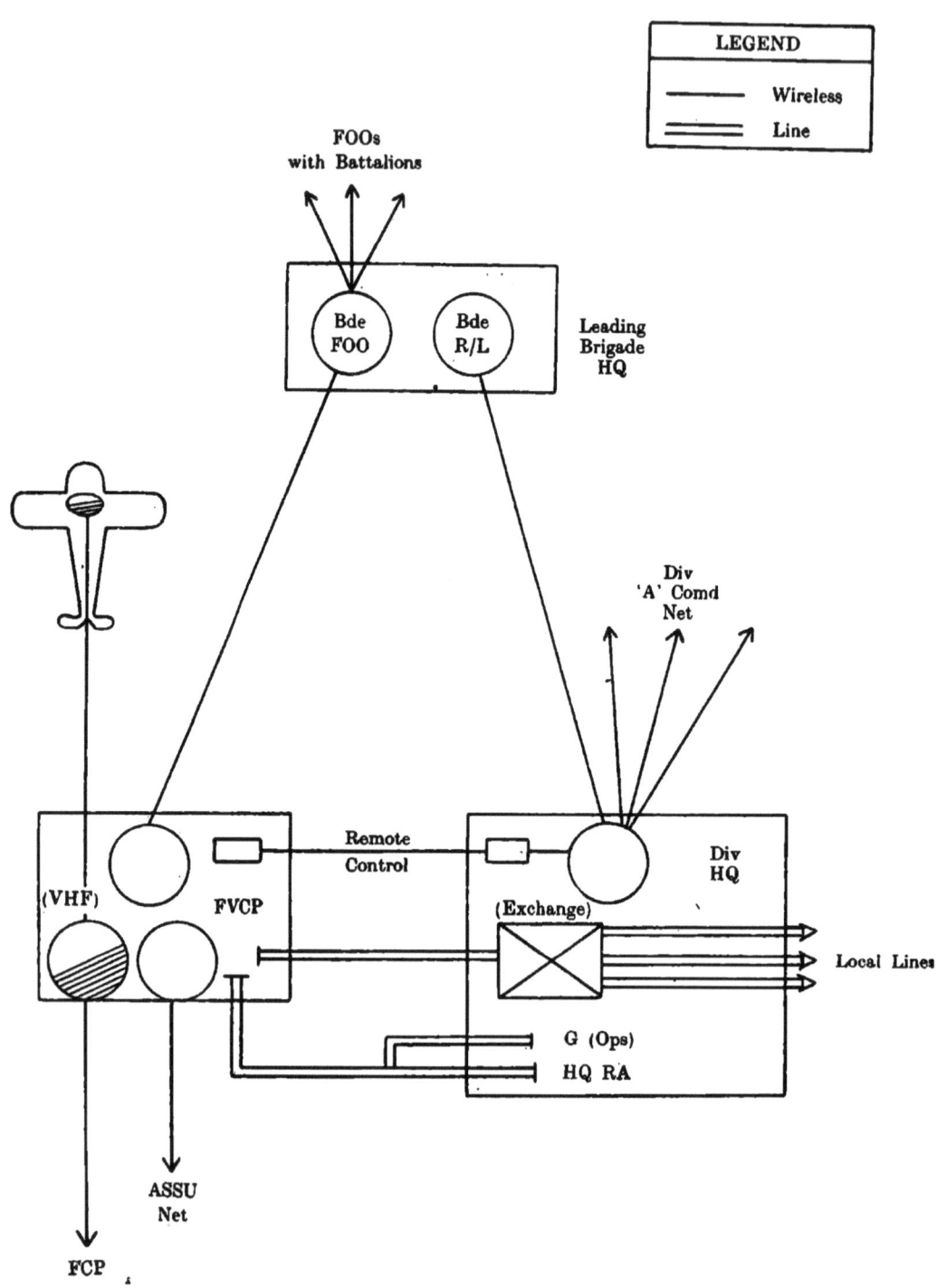

SECTION III

OPERATIONS 25 MARCH

A. CORPS COMMANDER'S ORDERS FOR 25 MARCH

Commander XVIII US Corps (Airborne) had visited HQ 6 Brit Airborne Div at 2245 hours on 24 March with Commander 17 US Airborne Div and issued his orders for the following day. His instructions were for 6 Brit Airborne Div to maintain the positions it was then occupying: for 6 Airlanding Bde to be relieved by 157 Inf Bde (of 52 (L) Div) under command 15 (S) Div during the night 25/26 March and for the Division to be prepared to advance at first light 26 March to secure phase line PARIS (see map 5). 17 US Airborne Div was to secure phase line LONDON on 25 March.

B. 6 BRIT AIRBORNE DIV

3 Para Bde

3 Para Bde spent a noisy first night though the enemy was chiefly concerned with trying to escape from his position in the woods. During the night considerable traffic from the RHINE crossings passed through the brigade area, and the Commanding Officers of 44 R Tks and 3 Tk SG visited Bde HQ.

Soon after first light 25 March, the enemy launched a counter attack with infantry and about four tanks against 1 Cdn Para Bn, but was easily driven off. The rest of the day passed comparatively quietly.

5 Para Bde

5 Para Bde spent a quiet day. Contact was made between the patrol of 7 Para Bn and 6 KOSB (15 (S) Div) at 0900 hours, at FORTNUM cross roads.

6 Airlanding Bde

During the night 24/25 March the enemy was active against the Northern part of 6 Airlanding Bde front. At 0230 hours tanks and infantry attempted to rush the bridge immediately West of RINGENBERG. After obtaining permission from Div HQ, 2 OXF BUCKS blew this bridge at 0240 hours. Shortly before dawn small parties of enemy infiltrated into the Northern edge of 2 OXF BUCKS area and set light to buildings there. In spite of efforts to clear them out some enemy remained in that area most of 25 March.

Fighting patrols were sent out at first light 25 March by 5 Para Bde to close the gap between its area and 6 Airlanding Bde. 5 Para Bde was also warned to be prepared to relieve 6 Airlanding Bde of responsibility for the defence of HAMMINKELN should 12 DEVON have to be used to restore the situation in 2 OXF BUCKS area. This did not however prove necessary. At 0730 hours two enemy tanks attempted to rush the bridge in 1 RUR area, but were driven off, one tank being destroyed and the other damaged by a 17-pounder covering the bridge.

During the day a continuous air "cab rank" was maintained over the area and a total of about twelve targets was attacked with good results. Tac R later reported only slight movement on the roads leading in to the bridgehead.

At 1045 hours, B Sqn 44 R Tks (DD) arrived in the area and moved into the vicinity of 6 Airlanding Bde HQ. One battery of SP anti-tank guns also arrived and a troop was positioned to protect each of the bridges.

Further attacks on enemy tanks were made by Typhoons during the afternoon.

During the evening HAMMINKELN was shelled by an enemy SP gun in position to the East of 1 RUR.

During the evening the brigade area was handed over to 157 Inf Bde (52 (L) Div) under command 15 (S) Div. The latter assumed command at 0600 hours 26 March, to enable 6 Airlanding Bde to continue the advance.

6 Gds Armd Bde

Left Flank Squadron 3 Tk SG arrived at HAMMINKELN about 1700 hours and was followed three hours later by the rest of the battalion, which was kept under command 6 Brit Airborne Div in reserve.

C. 17 US AIRBORNE DIV

Part of this division was employed in the morning in helping to tidy up the situation in WESEL (see paragraph D below).

17 US Airborne Div launched an attack with 194 Glider Inf Regt and 507 Para Inf Regt at 1500 hours to seize phase line LONDON. 194 Glider Inf Regt advancing against light resistance with no enemy artillery or mortar fire reached its objectives by 1800 hours. 507 Para Inf Regt met stiffer resistance in the vicinity of WESEL, but had two battalions on LONDON before midnight.

D. 12 CORPS

1 Cdo Bde

The position in WESEL on the morning of D+1 was not entirely satisfactory. 1 Cdo Bde was having some difficulty in getting heavy weapons across the river. The crossing was being shelled and the Buffaloes which had been working continuously for 24 hours were in need of maintenance. The enemy was still sensitive about our hold on the place and during the early morning had put in a counter attack against 45 (Royal Marine) Commando in the factory area North East of the town.

To tidy up the position, 507 Para Inf Regt of 17 US Airborne Div was ordered to make firm contact with 1 Cdo Bde North West of WESEL. This link up took place at 1330 hours. 46 (Royal Marine) Commando then pushed South through the town to meet the men of 1 CHESHIRE who were trying to make contact with the Americans on the South bank of the River LIPPE. At 1400 hours 1 Cdo Bde passed to under command XVIII US Corps (Airborne), and was attached to 17 US Airborne Div.

15 (S) Div

In the Centre during the night the enemy reacted again to 12 Corps extension of the bridgehead and attempted a counter attack on MEHR. As in his previous efforts, this merely attracted increased artillery fire and the attack was broken up, but not before some infiltration had occurred.

At 1100 hours a mobile force of 6 KOSB and the DD regiment (44 R Tks) attacked North East with the object of capturing the bridge over the River ISSEL at GERVERSHOF (marked 'B' on Map 11), passing through the North West corner of 3 and 5 Para Bde positions. By 2300 hours good progress to within one mile of the bridge had been made. A sharp battle was fought during the morning against an enemy defensive position at the edge of the wood North West of 13 Para Bn; this position was held by SP guns which blocked the route of advance. 46 (H) Inf Bde found progress slow in the woods East of HAFFEN, but 2nd Battalion The Glasgow Highlanders (2 GLAS H) cleared the Southern area and made a firm base for 2 A and SH, which was temporarily under command 46 (H) Inf Bde, to attack to the North through the woods.

By midnight, 6 KOSB had crossed the autobahn and was approaching the bridge. 46 (H) Inf Bde cleared the woods East of HAFFEN and 2 GLAS H made contact with 7 SEAFORTH at the bridge over the water obstacle (marked 'C' on Map 11). 9th Battalion The Cameronians (Scottish Rifles) (9 CAMERONIANS) spent the day in perhaps the heaviest fighting on the divisional front, in an attempt to clear the small villages North of MEHR.

E. ENEMY

Although there was more opposition to 12 Corps and XVIII US Corps (Airborne) on 25 March than on the previous day, this was mainly on the flanks, and was not very determined. The Germans had committed 15 PG Div, one of the divisions of 47 Pz Corps, against 30 Corps in the REES sector, where resistance had been very much stronger.

F. SUMMARY

Progress on 25 March was again satisfactory, although for the most part the airborne formations maintained the positions they had occupied the day before, with only slight adjustments. The enemy had still not been able to seal off the bridgehead, and the build-up was proceeding according to schedule.

In his report on Operation VARSITY, Commander XVIII US Corps (Airborne), Major General RIDGWAY, came to the following conclusions:

1. *Concept and planning were sound and thorough, and execution flawless.*

2. *The impact of the airborne divisions, at one blow, completely shattered the hostile defence, permitting prompt link-up with the assaulting 12 Corps, 1 Cdo Bde and Ninth Army to the South.*

3. *The rapid deepening of the bridgehead materially increased the rapidity of bridging operations, which, in turn, greatly increased the rate of build-up on the East bank, so essential to subsequent successes.*

4. *The insistent drive of the Corps to the East, and the rapid seizure of key terrain in the DULMEN and HALTERN areas, were decisive contributions to this operation, and to subsequent developments, as by it both British and US armour were able to debouch into the North German plain at full strength and momentum.*

5. *In planning and execution, the co-operation of participating air forces, both British and American, I consider completely satisfactory. There was no enemy air interception. The fighter bombers, in their counter-flak role, were as effective as could have been expected. The air re-supply by heavy bombers was timely, and met a critical need. Troop delivery by IX Troop Carrier Command was on time, and with minor exceptions, in the correct areas.*

6. *I wish particularly to record that throughout both planning and execution, the co-operation and actual assistance provided by the Commanders, Staff and troops of the British formations under which this Corps has served, which it commanded, or with which it was associated, left nothing to be desired. For my part, I have never had a more satisfying professional service in combat, nor more agreeable personal relations with participating commanders.*

SECTION IV

SUBSEQUENT OPERATIONS

After 25 March operations proceeded rapidly according to plan. Phase line NEW YORK was reached on 26 March and phase line PARIS on 27 March : by the time the latter was reached enemy resistance was very weak and XVIII US Corps (Airborne) was ordered to advance on the line DORSTEN—WULFEN—LEMBECK. On 28 March 6 Brit Airborne Div captured ERLE and later that night LEMBECK. It then passed to command 8 Corps. 17 US Airborne Div captured WULFEN.

Before daylight on 29 March 507 Para Inf Regt had relieved 6 Gds Armd Bde in HALTERN and by 1000 hours the latter formation had captured DULMEN.

HQ XVIII US Corps (Airborne) closed down East of the RHINE at 0600 hours 30 March, all remaining British units under command passed to command 8 Corps and American units to command XIX US Corps (Ninth US Army).

The progress of Second Army up to 31 March is shown by the following extract from its own history :—

There were East of the River RHINE, under command of Second Army, eight infantry divisions, four armoured divisions, two airborne divisions and four independent armoured brigades. All initial objectives had been gained, the defence lines of the enemy had been broken and Second Army was 40 miles on from the river.

It was estimated that 30,000 casualties were inflicted on the enemy during these operations while in the period 24–31 March, Second Army incurred losses to the extent of 233 officers and 2491 other ranks.

Only one week after the assault crossing the Commander-in-Chief was thus able to give as his intention :—

To exploit the present situation rapidly, and to drive hard for the line of the River ELBE so as to gain quick possession of the plains of Northern GERMANY.

Second Army will operate strongly to secure the line of the River ELBE between WITTENBERGE and HAMBURG.

In less than six weeks the war with GERMANY was over.

PART III

Personal Accounts of Actions for Study

SECTION I

INTRODUCTORY LECTURE

The Introductory Lecture to be given before the tour of the VARSITY Battlefield may be based on the accounts given in this section. The appointments held at the time of the operation by the officers who wrote the accounts are also shown where applicable. The total time taken to give the Introductory Lecture if all the accounts are included would be about forty minutes.

A. BACKGROUND OF OPERATION VARSITY
Notes prepared by
Major General E. L. BOLS, CB, DSO,
(General Officer Commanding 6th British Airborne Division)

"1. Operation VARSITY was the last major airborne operation of the war and was, therefore, an endeavour to profit from the experience and lessons of all the previous airborne operations, both the enemy's and our own.

"2. It took place at a stage in the war when the ultimate victory was no longer in doubt. The enemy morale allowed chances to be taken, giving rise to opportunities to be seized, which could not have been prudently planned for earlier in the contest.

"3. The 28 days for final planning and preparations were, thanks only to the excellent weather throughout, time enough, but only just time enough.

It was possible to give the whole division re-training in its airborne role. In this connection it should be noticed how wise it had been to take in 'theatre reinforcements', who were untrained in the airborne role, during the ground fighting. These were shed before the preparations for VARSITY and replaced by ready trained airborne reinforcements in the U.K. who then only had to be integrated into experienced units and sub-units.

Had it not been for the good weather, commanders and staff might have found it impracticably difficult to attend the many necessary co-ordinating conferences at the HQs concerned in the U.K., FRANCE and BELGIUM.

"4. A planning factor, which may become indistinct with time, is the practical difficulty of last minute co-ordination, briefing, control and security when the formation has of necessity to be dispersed to such a large number of airfields covering a wide area some time before take off.

"5. In spite of the intelligence available about it, and the positive action to neutralize it, the enemy light flak proved an uncomfortable factor.

Tactical landings close to the objective, with their obvious advantages in speed and surprise, can easily be thrown into confusion if the enemy flak is too effective.

Conversely, if the means employed to overcome the flak immediately before the 'fly-in' cause too much smoke and dust to rise, the bad visibility thus caused may also confuse the tactical landings.

Even when things go well, a number of landings are made in the wrong place due to unpredictable causes. For these misplaced personnel to rejoin the main battle quickly and effectively it is necessary for them to have studied, and to have in their possession, maps covering a far wider area than that selected for their dropping and landing zones.

"6. Formation headquarters need battle experience every bit as much as do the fighting troops. In this connection it should be noted that XVIII US Corps HQ was a well experienced fighting formation HQ, so very necessary for the successful outcome of this quickly planned fast moving operation.

"7. It is a platitudinous fact that no two airborne operations have been or are likely to be ever similar in detail. The battle winning factor in any 'quick link-up' type of operation has been and will be, concentration on the ground in sufficient numbers to overwhelm the opposition in spite of the initial handicaps of reduced mobility and light armament inherent in the vertical assault."

B. AIR BACKGROUND AND MAJOR PLANNING
Notes prepared by
Group Captain K. B. B. CROSS, CBE, DSO, DFC,
to cover points not included in Part I, Section VII.

Air Superiority

"Air superiority is the first factor to be considered in the planning of any airborne operation, and this was well appreciated by the Commander-in-Chief 21 Army Group who had written previously :-
The first and basic principle is that you must win the Air Battle before you embark on a land or sea battle. If this is not done then operations on land will be conducted at a great disadvantage. Once the Air Battle is won, then Air power is available to provide the ground forces with direct forms of assistance.

"The term Air Battle is slightly misleading, in that it implies that at some stage in a war a decisive result can be achieved, whereas in fact, the Air Battle is continuous and can only be completely won when all the enemy's combat aircraft are destroyed together with his capacity to produce more. It would therefore seem to be more correct to say *that a satisfactory situation in the air must be achieved before you embark on a land or sea battle.*

"At the time this operation was contemplated a satisfactory situation in the air had been achieved and considering its overriding importance, it is as well to examine how it had come about.

"The brunt of the air fighting in North-West EUROPE had been borne for at least two years previous to 1945 by the strategic Air Forces of the Allies in particular RAF Bomber Command and VIII USAAF. By striking at targets inside GERMANY they had in effect ensured that the main air battle took place away from the area of land operations. This was particularly true of the period under review, when highly successful campaigns against the German oil and transportation system had made it essential for the enemy to retain what was left of his air forces, for the defence of the REICH. In addition, the direct effect of the attacks on oil and transportation on the mobility of his armed forces should be remembered.

"The Tactical Air Forces part in obtaining this "satisfactory situation in the air" must not be overlooked. While the bulk of the air fighting had taken place in GERMANY before March 1945, it had been their responsibility to maintain a satisfactory degree of air superiority over the Allied Land bases. This task had been faithfully discharged and by March a degree of air superiority amounting to air supremacy was being maintained over the battle area.

"It is quite certain that had this satisfactory situation not existed, it would have been impossible, on the air side, to execute an Airborne operation of the magnitude of VARSITY with much hope of success. No acceptable degree of security to the long stream of transport aircraft, tugs and gliders could have been guaranteed by means of close fighter escort, fighter cover or by purely local air operations alone.

Landing of gliders

"In selecting the LZs for the gliders and the DZs for the paratroops, the aim was to land the troops in tactical groups as near as possible to their initial objectives. This was the first time this method of landing had been used for a complete division. In addition the troop-carrying gliders were planned to land on the outside of the LZs, and so give protection during the unloading of the heavy equipment which was to land in the centre of the LZs.

"The planned tactics over the LZs were different for British and American aircraft. The British aircraft approached and released at 2,500 feet, whereas the American aircraft were at 500 feet. The greater height of release for British aircraft was made possible by a timed glide, turn and approach drill evolved and practised after ARNHEM.

Re-supply

"To guard against the possibility of dropping re-supply equipment outside the perimeter of our own airborne troops, five Supply Dropping Points (SDPs) were selected beforehand. Immediately before any re-supply the airborne troops were to signal which SDP was to be used.

Weather

"In airborne operations the weather is a vital factor. Reasonable conditions of wind, visibility and cloud base are required at the Base, throughout the route and at the objective. To reduce the good weather area at bases in the UK all the aircraft for 6 Brit Airborne Div were concentrated in EAST ANGLIA. This concentration also simplified communications and control, but at the same time caused some congestion in forming up the aircraft and gliders in the ESSEX area."

C. PARTICIPATION OF TACTICAL AIR FORCES

Notes prepared by
Wing Commander P. E. ROSIER, DSO, OBE, RAF.
(Group Captain, Operations, 84 Group, RAF)

Introduction

"From the point of view of RAF planning at Tactical Group level, Operation VARSITY was considered an integral part of Operation PLUNDER. The preliminary phases in the air operations were destined to facilitate the task of the ground forces in both operations. It was agreed however that the Tactical Air Force would need to plan definite operations to take place on D-Day in support of Operation VARSITY.

"During the planning stage it was apparent that various air problems would arise which would require detailed co-ordination not only between air and ground forces, but also between the various air forces employed in support of the operation. These notes detail these problems as they occurred to the Air Staff at 83 Group and explain how they were overcome.

Responsibilities of 83 Group, RAF

"The 2 TAF Air Plan outlined the responsibilities of 83 Group, the RAF Tactical Group allied to the Second Brit Army, in support of this operation. These responsibilities included:—

(a) The provision of air cover over the area of the airborne landings.
(b) An anti-flak programme.
(c) The provision of direct air support (impromptu).
(d) Armed reconnaissances.

"It was considered that the resources of 83 Group were insufficient in themselves to complete the above tasks and it was therefore decided that additional forces from 84 Group and 29 US Tactical Air Command (29 USTAC) should be made available. 83 Group was then given the further responsibility of co-ordinating the operations of these additional forces.

Air Cover

"The protection of the airborne forces from air attack on their way to the landing and dropping zones was entrusted to aircraft of Fighter Command RAF, IX USAAF, and 2 TAF. In order to avoid confusion between aircraft of these different air forces, and to facilitate control, it was decided that fighter aircraft of Fighter Command and IX USAAF should escort the airborne stream as far as the West bank of the RHINE and that 83 Group should be responsible for its safety East of the RHINE.

"83 Group carried out this task by covering the area with fighter patrols besides carrying out sweeps well to the Eastward of the dropping zones. At the same time, operations were so co-ordinated that aircraft from 84 Group and 29 USTAC were also playing their part in this task.

Anti-Flak Programme

"It was appreciated that enemy anti-aircraft fire might well be one of the greatest obstacles to the success of this operation. An anti-flak committee, composed of representatives from the Army and Royal Air Force was set up at HQ 83 Group to study the disposition of enemy anti-aircraft guns within the area. Anti-aircraft positions were plotted from air photographs and other intelligence and flak maps were produced.

"The anti-flak programme consisted of counter battery-bombardment by artillery, the dropping of fragmentation bombs by medium bombers, and direct attacks on gun positions by fighter bombers using cannon and rocket projectiles. 83 Group was responsible for co-ordinating the anti-flak activities of the air forces placed under its operational control. The attack by fighter bombers was timed to coincide with the arrival of the airborne stream over the battle area. Attacks had to be confined to an area East of the dropping and landing zones and the uncompleted autobahn East of the River ISSEL was made the bomb line.

Direct Air Support

"Arrangements had to be made whereby the airborne forces could be provided with the air support they required. This was accomplished through the medium of contact jeeps and aircraft at readiness in the air. Controllers were provided by 83 Group to take charge of the available contact jeeps within 6 Brit Airborne Div. Sufficient communications were made available to enable these controllers not only to ask for air support, but also to brief pilots in the air for attacks on particular targets. To provide the quickest possible air support during the actual operation, 83 Group laid on "cab ranks" of aircraft which were on call for any support needed by the airborne forces.

Armed Reconnaissances

"A heavy programme of armed reconnaissance carried out by aircraft of VIII USAAF, 83 Group, 84 Group and 29 USTAC, was maintained in support of this operation. 83 Group was given an area extending to approximately fifty miles East of the battle area, within which it had the task of co-ordinating the armed reconnaissance activities of its own aircraft and aircraft of 84 Group and 29 USTAC: 84 Group was made responsible for the Northern part of the area, 83 Group the central part and 29 USTAC the Southern part."

D. FIRE SUPPORT BY 12 CORPS

By Major G. S. HEATHCOTE, MBE
(GSO II HQ RA 12 Corps)

Fire support before H Hour

"The artillery resources and the actual details of the fire plans CLIMAX and CARPET are given in Part I of the book, Section VIII.

"CLIMAX was intended as a softening bombardment directed against known enemy localities in the area of the drop. The targets were to be selected by CsRA of the Airborne Divisions. In the event the Artillery Commander of 17 US Airborne Div drew three "goose eggs" on the map and left the selection of individual targets within that area to RA 12 Corps. This worked fairly well as planning was being done from defence overprints available to both HQ and resources were liberal. 6 Brit Airborne Div made a more detailed plan but this arrived at HQ RA 12 Corps on 22 March, after the fire plans had had to go to press. It was implemented by telephone and was not as satisfactory as it might have been had it arrived earlier, or if it had been possible for more frequent contact to have been made between divisions and RA 12 Corps.

"CARPET was an anti-flak bombardment. It was due to last for thirty minutes, but on the day it lasted only twenty-two minutes owing to the early arrival of the fly-in. There was a very large number of targets and it was not possible to do a "milk round" but only to spread the effort over all targets. Owing to the fact that some targets were very distant, only certain guns could engage them. New targets were being added right up to P Hour and had to be included in the fire plan by issuing amendments by R/T.

Support of the Airborne Forces after landing

"The regrouping which took place at P Hour has been covered in Part I of the book (Section VIII, paragraph B (iii)). CsRA 52 (L) and 53 (W) Divs were in fact "purveyors of fire power" from the West bank for their opposite numbers in 6 Brit and 17 US Airborne Divs respectively. They were able through their communications, not only to call for the fire of their own guns but also those of the rest of the Corps artillery if necessary. It should be noted also that each of these divisional artilleries had a medium regiment (two in the case of 52 (L) Div) deployed well forward. In the case of 6 Brit Airborne Div it was the medium regiments of RA 52 (L) Div which alone were able to provide direct support to 5 Para and 6 Airlanding Bdes. Airborne FOOs were able to communicate direct with regiments of RA 52 (L) and 53 (W) Divs, as well as via the link from artillery commanders of the Airborne Divisions to the CsRA on the ground, West of the RHINE.

Subsequent Movement and Regrouping

"An early priority to cross the river was given to guns of 17 US Airborne Div (land tail), and to 6 and 25 Fd Regts and 146 SP A Tk Bty, which were to join 6 Brit Airborne Div. In addition a number of changes of command were taking place about this time. Three Corps Artillery HQ were acutely interested in these actions—RA 12 Corps, RA 8 Corps and Artillery HQ XVIII US Corps. The result was a "telephone battle" which continued for some time until the re-grouping was completed."

E. FIRE SUPPORT PROBLEMS OF 6 BRIT AIRBORNE DIV

By Colonel W. McC. T. FAITHFULL, DSO
(CRA 6th British Airborne Division)

"From the outline plan it was obvious that the maximum number of infantry would be necessary for the job; at the same time the available air lift was limited.

"3 Para Bde would be in range of field guns from the West bank of the RHINE, whilst the area was thickly wooded. For this brigade, therefore, it would not be necessary to provide airborne field artillery support, nor would the anti-tank problem be very acute.

"However, neither of the other two brigades would be within range of any guns from the West bank of the RHINE except medium and heavy. Therefore the Airborne Light Regiment would be essential for the purposes of defensive fire, counter-mortar and close support of any minor attacks. And although the Glider Brigade had its own 6 pounders, a full anti-tank layout would have to be flown in, for 5 and 6 Bdes and divisional reserve.

"In spite of this, the air lift being so limited, it was obvious that gunners as well as RAC and RE would have to be cut to a scale below that which was desirable.

"The whole of the Airborne Light Regiment was necessary, and a saving in gliders was effected by flying in two batteries, each of twelve guns instead of the normal three batteries each of eight guns. At the same time a saving was effected by flying in only two of the three anti-tank batteries; one of these batteries gave additional support to the Glider Brigade and at the same time provided a minimum amount of support for 3 Para Bde. It was however realised that this was cutting things rather fine so a re-supply of 6 pounders by parachute drop was arranged for the evening of D Day.

"The Forward Observer Battery had to be flown in complete to take advantage of the fire power available in the massed guns on the West bank of the RHINE.

"In short, therefore, close support was provided by the one Airborne Light Regiment only for two of the brigades, whilst that for the third brigade was provided by RA 52 (L) Div from West of the RHINE.

"The Forward Observer Battery is a parachute unit of FOOs and signallers who land with brigades, providing one FOO per battalion. It is the unit responsible for the entire fire control from supporting ground force artillery for the airborne forces; as a secondary role it can shoot the guns of the Airborne Light Regiment. Communications are, of course, one hundred per cent R/T, and the wireless ranges involved are much greater than in normal artillery work.

"It should be realised that the airborne battle differs from normal in that all three brigades are "up", or in the line. This makes the artillery problem all the harder because the Forward Observer Battery can only provide a total of nine FOOs—with the Airborne Light Regiment providing a further three or four. Taking into account the possible casualty rate the number of available OPs is none too large.

"The planning was rather complicated because 12 Corps had under it three, so to speak active, divisions all of whom were to be engaged in the battle at the same time, i.e. 15 (S) Div, 6 Brit Airborne Div and 17 US Airborne Div. The dovetailing of fire plans therefore presented some difficulty.

"The airborne fire plan in terms of task traces and communications cannot be finalised until after each of the three brigade plans is firm. This final airborne plan then had to be submitted to 12 Corps for final agreement and necessary adjustment to make it fit in with the other two divisions. The fact that such planning was done in ENGLAND whilst 12 Corps was in HOLLAND made things no easier.

"A word about the planning within the division. Because the division fights three brigades "up' the CRA has to plan with the three brigadiers simultaneously. Co-ordination is correspondingly more difficult than is the case in a normal land battle when it may be expected that only one or at the most two brigades are involved at any one moment.

"The smallness of the airborne perimeter presupposes congestion, and in the planning one even goes so far as to site individual anti-tank gun positions from air photographs, a procedure which has been found to be about 80 or 90% effective.

"A further complication arises from the large number of airfields from which the gunner units take off. Whereas the guns of the Light Regiment may take off from only two airfields and land on one LZ, its OP parties may take off from different airfields in order to fly in and land with the appropriate brigades and battalions.

"The Forward Observer Battery will be split up on to as many airfields as the nine battalions may take off from. Similarly the anti-tank batteries will take off from several airfields with a view to landing in the vicinity of each brigade DZ. This all leads to difficulties of briefing and control.

"It will be of interest to hear the times at which the various artillery communications were through and established.

"The FOOs with 3 Para Bde were through to the guns on the West bank of the RHINE by P+15 (P was the Hour at which the first aircraft appeared over the area); 5 Para Bde was through at P+35 minutes, whilst 6 Para Bde was not through until P+45 minutes thanks to casualties and the fact that the FOOs were travelling in gliders which did not appear over the area until something like P+30 minutes.

"The control set at HQ RA did not land until P+40 minutes, but had reached its station and got through by P+60 minutes having the whole group on net at P+80 minutes. These timings were better than had been expected and were the result of much hard training.

"It is sometimes forgotten how vitally important R/T communications are to airborne troops. The loss of one or two key nets when landing by parachute, or because of a damaged glider, may create an impossible situation. It is therefore considered essential to fly in a duplicate set for every station considered important. This might seem expensive in air lift but has been proved correct in every airborne operation and cannot be ignored. Actually the loss of gunner R/T sets in this operation was something just under 50%."

F. RAF ASPECT OF AIRBORNE PLAN

By Squadron Leader I. C. MUSGRAVE, OBE, DFC, RAF

(Commanding 296 (Airborne Forces) Squadron RAF)

"This report deals only with the part played by 296 and 297 Sqns, each supplying thirty Halifax/Horsa combinations, and operating from RAF Station EARLS COLNE, ESSEX. These two squadrons were the first Airborne Forces squadrons to be formed, and were associated with the airborne operations in SICILY, NORMANDY and ARNHEM, apart from their Special Operations Executive and Special Air Service experience. Due to the shielding of personnel by the Air Council, the knowledge of airborne technique was not dispersed by normal RAF "operational tour" postings and consequently the standard of efficiency had reached its peak by March 1945. It will be exceedingly difficult to attain this standard at an early stage in any future war due to the limitations of aircraft availability for airborne exercises, and the dispersion of personnel with the necessary knowledge at low level.

"For Operation VARSITY therefore, the organisation before take-off, which often determines the efficiency of the whole operation, ran very smoothly. Briefing, which was attended by the Deputy Supreme Commander AEF, was most comprehensive, and he expressed the opinion that it was the best he had ever heard. I consider that the briefing played a very large part in the Station achieving the highest success figures of the Group. Of the sixty Horsas to be delivered, fifty-nine released at the correct point, and the remaining one suffered a broken tow rope and landed behind our own lines. The failure was due to slipstream from preceding aircraft, and the remnants of the rope still attached to the Halifax were brought back for examination in accordance with the briefing.

"To revert to the take-off, sixty combinations took off in fifty-six minutes, of which thirty had been pre-marshalled using 500 yards of our 2,000 yard runway. There was a tendency to overload Horsa gliders by soldiers, not unnaturally, adding extra ammunition. This practice will not occur in future. The organisation necessary to ensure the successful take-off of such large numbers of combinations is too long to be discussed here, but suffice it to say that the direction of take-off decided by the weather decision on D-1 was most fortunately the right one. Moving one hundred and twenty airframes when aircrews should be resting is not a good start for an operation and wind forecasts so far in advance are not always accurate.

"The form up was fairly good, but with the usual tendency to straggle at the back. Course was set on time, in excellent weather with no cloud, and very good visibility. On joining the main stream behind some hundred Stirlings it was observed that they were also strung out, intermingling their Station serials. Aircraft varied in height by some thousands of feet in an effort to avoid slipstream but a fair effort was made to close up and release at the right height at the target.

"The route was simple, with simple navigational aids. When crossing the Channel, DUNKIRK was clearly visible due to the enormous visibility. Since airborne forces flying East could have only one significance for the enemy, it is apparent that if the enemy forces in DUNKIRK had made the right signal, and it had reached the right person, it might have had a most unpleasant effect.

"Visibility was good up to the RHINE, but the East bank was fairly thick with a grey/white smoke, streaked with black in places. This was, as nearly as I can remember, at 1033 hours, as my serial was three minutes early. The head of the stream had been eight minutes early, and it was almost impossible to lose this three minutes without some forms of dog-leg. The effect of this early arrival on the gunners fire plan has been discussed elsewhere. The cause was partially a tail wind, and partially a slight miscalculation of airspeed in the planning stage.

"The visibility at 2,500 feet over the LZ was excellent, with the smoke cloud well below. Flak was moderate, although my third aircraft was shot down in flames immediately after he had released his glider at the correct place. It was my impression that flak was being directed at the gliders, going in to land through the fog of war, and not at the aircraft to the same extent. This was confirmed by the casualty percentages. Out of four hundred and forty aircraft at 2,500 feet, seven were lost, but the glider pilots suffered 29% losses. The Americans at 600 feet lost forty-six aircraft, but their glider pilots suffered only 11% losses. (This was out of a total of some eleven hundred and fifty aircraft)."

SECTION II

ITINERARY

(Time has been allowed at each Stand for debussing and embussing)

Time	Event/Account	Speaker
0930	*Arrive STAND* 1 (188479)	
	A. Description of ground	Conducting Officer
	B. Relation of divisional plan to ground	Comd 6 Airlanding Bde
	C. Action of HQ RA and RA units 6 Brit Airborne Div	CRA 6 Brit Airborne Div
	D. Establishment of Div HQ and development of signals plan	CR Sigs 6 Brit Airborne Div
	E. Practical Administration	Col 'Q' (Plans) HQ 21 Army Group (Acting AA & QMG 6 Brit Airborne Div on Operation VARSITY)
	Questions	
1020	*Depart STAND* 1	
1040	*Arrive STAND* 2 (159480)	
	A. Description of ground	Conducting Officer
	B. Action of 3 Para Bde and, in particular, 8 Para Bn	CO 8 Para Bn
	Questions	
1120	*Depart STAND* 2	
1130	*Arrive STAND* 3 (193495)	
	A. Description of ground	Conducting Officer
	B. Relation of 5 Para Bde plan to ground, and action of 5 Para Bde	Comd 5 Para Bde
	Questions	
1200	*Depart STAND* 3	
1220	*Arrive STAND* 4 (191509)	
	A. Description of ground	Conducting Officer
	B. Action of 7 Para Bn	CO 7 Para Bn
	Questions	
1245	Lunch	
1335	*Depart STAND* 4	
1345	*Arrive STAND* 5 (201486)	
	Pointing out of LZs and relation of 6 Airlanding Bde plan to ground	Comd 6 Airlanding Bde
	Questions	
1405	*Depart STAND* 5	
1415	*Arrive STAND* 6 (213491)	
	A. Description of ground	Conducting Officer
	B. Operations by 123 (Typhoon) Wing RAF	Comd 123 Wing RAF
	C. Action of 6 Airlanding Bde	Comd 6 Airlanding Bde
	D. Action of 12 DEVON	CO 12 DEVON
	Questions	
1500	*Depart STAND* 6	
1505	*Arrive STAND* 7 (211479)	
	Account by Glider Pilot	Glider Pilot
	Questions	
	Summing-up	
1530	*Depart STAND* 7	

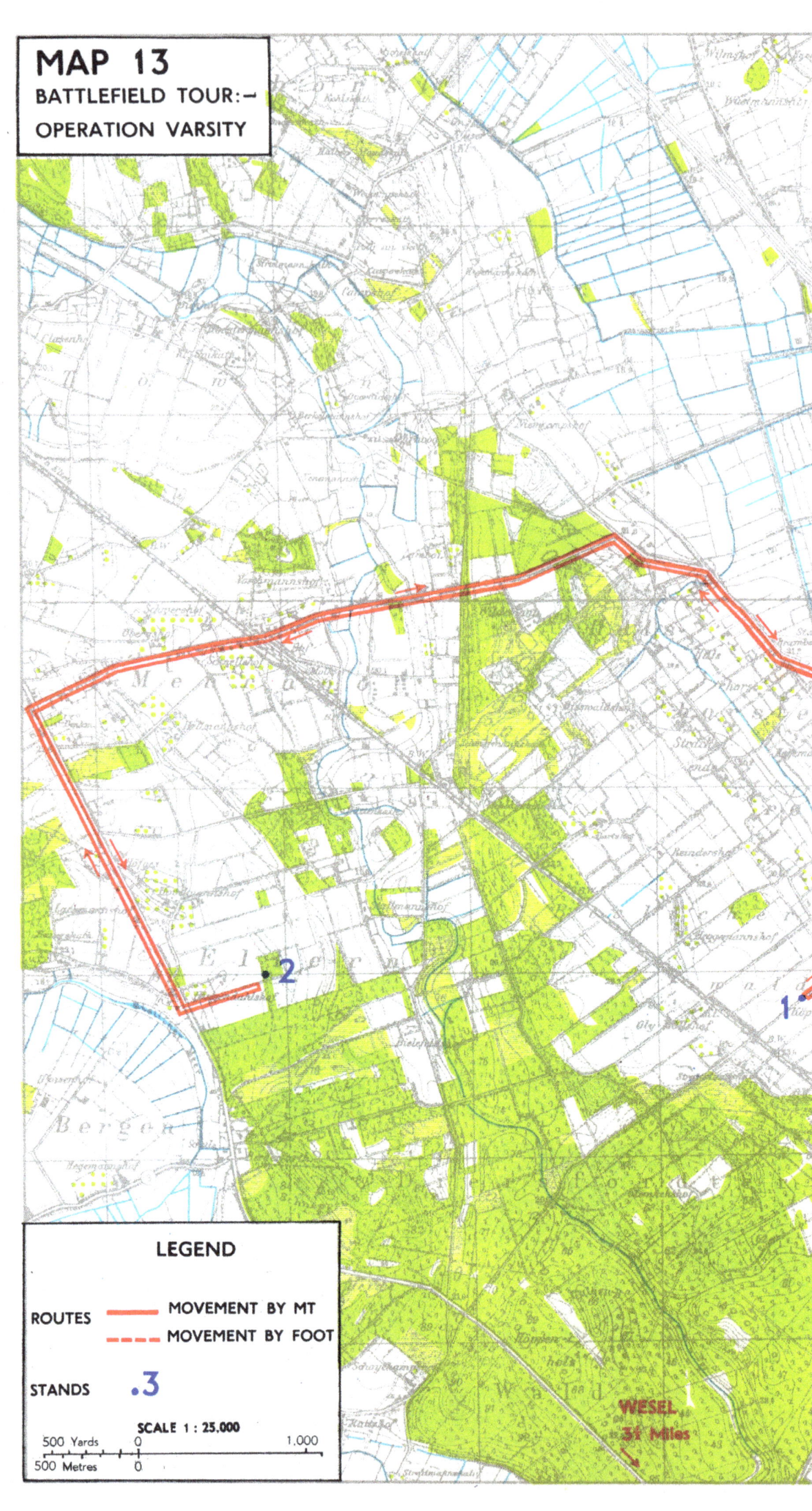

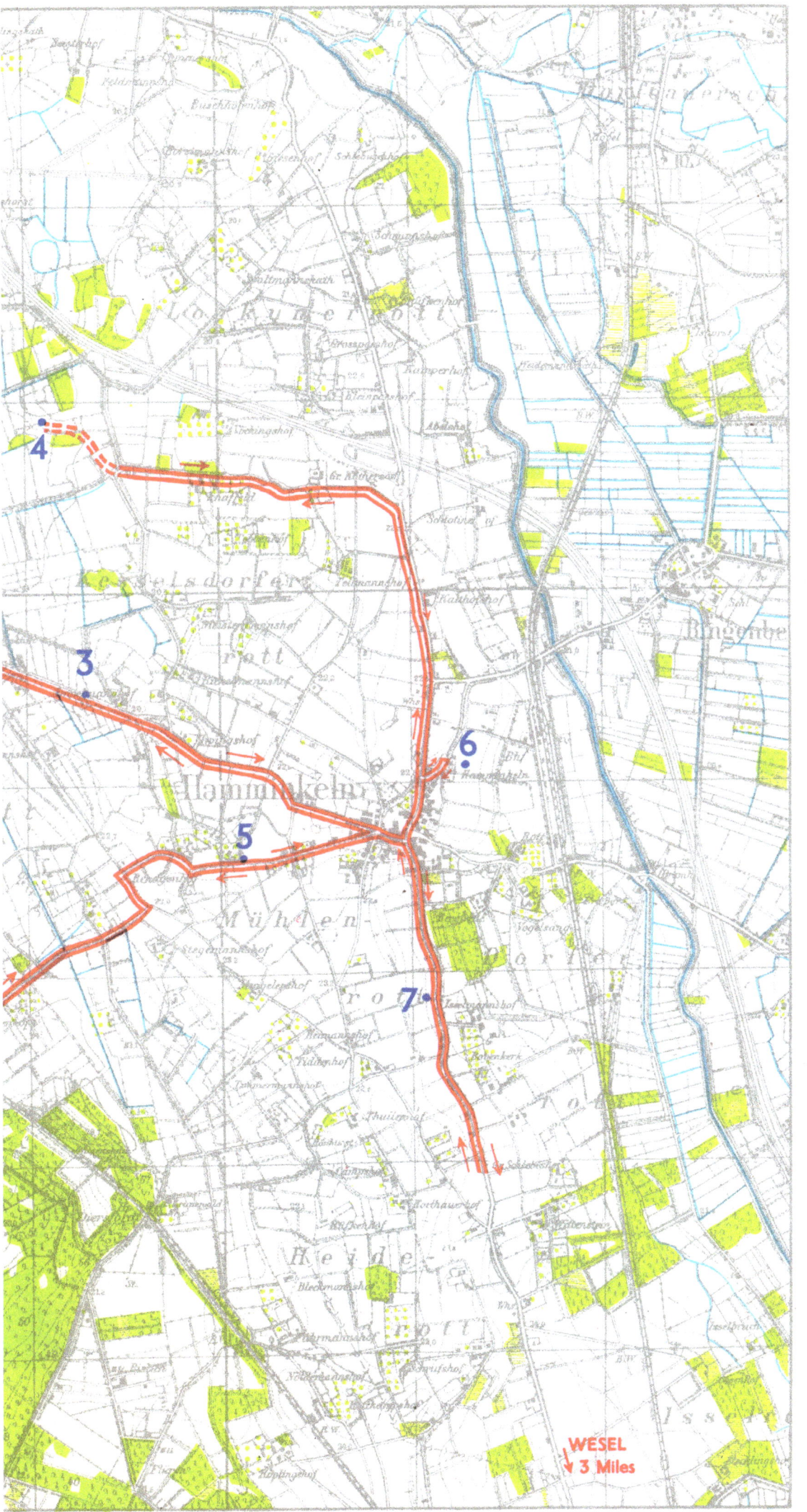

Stand 1

SECTION III

PERSONAL ACCOUNTS

(Note :—Officers' ranks and decorations are shown as they were in December 1947. Appointments shown are those held in March 1945).

STAND 1 (188479)
(Spectators stand facing North-West)

Object of Stand

    (a) To study the establishment of HQ 6 Brit Airborne Div, and development of the signal plan.

    (b) To study the action of HQ RA 6 Brit Airborne Div.

A. Conducting Officer

Description of ground

"The farmhouse in the orchard behind where you are now standing is called KOPENHOF (188479) and was the site selected for Main HQ 6 Brit Airborne Div. The open area in front of you was the Div HQ Landing Zone and the gun area.

"HQ RA was established in the small wood 200 yards to your Right front on the other side of the track.

"Looking down the track to the Left you will see about 300 yards away a level crossing. Following the line of the railway to the Right, you will see another level crossing; the buildings in the trees behind this were used initially as Rear Div HQ.

"Beyond the railway and running almost the whole length of the horizon is a thick wood, standing on rising ground : this is the DIERSFORDTER WALD. Opposite this point it is about 2,500 yards wide and the River RHINE is another 4,500 yards beyond it.

"The boundary between 6 Brit Airborne Div and 17 US Airborne Div crosses the railway about a mile South of the level crossing, running approximately from West to East."

B. Brigadier R. H. BELLAMY, DSO, Comd 6 Airlanding Bde

Relation of the divisional plan to the ground

(General direction of DZs and LZs to be pointed out on ground)

"The main tasks allotted to 6 Brit Airborne Div were :—

    (i) To seize and hold the high ground overlooking the West Bank of the RHINE in the DIERSFORDTER forest.

    (ii) To seize and hold HAMMINKELN, a main centre of communications.

    (iii) To seize and hold three bridges (one railway) over the River ISSEL to the East of HAMMINKELN.

    (iv) To contact 12 Corps to the Left and 17 US Airborne Div to the Right as soon as possible.

"In order to carry out this plan 3 Para Bde was to land on DZ 'A' and to seize the high ground overlooking the RHINE.

"5 Para Bde was to land on DZ 'B' and seize and hold the area to the North of the divisional sector and to link up with 12 Corps.

"6 Airlanding Bde in gliders was to seize HAMMINKELN and the bridges over the River ISSEL by landing tactically in battalion groups on three LZs.

"One point of interest is the tactical landings of 6 Brigade, and the use by them of coup-de-main parties to glide right up to the bridges over the River ISSEL."

C. Colonel W. McC. T. FAITHFULL, DSO, CRA 6 Brit Airborne Div

Action of HQ RA and RA Units

"The gunner landing plan was for the Light Regiment to use the LZ about 180486 and to come into action about 189485 for the purpose of supporting 6 Airlanding Bde and 5 Para Bde. They could in fact support 3 Para Bde—were it necessary—by turning the guns round through 180 degrees. One anti-tank battery was to land by glider on to 5 Para Bde DZ; whilst two troops of the other battery (mostly 17 pounders) landed on 6 Bde LZ, one troop on the 3 Bde DZ and one troop on the Div HQ LZ—the latter to act as divisional reserve.

Stand 1

"In the event the considerable haze together with AA fire caused many wide landings and considerable casualties. For instance, at dusk on the day of the landing the Light Regiment had only collected 50% of its guns and personnel, whilst two majors were killed and one wounded. The anti-tank battery in support of 5 Para Bde was badly shot up on the LZ, the major killed and only four or five guns out of sixteen survived. The other battery lost some 17 pounders in the Hamilcar gliders around HAMMINKELN whilst the troop with 3 Para Bde lost half.

"The Forward Observer Unit was lucky in that it only lost two officers killed and one wounded with a corresponding number of signallers. HQ RA was also lucky in that, having lost the Brigade Major, Signal Serjeant, etc. when their glider was machine-gunned from a farm house and wrecked, the CRA and IO survived the complete wreck of their own glider. Moreover the happy accident of a regiment from 17 US Airborne Div landing on the LZ of 6 Airborne Div HQ and proceeding to neutralise much of the opposition probably saved the day.

"The first four or five hours after landing were fairly quiet as might be expected. Because 17 US Div was still flying in for an hour or two after 6 Div had landed, there was not much artillery firing to be done, but as soon as possible the pre-arranged DF tasks were registered whilst no time was lost in re-organising OP parties and communications.

"The Light Regiment had arranged to have one regimental and two battery wireless nets. This proved unsound because the loss of each of the three control sets led to some confusion. It would have been better to have had the whole regiment on one net.

"Towards evening the enemy put in some small attacks which gave the fire control system a chance to settle down to its work. The Light Regiment fired a certain amount of coloured smoke from two 25 pounders specially flown in to indicate targets to Typhoons, but in general the afternoon passed in digging in and salvaging equipment and burnt out gliders. Continuous sniping was no help in this respect. However, with the help of a small bulldozer flown in in a Hamilcar and a number of reasonably willing German prisoners things became fairly shipshape that evening.

"It was about this time when the first re-supply aircraft appeared. They flew in rather too low causing many parachutes not to open and making everyone bolt for cover. Immediately afterwards every jeep had to be made available to recover the supplies and take them to a central dump.

"It was towards evening when it became apparent that the appreciation that RINGENBERG would be a forming-up place for enemy counter-attacks proved right. In anticipation of this the fire plan catered for a carefully spaced concentration by three medium regiments. This concentration was continually called for and probably prevented the enemy from pressing home his attacks more than he did. As it was 2 OXF BUCKS was hard pressed and had to blow a bridge. A few shells from medium guns fell short close in front of or amongst our own infantry, but considering the ranges involved and the closeness of the enemy this was to be expected, and the few casualties caused thereby were not a serious matter.

"The night passed as far as the gunners were concerned in arranging, and calling for, long range harassing fire on roads leading into HAMMINKELN.

"It was early next morning however when all three brigades called for fire at the same time, the major threat being a somewhat serious counter-attack on 1 Cdn Para Bn in 3 Para Bde. The flexibility of the fire control system did enable all calls to be met simultaneously.

"It was sometime next morning when to everybody's relief an SP anti-tank battery arrived together with a squadron of tanks and the recce parties of two field regiments, whilst 4 RHA came across the river and were in range of 5 Para Bde. It was now that wireless communications were at their worst and the fire control system of relay stations and step ups proved its worth. There was no case of a call for fire failing to be answered although sometimes there may have been delay; this was often caused by the extra care necessary at the guns because they were firing at such long ranges.

"Enemy mortar and shell fire was noticeably absent but this was because the landing had taken place plumb in the middle of his gun area. The enemy therefore had few, if any, guns or mortars to bring against us. Nevertheless the counter mortar organisation was going well, as was the Typhoon 'cab-rank'."

D. **Lieut Colonel P. E. M. BRADLEY, DSO,** CR Sigs 6 Brit Airborne Div

Establishment of Div HQ and execution of Signals Plan

"Before I describe the establishment of Div HQ in this farm, let us go back to ENGLAND on the early morning of 24 March 1944, where 6 Airborne Div is taking off. The scene is one of great activity.

"Our glider was "chalk number" 320, the sixth of the twenty-one Div HQ and Signals' gliders: the Divisional Commander's was 315. We took off from RIVENHALL aerodrome in ESSEX at about 0730 hours 24 March. My fellow passengers were the GSO I, the Chief Clerk, the NCO i/c "A" Command wireless detachment, a second operator and the GSO I's batman. In the glider were a jeep with the "A" Comd (R/T) set and charging engine, and a trailer with the 'G' office equipment. Already before we took off the sky seemed to be full of aircraft.

"The flight was a long one, but smooth. Anyway I had taken the precaution of swallowing the ADMS' famous air sick pills, which had the alleged additional property of making one less afraid. The sky was clear and one caught occasional glimpses of other aircraft and gliders through the porthole or by standing behind the pilots and looking through the perspex front. We talked a little, but it was difficult above the roar of the tug's engines.

Stand 1

"We crossed the RHINE soon after 1030 hours. I never saw it myself as I was too busy strapping myself in. Then we sat and waited. Everyone's face was tense and chalky white : it was a relief to realise that the feelings of my companions were much as my own. Suddenly there was a crack as the pilot cast off and the noise of the tug's engines died away, to be replaced by the rushing of the air. It was then that we realised more and more the presence of those other less pleasant noises, the crack of the AA fire, the automatic and mortar fire on the ground. We were in a steep dive and in my mind I can still see the pilot casting his eyes around looking for his landfall through the haze and smoke that covered the ground. There was a bump and we were down, bumping along the ground. The Chief Clerk and the Signals NCO had loosed their straps and were already trying to open the door. They were thrown all over the place. When we eventually came to rest, it seemed an age before the door would open—in reality only a few seconds. We all tumbled out and lay flat to get our bearings.

"Every glider had a briefed point of landing. Ours had been just in front of the KOPENHOF by that small wood to the right. In fact we had landed some way away beyond the big wood out there in front. The GSO I and the senior pilot lay on a pile of swedes and worked out where we were whilst the rest of us watched to either flank. There were mortars bursting at the far end of the LZ and spasmodic automatic fire round and about, but no one seemed to be paying any particularly unwelcome attention to us personally. Frankly I did not really know whether we were in TIMBUCTOO or CHINA, but the pilot gave us our location pretty well dead accurately and the GSO I gave us the order to unload. Meanwhile the sky seemed full of gliders coming in out of the haze in all directions. I think at that time I was more afraid of our own gliders coming in than of the attentions of the enemy. One HORSA landed only a few yards away and went crashing on through the fences. A HAMILCAR with a 17 pounder came to rest a short distance away on the other side of us. Unloading seemed to take an age : one's feeling of time was quite distorted. In fact within five minutes we were moving in open order across the LZ with jeep and trailer behind. We met little parties doing the same and a few American parachutists of 17 US Airborne Div, who had landed on our zone in error. It was an error that was very fortunate for us, because the company of 12 DEVON that was meant to land ahead of us to clear the LZ area was missing and if the Americans had not already started clearing operations when we landed, our casualties would have been much heavier. The Americans wore "Stars and Stripes" brassards for identification purposes. I remember thinking at the time how effective they were. It was all very strange, almost like a dream, this sudden change from the quiet ESSEX countryside to a battle in the middle of GERMANY. My OC 'O' Section, relates how he met a lone American on the LZ and said 'Good morning' : 'Good morning' said the American and passed on, much as if they had met on a stroll in the country.

"We skirted the big wood and made straight across the LZ towards the KOPENHOF, where we arrived soon after 1100 hours. Only twenty minutes had elapsed since we landed : it seemed a great deal more. The buildings of the KOPENHOF had already been cleared by a mixed party of Americans, HQ Defence platoon and Signals, with the ADC for good measure. He and the Commander had landed exactly as planned almost at the door of the KOPENHOF, in the field to the Right. The situation was not one in which the glider could be unloaded : it is not often that a divisional commander is involved in the fight for the capture of his own HQ ! There was a little knot of very frightened Germans under the trees to the Left of the farm and the Americans were establishing an RAP in the house. In the vicinity there were at least two gliders burning merrily like a fire work display as the ammunition was exploding. There was still spasmodic automatic fire in the wood all round, though the farm area was clear enough.

"The "A" Comd (R/T) set was brought in and opened at 1100 hours. Immediate contact was made with 3 and 5 Para Bdes, who reported all well. The Commander was there at the time and I do not know which of us was the more excited and pleased, when I reported the news to him. He had already seen the Commander of 6 Airlanding Brigade who had landed nearby and was in touch with his own brigade. The CRA and the FOOs were through to our guns. And so within half an hour of the landing of the first Div HQ glider, the communication situation was highly satisfactory : the only communication not yet available was direct to XVIII Corps, although that too was possible through RA channels. At that time, apart from HQ RA, the only wireless set available at Div HQ was the vital "A" Comd set that had come in with the GSO I and myself. OC A Section and the Signal Security Officer, were the only signal officers that had arrived besides myself. There was a handful of men. The "A" Comd set was through to 6 Airlanding Bde at 1128 hours. One of the FVCPs with its RAF crew was next to arrive and was through to the FCP on VHF soon after arrival, so air support also was now available to the division, but to land fighter pilots by glider into the middle of an airborne operation I feel is unkind to say the least of it ! By 1200 hours the Commander's Rover set was unloaded from its glider and as he had no immediate need of it, it was put onto a lateral link to 17 US Airborne Div, though no communication was established until 1600 hours. As it transpired the set and British crew with 17 US Airborne Div had met with a series of mishaps. The operators on either end of this link were brothers, so you can imagine the anxiety to establish communication.

"Div HQ was to rendezvous in two places. Main HQ at the KOPENHOF : Rear HQ at another farm the OLY-MOLLSHOF which has already been pointed out to your Left front. A private one-to-one link was established between them on SCRs 300. This link was invaluable. On it I learned that the Adjutant, and OC O Section had arrived. I immediately ordered the former to report to Main HQ with more men and equipment. There he arrived about 1200 hours in a fair state of dishevelment, his glider having been brewed up on landing together with his "destructor box" of secret documents ! The story of his landing is quite amusing. His glider was briefed to land very close to an enemy "strong point". This was marked as such on the defence overlays and photo interpretation successively showed it as steadily growing in size. He was naturally a little apprehensive. The glider landed exactly as briefed, almost on top of the "strong point" ; at that moment it went on fire. He hurled himself out right into the "defences" prepared for untold glories ! Imagine his slight embarass-

Stand 1

ment and even perhaps relief on discovering that the "strong point" was nothing more than an enormous heap of mangles that the local farmer had daily been piling up and increasing in size ! However he had an adventurous journey to his RV.

"At Rear HQ the area was by no means clear and sniping continued throughout the morning and early afternoon.

"Meanwhile at Main HQ the "Ops room" had been established in the air-raid shelter in front of the house, with the signal office in the building itself. An ASSU set had arrived and was soon through to Second Army. At 1315 hours, the first of our 52 Sets came in for the spare "Q" link to 12 Corps. It was opened as soon as possible with its flick frequency on the direct one-to-one link with XVIII Corps : communication being established at approximately 1335 hours. At Rear HQ the Base link to HQ 1 Brit Airborne Corps in UK was opened at approximately 1310 hours and was through first call. Early in the afternoon owing to the situation at Rear HQ that HQ was ordered to close and come in to Main HQ. The set working the "Q" link to 12 Corps arrived at Main HQ from Rear HQ at 1530 hours and was through at 1600 hours. The base set was closed during the move and contact was not re-established on arrival at Main. HQ 1 Airborne Corps was heard on and off during the night rather weakly through very heavy interference, but the link was not through again until 0500 hours the next morning on the day frequency. Communications for Base therefore had to be passed through XVIII Corps, a delay which might have proved serious. This was the only communication failure of the operation. On the "A" Comd net 3 Para Bde was through to the signals LO with 15 (S) Div, and the APM controlling the move of the Land Element across the river was through to Div HQ. This latter set caused an overload on an already busy net and was closed down early on the 25th. By that time of course 3 Para Bde was already in ground contact with 15 (S) Div. An SCR 300 salvaged from the Americans was opened on the Common Recognition Wave. A certain amount of conversation was intercepted, but little further value was obtained at Div HQ. On D Day only two operational links remained unopened, the American manned link to XVIII Corps and the "B" Comd (W/T): for neither was there a set available. The lack of the latter was never felt: indeed it was never opened until the arrival of the second build-up. In addition there was no Press link, as both Press sets had been brewed up. There was a certain amount of pressure to divert an operational set for the purpose, but I was not prepared to play. The Press were really very good about it. A short Press message was waiting on the Base link when it was re-established on the morning of the 25th : it was at the bottom of a pile of priorities and I am not sure that it was ever passed. The correspondents had had a very rough time and it was a very battered and bandaged party that attended the Commander's conference that evening. I couldn't help admiring them when I thought that it was at least the second if not the third airborne operation that many of them had done cheerfully and unarmed.

"One line detachment had arrived at Div HQ and during the afternoon and early evening of D Day, local lines at Div HQ and lines to 5 Para Bde and 6 Airlanding Bde were laid. The exchange was established in the farm. The route to 3 Para Bde was not clear and lines could not be laid to them until early on D + 1. The same of course applied to DRs.

"At first fair confusion existed in cipher matters. The cipher officer was very seriously injured when his glider crashed into the trees. In this same glider the DAAG was killed. The cipher operators were very scattered and it was a long time before the information could be ascertained and passed to higher formation as to what cipher pads had arrived, which was essential before we could receive from them any cipher messages. Both the US cipher machines had been destroyed. This caused further delay on messages from XVIII Corps.

"Fortunes in the Brigade Signal Sections had varied. In spite of losses in men and equipment there was little delay in opening satisfactory communications at HQ 3 Para Bde and HQ 6 Airlanding Bde. 5 Para Bde had suffered more serious loss. The OC Signal Section had been killed on the DZ and a great deal of equipment had been lost, as amongst other things all the Bde HQ gliders had gone astray. However, communications were established, initially on the short-range SCRs 536 (Walkie-Talkies), carried on the persons of the Brigade and Battalion Commanders : a system peculiar to this brigade, which paid an ample dividend. These sets were replaced as the WS 62 or 68 became available.

"At about 1300 hours on D Day, the first supply drop flown by Liberator bombers, flying magnificently low, came down very accurately all around us. From the signal point of view, the drop was disappointing as although ample quantities of signal equipment such as sets and batteries had been planned, very little was available in the dump even by D + 1. I was never able to discover why.

"Almost the last signals arrival at Div HQ on D Day was the 2 IC and OC 1 Coy, who came in at about 1600 hours, a filthy and dishevelled looking figure cheerfully asking if everything was through. His glider had landed somewhere in the 5 Para Bde area, had been hit as the men jumped out, and gone up in flames. By that time I had been mentally penning letters to his next of kin and I was mighty glad to see him.

"Div HQ had been digging in all day with the assistance of the sappers' bulldozer. By the evening, sets were underground, slit trenches had been dug and lined with parachute silk, and defence posts prepared. During the night 24/25 March there was a series of alarms and excursions as 8 Para Bn of 3 Para Bde cleared the woods to our rear, but nothing materialised. Commander XVIII US Corps, Major General RIDGWAY, literally fought his way through during the night via 17 US Airborne Div to see the divisional commander. He was the first man from West of the RHINE that reached Div HQ. The KOPENHOF that night was a strange mixture of HQ, signal office, RAP, mortuary and cowshed. I myself lay down in the hall for a few hours next door to another recumbent figure. It was not until the next morning I that discovered my companion was an American soldier who had died some hours previously !

Stand 1

"Early on the 25th, parties scoured the LZ for equipment, an operation that was well rewarded, as several sets were recovered from crashed gliders, also a number of glider batteries, which were of enormous value as by then the loss of charging equipment was causing anxiety as to the battery position.

"By 1000 hours 25 March, the leading tanks of 3 Tk SG had reached Div HQ and during the afternoon, the first build-up party had arrived, consisting mainly of line detachments and maintenance equipment. With them was OC 2 Coy, who had been acting as my representative with the ground forces. The link up was firm.

Lessons

"The signal lessons that may be learnt from this operation I think may be summarised as follows:—

(i) No amount of detailed signal planning to cover any and every contingency is too much. Unlike reconnaissance, signal planning is never wasted.

(ii) Signal officers must be in a position to ensure that the wireless equipment available is more than capable of doing the job. There is *no* room for doubt in this matter.

(iii) The value of airborne signals having been recently in active operations was very apparent. The division had only been withdrawn from the line in the middle of February, so the men were in an excellent state of training with their "ears" really "in". So often airborne signals had to be committed to an airborne operation after months of waiting at the base and no amount of ordinary training is a real substitute for operations.

(iv) 100% duplication of wireless detachments and other equipment is *not* over insurance. At Div HQ in this operation owing to limited airlift only about 60 or 70% reserve was possible. As has been seen, two planned links could not be opened on D Day and there was NOT one set in reserve. If Div HQ had been subjected to heavy mortar or shell fire after establishment as is more often than not the case, with consequent further loss of equipment, a breakdown in communications would have resulted. We were sailing very close to the wind indeed.

(v) The value of separating personnel and equipment from their duplicates in different aircraft was clear, as was the necessity for flexibility in briefing wireless crews and in setting up flick frequencies so that sets and crews might be allocated to links as the situation demanded.

(vi) The value of scouring the DZs and LZs for equipment was also clear. It must be remembered again that after the first hour or so, the LZ was comparatively free from fire, which is usually not the case."

E. **Colonel O. POOLE, CBE, MP,** Col Q (Plans) HQ 21 Army Group and Acting AA & QMG 6 Brit Airborne Div on Operation VARSITY.

Practical Administration

"I do not intend to repeat what is already set out on the subject of administration in Part I and Part II of the book, but only to emphasise some of the main points and to recall some of my personal experiences.

"As far as the planning of the operation was concerned, there was a considerable change of opinion as regards the administrative set-up, and proposals which had been turned down in the ARNHEM operation were accepted, the most important being that the airborne forces should be maintained by the ground forces after landing, and that no Airborne Corps HQ should be interposed in the administrative organisation.

"As I had no executive capacity in Div HQ, I was asked by Major General BOLS to undertake the organisation and general control of Rear Div HQ. After a most peaceful and enjoyable trip the glider in which I was travelling landed almost exactly where had been planned, and in spite of sustaining considerable damage no one was hurt. I was surprised to find everything was very quiet and soon found the reason why—some paratroops from 17 US Airborne Div had landed in the wrong place and had mopped up the two enemy guns operating in that particular sector. After unloading the jeep and trailer we made our way to the farm buildings where Rear Div HQ was to be established and made such defence arrangements as were possible with the Glider Pilots. Communications were non-existent, but I succeeded in finding a wireless operator with a portable set on his back and established communication with Main Div HQ. It soon became apparent that the AA & QMG and the DAAG were missing, so I arranged to remain at Rear Div HQ myself and sent the DAQMG (the only remaining AQ staff officer) out to make such contacts with Brigade Headquarters and the RASC section as he could. By means of him and other officers liaison was made with most Headquarters that afternoon and the maintenance area organised.

"At about 1 p.m. the first supply drop was delivered. No one was hit on the head which appeared to be quite inevitable. There was no difficulty in locating or recognising the different types of supplies, but owing to shortage of transport and sporadic sniping from woods and buildings, very little could be collected that afternoon.

"In the afternoon Rear HQ was mortared and the rifle fire increased, and at my request a platoon of the Defence Company was sent to reinforce the defence. I decided, however, that it would be preferable to join up with Main HQ for two reasons:—

(i) owing to lack of adequate communications and casualties on the Staff, Rear HQ was completely out of touch with what was going on, and unable to take effective action.

(ii) The defence was insufficient to hold the position against even the slightest attack.

Stand 1

"The RAP which had established itself in the farm buildings was evacuated and moved to Main HQ and the remainder of Rear HQ moved across under covering fire from the Defence Company. As far as I can remember, there were only two or three casualties.

"Once Rear HQ was established with Main HQ the Administrative Staff, such as it was, was in a better position to find out what was required and to take such action as was necessary.

"It was a pity that Rear HQ did not have time fully to establish itself before HQ 53 (W) Div took over the sector and occupied the same buildings for its HQ. It inevitably takes a little time for communications to be established and for the members of the staff who were with the seaborne tail to establish themselves in the HQ, and it would have been a great advantage if Rear HQ could have remained another twelve hours before side-stepping. However, this was done without any apparent disadvantage to the fighting troops although a certain amount of administrative "untidyness" must be expected.

"It will be realised from the foregoing that administration of an airborne force immediately after landing depends on :—

(i) the resourcefulness of the Staff and Services officers ;
(ii) careful briefing beforehand so that junior officers and services can take action without detailed instructions ; and
(iii) the establishment as soon as possible of communications.

"I think it could be said that, as a result of careful planning and the setting up of a sound administrative organisation, the difficulties of the first few days were overcome without any prejudice to the operation."

Stand 2

STAND 2 (159480)

(Spectators stand facing North)

Object of the Stand

To study the action of 3 Para Bde, with particular reference to 8 Para Bn.

A. Conducting Officer

Description of Ground

"You are now standing on the Southern side of the 3 Para Bde DZ (DZ 'A') which included the open ground in front of you. This part of it was where the brigade glider element was to land—you can still (November 1947) see the remains of one of the gliders on the edge of the wood behind you.

"This is the North-West corner of the 6 Airborne Div area—the boundary with 15 (S) Div (12 Corps) ran a short distance the other side of the main road to your Left, and turned East across the road about a mile North of here.

"The large wood behind you is the DIERSFORDTER WALD: the high ground in the wood further South is a spur overlooking the RHINE called the SCHNAPPENBERG feature.

"Your attention is particularly drawn to the ground which will come into the following account: the orchards and buildings to the North-West, at the North-West extremity of the DZ: the wood to the North-East (162485): and the tongue of wood 300 yards East (163480). You will appreciate that this DZ was a good one, but narrow, and as the aircraft were to fly-in from the West nine abreast, many parachutists were likely to land in the trees."

B. Lieutenant Colonel G. HEWETSON, DSO, OBE, CO 8 Para Bn.

(Positions indicated by map reference in the account will in most cases be pointed out on the ground)

Action of 3 Para Bde

Tasks

"The order of dropping of 3 Para Bde was 8 Para Bn, 3 Para Bde HQ, 1 Cdn Para Bn, 9 Para Bn, elements of 3 Para Sqn RE and 224 Para Fd Amb. The glider element would come in at P plus 60 minutes, P Hour being the time of the parachute drop.

"Each parachute battalion had been allotted thirty-five Dakota aircraft, two Horsa gliders and one Hamilcar glider. The total lift for the brigade was one hundred and twenty-two Dakotas, twenty-seven Horsas and three Hamilcars.

"8 Para Bn was to seize the DZ and establish a brigade rallying point in the tongue of wood to the East (163480); on the completion of the glider landing it was to come into reserve through the wood to the South-East (168473); and on orders from 3 Para Bde HQ it was to clear and hold the area of road and railway crossing (185476) to cover the rear of Div HQ.

"9 Para Bn was to clear and hold the SCHNAPPENBERG feature and to clear and hold the spur at 157461. Contact to the South had to be made with 2 Bn 513 Para Inf Regt, 17 US Airborne Div.

"1 Cdn Para Bn was to clear and hold area corner of wood you see to the South West (155477) and area of houses (156472), 1,000 yards through the woods to the South-West.

Enemy

"We had been informed that part of the area North of WESEL was held by elements of 7 Para Div. In the area were 3,500 VOLKSSTURM troops of fairly low morale and poorly equipped. The immediate battle reserve consisted of 116 Pz Div with thirty or more tanks in the area to the East of RINGENBERG (2250).

The Fly-in

"On 20 March the brigade moved into transit camps in ESSEX adjoining the take-off airfields. During the stay in the transit camps the weather was good and briefing continued all day combined with light exercise. On the evening of 23 March we were informed that D-Day was to be 24 March.

"The brigade emplaned at 0645 hours and the leading planes flew off at 0700 hours. The drop was timed for 1000 hours, 3 Para Bde being the first troops to drop.

"The flight was uneventful. It was a sunny clear day, and occasionally during the flight, I looked through the door and saw the most impressive stream of aircraft. Over the Continent we passed under the glider stream which would be released half-an-hour after the parachutists.

"In the leading aircraft, flown by the American Group Colonel, was the DZ marking stick who would be responsible for putting down the coloured smoke at the battalion RV.

"At 0946 hours we were given the order. "Five minutes to go". I remember feeling very apprehensive about this as according to the time given this would mean dropping on the wrong side of the RHINE. However at 0951 hours we crossed the RHINE with the usual sinking feeling of impending "baling out". I remember looking forward from the door and seeing the fog of battle on the ground, the aftermath of the terrific pounding from our massed artillery.

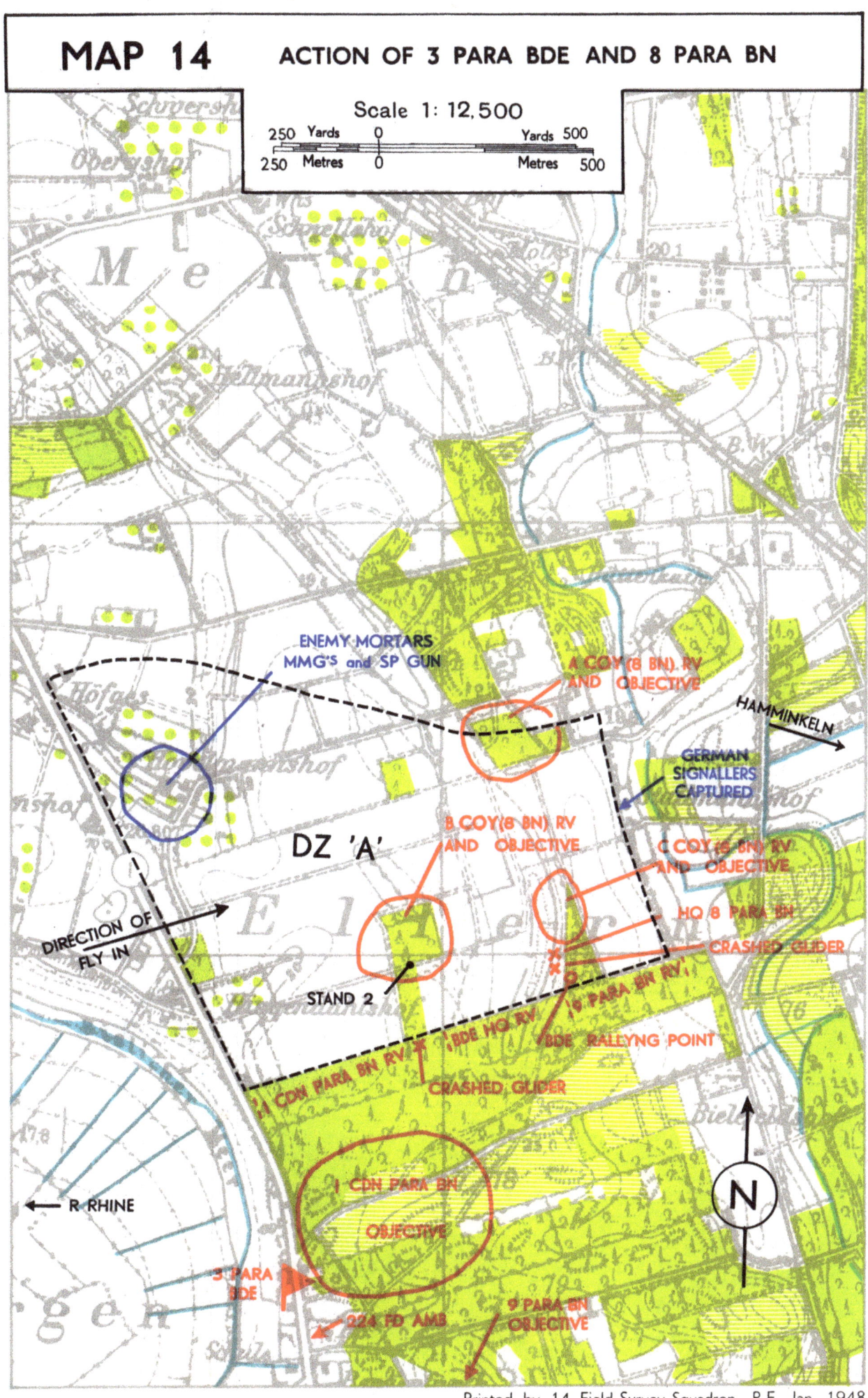

Stand 2

Landing

"Red light—green light—out—parachute open—ground fairly hard—sigh of relief! There seemed to be very little flak, bullets were whining across the DZ, nothing compared to the mental relief of landing safely. I landed 100 yards East of where we stand. The initial briefing and air photographs left no doubt as to the RV, in addition the blue smoke was already visible, the officer in No. 1 plane had dropped a few yards from the RV.

"As we stand here HQ of 8 Para Bn, whose action we will discuss in more detail later, was to RV in the tongue of wood 300 yards to the East. 9 Para Bn RV was in the wood to the South of 8 Para Bn; 3 Bde HQ and 224 Fd Amb in the wood West of 9 Bn (162477); 1 Cdn Para Bn West of Bde HQ.

"In approximately ten minutes the whole of the brigade was on the ground. The formation used by the American pilots gave a very concentrated drop, and very few sticks, except where there had been a hold up in the aircraft, dropped away from the DZ.

"Initially there was very little flak. One or two planes were shot down. I remember as I was getting out of my parachute watching a Dakota returning with flames streaming out of the engine; probably No. 1 plane flown by the Colonel, which crashed West of the RHINE.

"There was a considerable amount of shooting on the DZ, chiefly enemy, as at this stage of a drop it would be fatal for our own troops to open up.

"You can imagine from here the sight on the DZ. Thousands of parachutes drifting slowly to the ground and on the ground. Men getting out of their harness and opening kit bags with feverish haste, talking to anyone within call about the "jump", for at this stage in an operation to have landed safely is to be inoculated with 100% morale. Blue smoke going up from the East RV to guide in 9 Para Bn and Bde HQ. Yellow smoke from the Canadian RV to the West. A scene of indescribable chaos, yet rapidly men were moving off to the RVs and within thirty-five minutes 85% of the brigade had reported in. Above it all a continuous stream of aircraft flying East, the scream of 88 mm shells, the puffs of smoke in the sky, and the long lazy curves of tracer reaching at what looked a sitting target.

Enemy on DZ

"Let us pause here for a moment and see what the enemy situation on the DZ was at this time. Most of this of course is what we knew later but it will help you to appreciate the situation as it was.

"The tongue of wood where you now stand was occupied by approximately two platoons of German parachute troops, they were prepared to and actually did make a fight of it. The wood I pointed out to the North-East was also held and the orchards and houses to the North-West contained enemy mortars and an SP gun. Gun detachments were scattered round the DZ and through the woods to the South.

"Later an enemy officer taken prisoner in the wood told me that they expected airborne troops to be used for the RHINE crossing and it was appreciated that this DZ was one of the few places where we could safely jump. In consequence of this it had been strongly held, but when no paratroops appeared at 0900 hours most of them had been sent forward to counter attack the troops crossing the RHINE. I was very glad to hear it!

The Attack

"The clearing of the DZ by 8 Para Bn will be dealt with later.

"The Brigade Commander had landed safely and had joined the brigade in its RV. At approximately 1100 hours as the gliders were coming in he ordered 9 Para Bn and 1 Cdn Para Bn to carry out their respective attacks. Let us follow the 9 Para Bn.

"You remember its objective was the SCHNEPPENBERG feature and the spur to the South, at 156461. A Coy leading, it left its RV and moved South and West to track junction 165466. Here it formed up for the assault and by 1330 hours all objectives were taken against very limited opposition. Prisoners taken amounted to three hundred and some forty were killed. B Coy prior to the assault destroyed an SP gun which drove into their 'O' group. At approximately 1530 hours B Coy sent out a patrol which contacted the forward elements of 8 RS.

"By evening the battalion was established in slit trenches in the pine woods and all was quiet in the immediate neighbourhood.

"1 Cdn Para Bn which you remember had to clear the area from the South West of the wood to the houses at 157472 put in a spirited attack and by 1200 hours had taken the objective.

"At about 1400 hours forty-two Germans were seen moving East across the bridge at 154469. The MMGs were brought into action and all the enemy were killed.

"During the afternoon the enemy still holding the houses at the North-West corner of the DZ began to mortar and shell the Canadian position and tried to infiltrate along the main road. The Canadians counter-attacked. It was during this action that the only V.C. in 6 Airborne Div was won. Under intense mortar and machine gun fire in the open ground over there (South-West corner of DZ 155477) a medical orderly succeeded in removing the casualties from a burning carrier and repeatedly came out into the open to carry in wounded men.

"The Canadians were now firmly established on their objective. Bde HQ moved into this area and occupied the school at 156472. 224 Fd Amb with the responsibility of clearing all the casualties from the DZ established an ADS in the buildings at 157472.

Stand 2

Action of 8 Para Bn

"Let us now turn back to 8 Para Bn on the DZ.

"You will remember the initial battalion task was to seize and hold the DZ. The order of drop was A Coy, Mortar Platoon, MMG platoon, Bn HQ, B Coy, C Coy.

"A Coy's objective was the wood over there to the North-East (162485); B Coy and the MMG platoon the wood where we now stand; C Coy with Bn HQ and the mortar platoon in the tongue of wood to the East (163480). The South of this strip of wood was also the brigade rallying point. Companies had to RV on their respective objectives.

"A Coy succeeded with very little opposition, several prisoners being taken and the position was occupied by 1030 hours. Patrols were sent out to the North and East.

"C Coy and Bn HQ had little difficulty in occupying their positions. The enemy had dug trenches which were immediately taken over. Bn HQ with the 2 IC and the Adjutant was in the West edge of the wood there (see Map 14).

"B Coy, however, coming in disorganised parties of two or three men was unable to gain a footing in this wood. You can still see the trenches and strong positions held by the enemy (1947). I could see from where I was that B Coy was meeting with stiff opposition. Men coming into the positions from the North were being shot and there was still a fair amount of small arms fire across the DZ. Eventually, after great difficulty, the company commander collected about a platoon and attacked from the South through the narrow part of the wood. This attack was held up. The company commander and the platoon commander were both killed.

"In the meantime men were still coming in from the DZ. The stick of the anti-tank platoon with the platoon commander had jumped to the East of the DZ owing to a failure in the light signals in the aircraft. Returning to the DZ they had a short sharp engagement in the house over there (East 164484) and captured an officer and fifteen men of a German signal unit together with their 3-ton lorry. This vehicle was invaluable later when the DZ had to be cleared.

"The gliders began to arrive at 1100 hours. The LZ for the Horsas was the open space between the tongue of wood and the Bn HQ position. One of the first down, a 9 Para Bn glider, shot over the DZ and landed there (see Map 14. Parts still there 1947). Although it was badly damaged there were no casualties.

"My second-in-command had gone round to see Bde HQ and B Coy. I was standing at the entrance to the wood there (see Map 14), briefing the IO to keep in touch with Bde HQ on the wireless (at this time all companies less B Coy were in wireless communication with Bn HQ, and Bn HQ was in communication with Bde HQ), while I went down to see how B Coy was faring, and if it would be necessary to put in an attack with C Coy. Two serjeants, one from 9 Para Bn, were standing a few yards away. Suddenly with a terrific crash a glider came through the trees and I found myself lying under the wheel of a jeep. I managed to crawl out from the wreckage to find the glider, one of the medical Horsas of 9 Para Bn, completely written off. The crew had been killed and my IO and the two serjeants were also dead.

"At about this time the 2 IC reported back from B Coy. The wood had been taken by a platoon attacking from the North-East using No. 36 and 77 grenades and covered by the fire of the platoon from the South. The last phase of the attack was a hand to hand fight down a trench, led by the platoon commander. A considerable number of the enemy had been killed and one officer and twenty-six ORs were taken prisoner.

"It must be appreciated that during this phase of an airborne operation it is impossible to use artillery or mortar support on objectives within the area of the drop.

"At 1115 hours the Hamilcar glider of 8 Para Bn made a perfect landing at the North-East corner of the wood. This was very good news as it held the carrier which was soon being used, spare mortars, MMGs and wireless sets.

"The enemy now began to mortar and shell the DZ. The strip of wood where we are now standing came in for a great deal of attention and B Coy was moved South into the wood.

"Meanwhile the clearing of the DZ of jettison containers and equipment by parties provided by each company continued. By 1200 hours this was practically completed.

"I had now received the battalion casualty state. Up to this time four officers had been killed and three wounded. Twelve ORs had been killed and forty-three wounded and fifty ORs were missing. Of the missing men three arrived during the evening in a jeep. Their glider had made a forced landing West of the RHINE and they had crossed the river with 15 (S) Div. This was approximately 30% of the officers' strength and 25% of the ORs'. Fairly high casualties, but after all we had jumped on to the enemy and in such a position the first half hour of chaos on the DZ is bound to produce casualties.

"The brigade casualties were approximately three hundred.

"At 1200 hours the battalion was ordered into brigade reserve and moved less one platoon of C Coy (left to complete the clearing of the DZ and guard the dump) by way of Bde HQ into a position round road junction 168473. Two still active 88 mm guns were encountered. One inflicted a few casualties by firing into the trees causing shrapnel bursts. The crews were eventually eliminated.

"At approximately 1830 hours the Brigade Commander visited the battalion and ordered the move into a position covering the rear of Div HQ at KOPENHOF. The tracks through the wood ran in every conceivable direction, darkness was coming on, enemy groups in the wood were becoming quite active and it was soon very obvious that the battalion was utterly and completely lost. A decision

Stand 2

was made to stay put for the night and send out patrols. There were a few clashes with the enemy and prisoners were taken. This activity apparently startled Div HQ in no mean way and caused them to "stand to" most of the night.

"The battalion LO who had joined earlier had to return to Bde HQ and the Padre went with him to visit the casualties in 224 Fd Amb; they went with the escort conducting the prisoners. Unfortunately the party was ambushed in the wood and the LO and Padre were both killed.

"When day dawned the miracle of miracles had happened, the battalion was in the correct position!

Conclusions

"Personally, I think that this was the most successful airborne operation ever carried out, and the biggest one in that two complete airborne divisions were dropped simultaneously. The airborne operation in NORMANDY on D-Day was a night drop with dispersion over a wide area and 75% of the men were missing for a long time.

"At ARNHEM (September 1944) the DZ was some way from the objective which was strongly held. Owing to weather conditions the build-up was slow, and consequently the objective although taken by a small force could not be held.

"Parachute troops are extremely vulnerable on the DZ. There can be no co-ordinated control, weapons cannot safely be used and although morale at this period is at its peak the enemy can take heavy toll.

"On the RHINE crossing many parachutists landed in trees and were shot by the ground defenders below. Lieutenant Colonel NICKLIN of 1 Cdn Para Bn was killed in this way.

"I do believe that the sight of thousands of aircraft coming in has a very great morale effect on the enemy, and unless they are of the calibre of the Japanese they will not be prepared to put up very stiff resistance.

"The destruction of the enemy artillery in Operation VARSITY which had been dispersed in the woods and hedges presented a very difficult problem. It is difficult to pin point from the air and a terrific weight of counter battery fire is necessary to destroy it. Very few guns in this area had in fact been destroyed. The answer is no doubt to be found in guided missiles and the atom bomb of the future.

"On looking back on this operation I think I made a mistake in ordering companies to RV on their objectives. A and C Coys were successful, but B Coy could have fought a much more successful battle and had fewer casualties if the attack could have been put in as a company from the East or the South."

Stand 3

STAND 3 (193495)

(Spectators stand facing North)

Object of Stand

To study the action of 5 Para Bde.

A. Conducting Officer

Description of Ground

"HQ 5 Para Bde was established in the farm house on your Right.

"The village of HAMMINKELN is about a mile down this road to the Right—the church spire is visible from here.

"The dropping zone and landing zone of 5 Para Bde Gp was on the flat ground you can see in front of you. The whole of the divisional area contained the administrative echelons and the gun positions of the enemy defending the RHINE due West. Many of the gun positions and enemy posts had been identified by aerial photographs. The bulk of the enemy in this rear area was on the slightly more enclosed ground to the West of this road but there were a number of guns and entrenchments which appeared to have been sited with a view to covering this DZ area which the enemy realised to be suitable for airlanding operations.

"You have heard the plan for neutralising these enemy positions both by preliminary bombardment and from the air. The limiting factor in this programme was that for technical reasons it had to finish some 10–15 minutes before the arrival of the paratroops. This period was so long that the neutralising effect of the very heavy bombardment had worn off except for the positions which had actually been destroyed by direct hits or near misses. You will hear the implications of this when we come to consider the execution of the plan."

B. Brigadier J. H. N. POETT, DSO, Comd 5 Para Bde

Action of 5 Para Bde

(Wherever possible positions described by map reference in the account
will be pointed out on the ground by the speaker)

"You have already heard the task of 6 Airborne Div. The task allotted to 5 Para Bde was to seize and hold the ground astride the road on which we are standing from inclusive the road junction 197493 to inclusive the road junction 187497 and to deny movement to enemy reserves through the area.

"The Brigade Group consisted of :—

    7 Para Bn
    12 Para Bn
    13 Para Bn
    4 Airlanding A Tk Bty — 8 guns being 17 pounders and 8 guns 6 pounders
    Detachment of the FOU
    One tp of 591 Para Sqn RE
    225 Para Fd Amb.

"The brigade had a call on one medium regiment from the West bank of the river and one battery of 53 Airlanding Lt Regt which was to come down in gliders. The brigade objective was beyond the range of the field artillery on the West bank.

"The brigade plan was divided into two phases. The first phase was the landing by parachute and glider and the rallying of the troops on the dropping zone and landing zone.

"The second phase consisted of securing and consolidating the brigade objective.

"The DZ and LZ can be seen in front of you. In dry weather it is clearly very suitable for airborne operations. During the days of planning, however, there was some doubt as to whether the area would be flooded and we studied the air photographs with considerable anxiety. In the event, most of the surface water had drained off the DZ by 24 March.

"The parachute troops of the brigade group were to fly in in one formation in aircraft of the American Troop Carrier Command. The Americans fly in very tight formation of nine "ship" elements following close on one another. For a DZ of the size of the one you see in front of you it is possible for all aircraft in the group to commence dropping together and thereby achieve a much closer pattern on the ground.

"The parachutists of the brigade were to rally in the following localities :—

    (a) 7 Para Bn   in woods 190507
    (b) 12 Para Bn   North and South edge ⎫
        HQ 5 Para Bde   West end ⎬ wood 195502
        591 Para Sqn RE   South edge between 193502–194502 ⎭
    (c) 13 Para Bn   road junction 187497
        225 Para Fd Amb   road junction 189496
    (d) Glider Pilots and vehicle party   road junction 189496.

Stand 3

"The glider element of the brigade group was to land—surface water permitting—on the centre of the DZ and was to rally with the units under whose command they had been placed. The glider pilots and certain vehicles not required during the early stages of the battle were given a special RV.

"The tasks to be allotted to the various battalions for Phase II were as follows:—

7 Para Bn with under command one section of the field ambulance and in support one 6 pounder anti-tank troop were to:—

(a) (i) Secure area of woods 193507 and 190507.
    (ii) Protect the DZ.
    (iii) Deny enemy movement towards the Brigade objective from the North and East between inclusive road junction 183502 and inclusive wood 197507 until 12 and 13 Para Bns had consolidated their positions.

(b) on orders of the Brigade Commander move into brigade reserve in area from inclusive road junction 184492 to inclusive road junction 187485. It was to establish a standing patrol at cross roads 167492, strength one platoon, on landing. The CO was to be prepared to move the whole battalion to the area of these cross roads if ordered.

"12 Para Bn with under command one section of the field ambulance and in support two anti-tank troops (one 6-pounder and one 17-pounder) was to clear and hold the locality bounded by road junction 196504–point 198498–inclusive road junction 197493–West end of wood 193502 all inclusive.

"13 Para Bn with under command one section of the field ambulance and in support one anti-tank troop (17-pounders) was to clear and hold the locality bounded by point 194495–road junction 187494 –road junction 187497–road and stream junction 186493–buildings 193493.

"The artillery was given certain pre-arranged tasks to be fired on call. All calls for artillery support were to be made through Bde HQ. Each battalion had a FOO in communication with the FOO at Bde HQ. The Forward Observation Unit also undertook counter-mortar duties.

"The anti-tank layout had been planned through careful stereoscopic examination of air photographs and a trace had been prepared showing the tasks and approximate position of each machine-gun platoon. The battalion localities described had been planned so as to include the areas from which the anti-tank defence could best be arranged.

"The 4.2" Mortars of the Airborne Reconnaissance Regiment were under command of the CRA through whom calls for fire were to be made.

"The task of the Royal Engineers was largely on a divisional basis. Their first function was to open up the roads within the divisional area to wheeled traffic.

"Very strict orders were issued in respect to mining. No anti-personnel mines were allowed, and other minefields were confined to denying to the enemy egress from roads which were already planned to be blocked by necklaces of 75 grenades to be placed in position only when the approach of enemy vehicles appeared imminent.

"Various standing patrols were to be sent out from each battalion to give early warning of enemy movement. Contact patrols were also to be sent out to contact 3 Para Bde, 6 Airlanding Bde and Div HQ. 7 Para Bn was also instructed to send out a patrol immediately on landing to see whether 15 (S) Div had reached the crossroads some miles away due West of us about 167492.

"Arrangements for recognition of our own troops were by the display of yellow celanese triangles. In addition red berets were to be worn after the initial drop.

"There was no air support channel with Brigade HQ. Calls for air support were to be made through artillery channels.

"The wireless communications were duplicated throughout and complete arrangements were made for alternative methods of communication. These have been explained during the discussion of the signal plan. 5 Para Bde, however, had one extra link which proved of great value. The Brigade Commander and each Battalion Commander carried an American Walkie-Talkie set. It had been found in the earlier parachute operations that no matter how quick the normal signal communications, there was bound to be a period of time while the operators were marrying up their sets and batteries during which communications were impossible. From the very nature of this operation this period came at the most vital stage. By carrying these Walkie-Talkie sets, the Brigade Commander was able to gain contact with two of his battalions very shortly after the landing. The third battalion for some unexplained reason did not come on the air. I consider the sets were of the utmost value and would strongly recommend them in any future operation.

"So much for the plan. I will now give you a picture of how this plan worked out.

"The troop carrying formations arrived over the DZ a few minutes after 1000 hours on the morning of 24 March. The parachute drop was effected with very reasonable accuracy. The dropping zone had been obscured to some extent by the smoke of the battle further West and considerable credit is due to the navigation of the leading American pilot for the accuracy with which he identified the dropping zone. There was a fair amount of flak but considering the vulnerability of the large slow moving Dakotas, comparatively few casualties were inflicted in the air.

"Once the troops reached the ground, they soon realised the difference between an opposed and an unopposed landing. As has been said before, the countryside was covered with smoke and identification of the land marks which had been carefully learnt during the preliminary briefing was made difficult. Furthermore, there was a considerable amount of small arms fire and of shelling throughout the DZ area. Although battalions were dropped with fair accuracy, the individual officers and men had considerable difficulty in identifying their exact positions and this caused some delay to the rallying. Nevertheless, the battalions were successfully collected in their RV areas by about one hour

Stand 3

after the initial drop. It is important to note the difference in time taken in rallying under these conditions to rallying on an unopposed landing where the same result could have been achieved in a third of the time.

"The enemy opposition on the ground was moderate. The enemy was occupying entrenched positions and was difficult to locate. The paratroops on the DZ, moving to their RV were conspicuous and vulnerable. Considerable casualties inevitably resulted. Once an enemy post had been located and determined action taken to deal with it, the enemy surrendered without serious fight. The casualties incurred were from the enemy posts and guns before they were located.

"Just as the parachute troops were reaching their RVs the glider element of the brigade group began to come in to the airlanding zone and also the gliders of 6 Airlanding Bde slightly to the South. This caused a considerable diversion of the enemy artillery fire and proved a welcome relief to the parachute troops already on the ground. It was, however, a most distressing sight to see the gliders picked off both in the air and on the ground. The losses among the gliders had been heavy and consequently only a comparatively small proportion of the anti-tank guns and vehicles carrying machine guns, mortars and ammunition reached the battalions at their RVs. There is no doubt that had a strong armoured counter attack developed, the brigade group would have been seriously embarrassed by the loss of anti-tank guns and of the ammunition reserves.

"Once the battalions had RV'd, the problem of securing their objectives was comparatively simple and was effected with dash and speed.

"7 Para Bn whose task was to cover the consolidation of the brigade position was not seriously interfered with throughout its period in the out-post area. It dealt with minor enemy patrolling activities only.

"12 and 13 Para Bns worked hard at the preparation of the main defensive position. It was expected that an enemy counter-attack would develop any time from two hours after the landing.

"Contact patrols successfully met the units to which they had been dispatched and Bde HQ learnt over the wireless that the divisional plan had worked with complete success.

"The main position was sufficiently consolidated in five hours to permit the withdrawal of 7 Para Bn to the brigade reserve area leaving only patrols in front.

"The enemy made no attempt to counter-attack through the divisional sector on anything approaching a large scale so that there was little fighting for the remainder of the period until contact was made with the troops of 15 (S) Div.

"Almost all the casualties incurred by the brigade were during the initial one and a half hours until the enemy gun positions and infantry posts in the vicinity of the DZ had been mopped up. The casualties of the brigade group amounted to some 300 killed, wounded and missing, approximately 20% of the total engaged in the parachute and glider part of the operation. I am unable to estimate the number of enemy casualties as no count was made on the ground and prisoners—who were in considerable numbers—were directed back to a divisional PW cage."

Stand 4

STAND 4 (191509)

(Spectators stand facing East)

Object of Stand

To study the action of 7 Para Bn.

A. Conducting Officer

Description of ground

"You are now standing at the Northern end of 5 Para Bde area; the wood to your Right rear was the site of 7 Para Bn HQ. 700 yards to your front is another small wood, and just beyond and to the Left of it a bank of sand can be seen — that is the uncompleted autobahn. The last stand — 5 Para Bde HQ — is about one mile away to your Right".

B. Lieutenant Colonel R. G. PINE-COFFIN, DSO, MC, CO 7 Para Bn

Action of 7 Para Bn

"My battalion was ordered to establish itself at this end of the DZ and to take on all opposition which might interfere with the other two battalions, which were to capture the brigade objective (indicate on ground). In short 7 Para Bn came down looking for a fight, which is not a bad role for any battalion.

"The enemy in this area would be automatically taken on during the forming-up process and it was hoped that the sight of the massed drop would so lower his morale that this would not be too difficult. We all hoped very hard that this would be so because a parachute battalion is very vulnerable indeed until it has formed up — in fact it doesn't exist at all; it is just a collection of individuals, or at best small formed armed bodies of men, moving in the general direction of the RV. To land on top of, or even within small arms range of, an enemy position had long been a parachutist's nightmare. But on this occasion we did it and got away with it too.

"Once the forming-up was completed we could turn our attention to the most likely direction of attack. This was from either the North, North-East or North-West so that is why the battalion was here — the North end of the DZ. The layout was:—

A Coy, the 3" Mortar platoon and a single MMG in the small wood just to your Right front.

B Coy and a single MMG in the wood to your Left astride the autobahn.

C Coy and the two other MMGs about five hundred yards behind you.

"A parachute battalion only had three rifle companies then and not four as it has today.

"The drop was at 1010 hours and was from rather higher than we like for an operational drop; it must have been from nearly 1,000 feet. This would normally have been an advantage as it seems that one is in the air for longer than you expect and get a good chance of spotting a landmark as you come down, but in this case everyone was getting pretty anxious to get down quickly because it was far from healthy in the air. The German flak gunners weren't getting much success in shooting down the Dakotas so a lot of them switched and burst their shells amongst the parachutists instead; this was most unpleasant and we suffered a number of casualties before we even reached the ground. There was mortar bombing and shelling on the ground but it was a great relief to get there just the same.

"We tried out three experiments on this operation and two of these had to do with the drop and the forming-up, so I will tell you about them now.

"The first one was in the actual allocation of aircraft to companies. Originally the aircraft used to fly-in singly in line astern and each would drop its parachutists as it passed over the DZ. This was quite effective but it took a comparatively long time to get the whole force on the ground. The Americans had a quicker way which was very suitable for daylight drops. They flew their planes over the DZ in a tight formation and all the parachutists jumped from their aircraft at the same time with the result that practically the whole force was in the air together and a great deal of time was saved. Viewed from the ground it was most spectacular as the air seemed completely filled with parachutists and it had many advantages from the airborne point of view too. The snag lay though in the muddle you got on the ground. There was a most appalling mix-up of units and sub-units all over the DZ and our experiment was aimed at lessening this problem.

"The normal method of allocating aircraft for these saturation drops, as they were called, was to give the first nine aircraft to one company, the next to another and so on. This was very neat on paper and it looked good in the air too because the formation was made up of waves of nine aircraft. In the air the formation looked something like a battalion in close column of companies but on the ground it was worse than the practical exam. for Certificate 'A'.

"We found out this weakness on a practice jump shortly before the operation; on this exercise we couldn't go to our RV at all because the 'enemy' was holding it, so we had the job of trying to work out the muddle before attacking them. It was an almost impossible job so we put on our thinking caps and next time we allotted all the aircraft along one flank of the formation to one company and all down the other flank to another. Bn HQ and the third rifle company were put in the middle but their aircraft also ran from front to rear of the formation rather than across it. The result was that although everyone was still pretty muddled up on the ground the bulk of those in any one area were from the same company. It worked extremely well and was particularly useful to A Coy who, for some odd reason, were nearly all dropped well beyond the DZ. When he saw what had happened, the company commander collected together everyone who was near him and brought them in as a formed body. Thanks to the experiment he found that he had collected nearly all his own company. A Coy was late getting to its positions and this had repercussions which I will mention in a minute, but it was able to keep together.

Stand 4

"Another of the experiments was in the forming-up. It is usual for a parachute battalion to form up in a battalion RV and then to set out on its job from there, but in this operation speed was even more important than usual and particularly so in the case of this battalion. To save time the companies were told to form-up by themselves and in the positions they were to hold; this meant that the positions were manned about thirty minutes sooner than they would otherwise have been. In the case of this little wood the first man to arrive was the commander of HQ company. He had worked out his jumping order with very great care so as to land as close to the RV as possible; he got it a bit too accurate because he came down actually on it and got caught up in one of the trees. He got down all right and was busy searching it when the next arrivals came in. They said that he was doing this quite thoroughly except that he had forgotten to put a magazine on his Sten. Luckily there were no Germans here but they had been here a short time before and had dug some good slit trenches which saved us a lot of bother.

"The suddenness of the drop had the desired effect and we found the Germans slow to react. The battalion was in this position for five hours and during that time there was no really serious attack put in on us. There were various attacks on the B Coy position by parties of about a platoon strong or slightly more and, at one time, C Coy on the Left (looking North) took on about a company that was working round their way. It was the A Coy position that came in for the worst time. You remember A Coy came in rather late and when they arrived they found that their area was a very nasty spot. Their casualties were high and so were those of the mortars and MMG men who were with them. The trouble came from that little wood you can see straight in front of you about 700 yards away and just this side of the autobahn.

"A troop of 88 mm guns was located there and they were commanded by an officer that one could not help but admire. When the drop took place it appears that the gun crews panicked and ran away but this officer managed to turn enough of them back to man one of the guns. He was of course, in a hopeless position but he kept that gun firing and did an immense amount of damage before he was rounded up. Although A Coy suffered badly 12 Para Bn and Brigade HQ in the wood over there to your Right (194501) got it worse. It was 12 Para Bn that sent out the party that rounded him up; A Coy, of course, should have done it but they were late getting in and it had to be done quickly. We got our share of it here at Bn HQ and had quite a few casualties as I well know because I got a splinter in the face myself. If anyone sees the tip of my nose lying around near here I would be grateful to have it back. It was just about here that I lost it.

"The third of our experiments was a signal one. We decided that the Walkie-Talkie set would be of use as the distances were so small. We carried these in addition to the normal sets with the object of having communication from the very start. They were carried personally by commanders — the Brigade Commander had one, the Battalion Commanders and all Company Commanders. We had our own system for using them and dispensed with all the usual mumbo-jumbo of RT procedure. There were no link signs or code signs and no station acted as control, it was, in fact, a signaller's horror but it worked and worked well too. Everyone used their own christian names and you just spoke up when the air was clear. The Brigade Commander estimated that he was getting information from his battalions quite half an hour before he would otherwise have done. I remember calling him up to tell him that all my battalion were in except for Frank, that was A Coy, and having to say it again about three times. The atmospherics were very bad and I could hear that he was trying to say something to me too but could not get the words so made him repeat it several times. When eventually I got it I found that he was only saying "Don't talk so loud or so fast". After this I handed the set over to my Adjutant.

"There was one independent task which the battalion had and which I had left to the last. This was the holding of an important road and rail junction in an opening in the big wood between the two parachute brigades (167492). One platoon was the force for this job and they were to be out considerably longer than the battalion expected to be in this position. Like every part of the operation, speed into position was an essential but the distance from the DZ, in this case, was something like 3 miles and that through territory which was likely to be occupied and which had not been touched by the landing. To send the platoon off at the double seemed the obvious way to tackle it but this might have turned out to be the slowest way unless they got a clear run. I decided therefore to send off a small party with a wireless set and under an officer to spy out the land and then to send off the platoon when I knew which was the best way for it to go. The officer who was to take this party, however, was killed on the DZ and, as I had lost more than I like to think about the same way, I had no option but to send off the platoon without any preliminary reconnaissance. It was commanded by a Lieutenant PATTERSON, who was one of two Canadian officers that came to me in NORMANDY as non-jumping reinforcements, but who stayed with the battalion throughout and became qualified parachutists at the first opportunity. He reached the position after many adventures and scares and hung on there for 22 hours before he was relieved. It was one of the platoons of A Coy and they did a wonderful job.

"The Germans attacked him frequently but he competed with these most successfully using his own rather unorthodox methods of defence. Whenever an attack developed he sized it up as quickly as he could, and if he decided that it was only a weak one he would stay where he was and beat it off in the ordinary way, but if it seemed stronger than he could hold off, he would use the "Patterson Method", which was as follows. He would leave his position entirely and move his platoon round to one of the flanks; then, when the enemy had struck their blow at nothing and were wondering what to do next, he would rush them from the flank. In this way he killed a great number of Germans and captured many more; he also made contact with 3 Para Bde and later with 15 (S) Div. Altogether his was a very fine independent platoon action.

"The battalion, in these positions round here, took several hundred prisoners during the day. We used to collect them in this area until we had a really substantial number of them and then send them back to Brigade HQ with an escort.

Stand 4

"It is difficult to generalise about the opposition because, like the curate's egg, it was good in parts; one cannot say that it was generally good or generally bad. Some Germans fought extremely hard and others seemed to regard the war as lost already and to fight accordingly. Some of the German paratroops, who had fought so well on the other side of the RHINE, were in this area and we expected a harder tussle than they gave us. At the risk of creating a wrong impression about the opposition I would like to tell you the story of one of my NCOs who was dropped in the country beyond the DZ. As this man was coming down he could see someone on the ground just about where he expected to land, and, as he got lower, he could see that it was a German parachutist and that he had a Schmeisser in his hands. There was really nothing he could do about it and so he just cursed his luck and landed in a heap, as one does, at the German's feet. He told me afterwards that he shut his eyes and waited for the burst from the Schmeisser but it was so long in coming that he opened them again to see what the hitch was. He found that the German was busy collapsing his 'chute for him and when he had done this he helped him out of his harness and unpacked his Bren gun from the kit bag — he then surrendered to him. When he had got over the shock of all this the NCO noticed that about twenty more Germans had arrived and they all surrendered to him too. At the same time and within a mile of all this, other parties of Germans were putting up desperate fights.

"7 Para Bn was to operate in this position, you remember, to assist the other battalion to seize the Brigade objective; it was not intended that it should stay here indefinitely. I am glad to be able to say that the only Germans encountered on the main objective were those that were there when the landings took place; any that went there from this direction went as prisoners. The objective was captured by 1500 hours and 7 Para Bn was ordered to start withdrawing at 1545 hours.

"The withdrawal was not particularly easy because both B and C Coys were in contact at the time. A withdrawal is not an easy manoeuvre and it seemed a most unlikely thing for a parachute battalion ever to be called upon to do. Not because we thought that we could never get the worst of a battle but because there is, normally, nowhere for it to withdraw to. It has no rear. We had never practised it anyway and knew very little of the method, however we managed it all right and without loss too. Our next position was in reserve on the other side of the road.

"The casualties of 7 Para Bn had been high and were chiefly caused by the flak fire while we were in the air and the shelling and mortaring of the positions during the day. Once the drop is over it is better to get as far away from the DZ as you can because it soon becomes the target for every gun and mortar that can be scraped up but, in our case, the job was on the DZ and we had to stay put and take whatever was sent over. The total casualties were 92 out of just over 500 dropped — that is just under 20%."

STAND 5 (201486)

Object of Stand

(a) To see the area of 6 Airlanding Bde LZ.

(b) To relate 6 Airlanding Bde Plan to the ground.

Brigadier R. H. BELLAMY, DSO, Comd 6 Airlanding Bde

Plan of 6 Airlanding Bde

"The tasks allotted to 6 Airlanding Bde were :—

(i) To seize one railway and two road bridges over the River ISSEL.

(ii) To seize and hold HAMMINKELN.

"Bridges were to be prepared for demolition but were only to be blown on orders of the Brigade Commander.

"The brigade area was to be held at all costs.

"Formation was to be Right 1 RUR, Centre 12 DEVON, Left 2 OXF BUCKS.

"Three LZs were chosen, one for each battalion, Bde HQ landing in the centre with 12 DEVON. 1 RUR and 2 OXF BUCKS each detailed 'coup-de-main' parties of company strength to seize the ISSEL bridges. These parties were to land as near the bridges themselves as possible (1 RUR bridge 223485, 2 OXF BUCKS bridges 217497 and 217500).

"The plan was based on tactical landings, i.e. getting the troops right on to their objectives. 12 DEVON LZ was West of HAMMINKELN; the battalion was first to seal the place off from the North, West and South and then attack and capture it. This battalion had only three companies as one had to be detached for duty at Div HQ.

"Enemy flak positions were known but not as fully as they might have been as it turned out. 24 hours before the operation an up to date flak map was received at Bde HQ which did not raise morale and boded ill for the Left battalion! Infantry positions were not known in great detail.

"Landing in the Rear of the enemy's main positions led to the appreciation that resistance would be slight at first increasing in 24 hours when reserves came up. This was not correct and opposition in the brigade area was strong from the start.

"Bde HQ was established in this farmhouse on your Left".

Stand 6

STAND 6 (213491)
(Spectators stand facing East)

Object of Stand

(a) To study anti-flak operations by RAF Typhoons.

(b) To consider the action of 6 Airlanding Bde and in particular 12 DEVON.

A. Conducting Officer

Description of ground

"Beyond the railway to your front and about 800 yards away is the River ISSEL running North and South. It is not possible to see the 1 RUR and 2 OXF BUCKS bridges from here (indicate general direction)".

B. Wing Commander J. R. BALDWIN, DSO, DFC, Comd 123 (Typhoon) Wing RAF.

Operations by 123 Wing, RAF.

"For this operation 123 Wing consisting of four Typhoon Squadrons was moved from GILZI RIJN to NIJMEGEN. Three squadrons of the Wing were armed with rocket projectiles and the other with bombs.

"During the days preceding the river crossing the Wing was concerned with armed reconnaissance to the North-East of the battle area, with interdiction, and with certain pre-planned targets designed to disrupt communications and generally help to isolate the battle area. Among the targets chosen were a telephone exchange and Divisional and Corps HQ. They were attacked with considerable success.

"For Operation VARSITY, the Wing was selected for an anti-flak role in support of the airborne landings, and for this the squadrons were armed as follows :—

164, 198 and 609 Squadrons	4 × 60 lb. HE head rockets
	4 × 60 lb. fragmentation head rockets (anti-personnel)
183 Squadron	"Cluster" bombs, including a proportion of air-burst bombs for better anti-personnel effect.

"The squadrons were briefed to fly in sections of four at ten minute intervals — the first section to arrive half an hour before the first wave of transport machines was due. The pilots were to remain overhead until they had finished their ammunition of rockets or bombs, and their cannon ammunition. The bombline given was the half-constructed autobahn which runs North and South just beyond the River ISSEL. No attacks were to be made West of this line.

"I arrived with my section of four aircraft armed with cluster bombs and cannon about two minutes before the first wave of transport aircraft. We spotted a large gun position which we all attacked with cluster bombs — securing two or three hits on the position. This appeared to have been silenced. By this time the first wave was within range of light flak which was coming up very thickly indeed but mainly from West of the autobahn which was our bombline. In actual fact we attacked two positions with cannon fire, which were West of the bombline. This was as the first troops were actually being dropped. The thick haze of the battle made sighting of the gun positions very difficult, and until the tracer actually came up, most of the pits could not be seen. It was noticed that as soon as a dive was was made fire almost always stopped immediately.

"My impressions of the operation were these :—

(i) The smoke and haze of the battle made the picking out of the gun positions very difficult until they actually opened fire which was held until the transport machines arrived.

(ii) Most of the flak that caused the trouble was in fact outside the bombline and so could not be attacked by the Typhoons.

(iii) The gun positions which were attacked were nearly always silenced at least temporarily.

(iv) The anti-flak operation appeared at the time to have more success than operational research teams considered to be the case later on.

"123 Wing alone carried out ninety-seven sorties while the airborne attack was going in. No pilots were lost although some flak damage was suffered".

C. Brigadier R. H. BELLAMY, DSO, Comd 6 Airlanding Bde

Action of 6 Airlanding Bde

"The flight to the brigade objective was uneventful, taking place in beautiful weather, and the take-off arrangements in UK were excellent. All pointed to the plan being executed to order but two factors stepped in which changed the whole outlook.

(i) After crossing the RHINE the Air stream ran into very hazy conditions which obscured the Brigade area.

(ii) The flak map which had arrived only 24 hours previously was only too true and light flak was intense, as you heard from the last speaker.

Stand 6

"As a result, after the gliders were released at 2,000 feet, the pilots had a most difficult task trying to pick up landmarks and their right LZs. What was worse was that the gliders were silhouetted against the haze and stooging around looking for their areas made them a sitting target.

"However, sufficient troops of each battalion were landed in the correct places, and most important of all a percentage of the coup-de-main parties landed by the bridges. All important objectives were either in our hands or neutralised and ready for "plucking" by 1130 hours (one hour after the landing began). By 1300 hours HAMMINKELN was consolidated and it was possible to take stock of the position.

"Before doing this, a few words on the opposition. The flak had been heavy and taken its inevitable toll, ground opposition was stronger than anticipated, every farm house was a strong point and there was a considerable number of SP guns and half tracks milling around the brigade area. The enemy fought well but by 1300 hours realised it was hopeless and either gave up or got outside the perimeter.

"The position in the brigade on the afternoon of D-Day was fair. 1 RUR (Right) and 12 DEVON (Centre) were over half strength and not being unduly worried. 1 RUR had a number of skirmishes with tanks from the East but dealt with them effectively. 12 DEVON was peaceful in HAMMINKELN.

"2 OXF BUCKS on the Left and dangerous flank was not in a good position. Its total strength was in the vicinity of 200 only and it was becoming evident that the enemy were quite strong opposite it. This threat developed and during the night orders were given to this battalion to blow the road bridge, while one company of 12 DEVON was placed in support, but under command of the Brigade Commander.

"Enemy infantry infiltrated across the river throughout the night, set fire to unoccupied houses and 2 OXF BUCKS had quite a time throwing them out. By the morning of D+1 however no worse damage had occurred than the blowing up of the bridge and from then on enemy attempts to break the perimeter were confined to tip-and-run attacks with tanks and infantry which were dealt with by RA and the RAF "cab-rank".

"The question of control is inevitably difficult in any airborne operation and particularly when landing into defended areas. Wireless is all important and sufficient sets must be brought in to ensure that all links work. In VARSITY control was exercised from the start although many key personnel, including myself, landed in many peculiar places. What is essential is that briefing must be simple and designed so that every company and platoon can fight according to the intention and effect a link up as soon as possible.

"This was done and as the day wore on so control and the strength of units increased. The losses in personnel were high, but the losses to equipment were higher due to the great vulnerability of the glider in an enemy defended area. The nature of the fighting can best be described by the fact that probably the first casualty was the CQMS of Bde HQ leading his command to attack a farm building which had been selected in the UK as the area for the administrative element of Bde HQ."

D. Lieutenant Colonel P. GLEADELL, DSO, CO 12 DEVON

(Wherever possible places referred to by map reference in
the account will be pointed out on the ground by the Speaker)

The Battalion Plan

Intention

"The task allotted to my battalion, 12 DEVON, less one company, was to land on LZ 'R' and isolate the village of HAMMINKELN by preventing any enemy movement in or out of the village West of the main road running North and South through the village. Having achieved this, HAMMINKELN was to be seized and cleared as soon as possible, and held at all costs. One section 195 Airlanding Fd Amb was under command, and 3 Airlanding A Tk Bty less three 17-pounders was in direct support for the operation.

"C Coy, with one section 53 Airlanding Lt Regt in support, was given a separate task under Div HQ to clear the divisional LZ ('P') and concentration area (copse 190479), which you saw at Stand 1, and to cover the forming up of Div HQ.

"It was not known at that stage how many gliders were to be allotted to the Battalion. Alternative glider load tables, had however, already been drawn up catering for allotments from between 72 and 60 Horsas. In the event, the Battalion flew in on a 65 glider scale of which 36 were the new nose-unloading HORSA II type.

Method

"The Battalion plan was divided into two phases ; Phase I being the immediate isolation of the objective, and Phase II the assault. The plan was such that Phase II could be put into immediate effect if the opportunity occurred.

Phase I

"D Coy, with No 26 A Tk Pl (less two detachments) and some pioneers, was the coup-de-main company. It was to land as close into the village on the West side as possible, seize the Western cross-roads 208487, and exploit to the road junctions 210487 and 208488.

"A Coy, with one anti-tank platoon, was to land South-West and South of HAMMINKELN and isolate the objective from the South and South-West.

Stand 6

"B Coy, with two 17-pounders, was to land West of the objective and isolate HAMMINKELN from the North and North-West.

"The Reconnaissance Platoon was to land with B Coy and patrol to the large copse 212484, liaise with 1 RUR and prevent infiltration between the copse and HAMMINKELN.

"Although DF and SOS tasks were selected beforehand, there could be little prospect of firing them owing to the positions of neighbouring units. The Mortar Wing was, therefore, given the following tasks :—

(i) The first platoon to land to get into action in area orchard 201487 with zero line on HAMMINKELN.

(ii) The next platoon to remain in reserve on wheels in the same area.

(iii) The remaining platoon to form a road block facing West in area of houses 198486 (close to HQ 6 Airlanding Bde).

"The MMG Pl was to cover the entrances North and South of HAMMINKELN, one section firing by observation on each arc.

"HQ Coy was to establish a checkpoint in the South-East corner of orchard 202486. Advance Bn HQ was to be established at the cross-roads 204487. The Glider Pilots were to assist in unloading gliders, evacuating casualties to the RAP in the Bn HQ area, manning the POW cage and controlling the civilians.

Phase II

"Phase II was to be undertaken immediately the opportunity arose. D Coy was to clear the centre of the village and be responsible for the defence of the objective to the East and South-East. A Coy was to clear and hold the South of the village, and B Coy was to assault and hold the North-East and North-West face of the village. C Coy when available was to concentrate in reserve at the houses 181486 and be prepared to counter-attack the objective. Road blocks were to be erected and manned on all approaches.

Administration

"It was planned to phase the land and sea tail over the RHINE, including the cook's lorries, between D+2 and D+4. Every man flew in with one 24-hour pack ; and gliders carried, in addition, two compo packs for handling by Div RASC. The air resupply for the Division was being duplicated by preloaded DUKWs to be phased forward on D Day.

"All vehicles carried one spare filled petrol jerrican. Unit first line reserve was carried by the Land Elements.

"Every vehicle and glider carried spare stretchers and blankets.

Briefing and Concentration

"Company Commanders were briefed at BULFORD on 19 March. On 20 March the Battalion moved by road to the transit camp at GOSFIELD near BRAINTREE. On 21 March and the morning of 22 March all vehicles, handcarts and cycles were loaded into the unit gliders on the airfields at GREAT DUNMOW, RIVENHALL and MATCHING. The station was sealed at 1430 hours on 22 March and the whole battalion was briefed.

Action of 12 DEVON

Flight

"A final handshake with the AOC the Station and then we closed the doors. Everyone strapped themselves in and put their cigarettes out. We were fortunate in having a Squadron Commander of Glider Pilots and his RAF Serjeant co-Pilot with whom we had flown on a recent Exercise. My Jeep and trailer were lashed amidships ; I had the first seat on the starboard side and then came my batman, and one of the Regimental Police. Opposite us were the IO and a Private of the Intelligence Section. "Tail-end Charlies" were my Signaller and Jeep driver. Our glider chalk number—188.

"Promptly at 0630 hours our Tug started up and we taxied forward behind one of the A Coy gliders to the head of the main runway. A pause, and then off we went—slowly at first and then quickly gathering speed, we bumped along the runway, until the gentle sway of the glider and the cessation of thuds indicated we were airborne. Everyone shouted the customary "Airborne" and then settled down to face the long journey. We had not been off the ground a few seconds before the pilot turned round and drew my attention to the leading glider, its tow rope broken, circling down to find a spot for an emergency landing. Flying at 2,000 feet, the crossing was comparatively smooth, except for the usual air-pockets. Standing in the pilot's cockpit and looking out along the tow rope over the Halifax, one could see the long procession stretching out into the horizon. Once BRUSSELS was reached, and the stream of American aircraft joined in at 600 feet the air seemed to be filled by the massive armada. Darting in and out of the vast convoy were the Allied fighters, keen eyed to mark any threat of enemy interference from the air.

"Visibility was excellent on the way, and the landmarks easy to pick up. Occasionally, one detected a lone glider circling down and one hoped that their forced landing would be a good one. The noise of air rushing through the glider made conversation difficult ; unless one stood in the cockpit, there was little one could see through the small portholes on either side of the fuselage ; the hours, therefore, slipped tediously by.

Stand 6

"At 1000 hours we cheered up as the tea-container was passed round, after which we strapped in. As we approached the REICHSWALD, scene of the recent fighting, visibility lessened. At last, the long winding silver riband of the RHINE hove into view—but beyond, one could see nothing. In fact, once over the river visibility was scarcely a furlong, as the whole of the LZ was covered with a thick pall of smoke, dust, and ground mist. That we were over the area was apparent from the flak, and with a sudden wrench we cast-off and drifted downwards. At first all was quiet, in marked contrast with the last four hours on tow. Then, as we came closer to the ground the sounds of battle could be distinctly heard.

"The heavy flak and, more particularly, the light flak, and the small arms fire was still active, and the glider shuddered as a shell burst nearby. The Pilot signalled that he was going to try a landing, but the restricted view made him level up again with a sudden jerk. A burst, and then another, of bullets pierced the glider hull; the first struck the Jeep, fortunately missing the petrol tank, and the second wounded one of the soldiers in the back. Again the Pilot tried a landing, and again he levelled up, losing height the while. A few seconds—they seemed hours—later, he turned round and said—"I can't see a darned thing, but I'll do the best I can for you". There was a crash, the floor boards were torn open and we found our feet being dragged along the ground for a few yards; at the same time the wounded man was hurled forward against the cock-pit. With a jolt we came to rest (at 218501), and according to our prearranged deplaning plan, the door was slid open and one of the men dashed out, Bren in hand, to take up a covering position. We had no idea where we were, except that we had stopped inches short of a particularly deep bomb crater. Bullets appeared to be coming from three directions, and a 20 mm opened up from the autobahn, 120 yards away. There was a rush of air as a great Hamilcar Glider slid over our heads and crashed in the smoke a few hundred yards beyond. We were overjoyed to be hailed, suddenly in English. It was a platoon of 2 OXF BUCKS and they were firing in our direction. There was no chance of extracting my Jeep and so between us we carried our one casualty towards our friends. We then realised that they were on the banks of the ISSEL astride the railway bridge, and that we had landed between them and the enemy from RINGENBERG. Some Germans came out from a nearby copse, and were rounded up. I was naturally anxious to get to HAMMINKELN as soon as possible, so we left the casualty with that Coy HQ of 2 OXF BUCKS and made our way South along the railway track. The sound of shellfire and machine-guns, coming from all sides, was deafening, and every now and again we came on a glider blazing furiously, one or two with their crews trapped within and little one could do to extricate them. One glider, or what was left of it, had wrapped itself round a massive tree. The whole situation seemed chaotic, and I wondered if we should ever get it unravelled. Every farm house appeared to contain a defended post and isolated battles were being fought out all over the LZ and beyond.

"Five gliders had force-landed en route including OC D Coy; personnel of two of these took off again, but only the D Coy HQ glider reached the LZ. Enemy fighter interference was negligible until the RHINE was crossed—and even then it was almost non-existent.

After Landing

"The enemy were in greater confusion than we were. A number managed to concentrate in HAMMINKELN, particularly on the North-East side. They consisted mostly of flak gunners, Luftwaffe Regiment, Volkssturm and Parachutists. Three SP guns, some tanks, armoured cars and half-tracks were cruising about the LZ and engaged troops who were deplaning.

"The area in front of you now was covered with Light Flak Gun positions, manned mainly by personnel of Battle Group KARST. This was a special anti-airlanding formation with small groups of men, mostly paratroops, SS or Waffen SS, in various places throughout the 84 Div area. The Germans had evidently appreciated the likelihood of an airborne operation in this area.

"Confusion appeared to reign everywhere and isolated battles at close quarters were being fought out by detached parties all over the LZ and far beyond. I myself joined up with a platoon of D Coy and we concentrated about the road junction 212495 and, after encountering some resistance, reached the Northern edge of HAMMINKELN. Touch was gained by wireless with Bn HQ and B Coy, and so I gave the order for Phase II at 1135 hours. Companies duly assaulted and the objective was taken by midday. Consolidation and mopping-up were vigorously carried out in anticipation of the expected counter-attack and to eliminate the remaining flak positions. A German strong-point of some forty men in this Windmill (213491) was accounted for by one NCO. OC A Coy with his CSM and batman put out of action one tank and two half-tracked vehicles, and drove off a second tank. OC B Coy, although wounded and the sole survivor of his glider which landed at RINGENBERG, fought off the enemy for twenty minutes before being captured.

"Battalion casualties during the morning were:—

	Officers	*ORs*	*Total*	
Killed	6	24	30	(excluding FOO)
Wounded (all evacuated)	5	25	30	
Missing	5	75	80	(50 subsequently found to be killed)
	16	124	140	

"For his part, the enemy casualties must have been heavy during the day, and altogether some 500 POW were brought into the battalion cage.

Stand 6

"C Coy, with only two platoons—one platoon glider had received a direct hit just after release and another landed and remained with B Coy—was also landed slightly off-target. The enemy, who had been holding the divisional LZ in some force, had, to a large extent, been cleared by troops from 17 US Airborne Div. There was still, however, spasmodic sniping and mortaring, and the company suffered some further casualties.

Consolidation

"The Battalion consolidated as planned for Phase II. German reaction was only slight and consisted mainly of shelling the centre of HAMMINKELN with 88 mm SP guns, and mortaring. Parties of Germans withdrawing from the RHINE during the night were captured. The panic-stricken civilians and the POW were excellently handled by the Glider Pilots under the Squadron Commander and were never an embarrassment to the fighting troops.

"During the night, A Coy were moved over to the North-East of HAMMINKELN in support of a very depleted company of 2 OXF BUCKS, which was counter-attacked by some infantry and tanks. Further attempts by the enemy to concentrate East of the ISSEL were frustrated by action from rocket-firing Typhoons; he, therefore, limited himself to digging-in on the East bank of the river.

The first troops from Second Army to reach the Battalion area were a troop of M.10s from 15 (S) Div, at 1030 hours on 25 March, followed at 1600 hours by advance parties of 6 KOSB which was to relieve the Battalion for its break-out of the bridgehead the following day. Nine jeeps and trailers from the unit Land Tail also arrived during the evening with reserve ammunition."

Stand 7

STAND 7 (211479)

(Spectators stand on West of road facing East)

Object of Stand

To hear an account of the landing of one of 1 RUR's gliders.

Lieutenant D. S. M. TURNER, Glider Pilot Regiment

"I was the pilot flying one of the gliders allotted to 1 RUR; the battalion LZ was mainly in the area to the West of the road.

"Prior to the operation, the Glider Pilot Regiment had been concentrating more on individual spot landings as opposed to the mass landing technique used on concentrated LZs on previous operations. This was done with a view to a tactical landing in the future. The Regiment was briefed to land 6 Airlanding Bde on LZs near HAMMINKELN and to land elements of 2 OXF BUCKS and 1 RUR in coup-de-main parties on the bridges over the ISSEL.

"All the squadrons involved attended the Battalion's briefings, the individual squadron briefings and finally the air briefing by the RAF.

"Several units of the Regiment were attached to 46 Group RAF and were moved to EAST ANGLIA into the 38 Group RAF area. This was to concentrate the force and to save time "forming-up" in the air as well as to save flying time.

"On the morning of 24 March the visibility was good and all the combinations were airborne except for one which was unable to take off owing to the tug undercarriage collapsing. The stream formed up over HAWKINGE and flew from there to WAVRE and thence in a double stream at 2,500 feet to the target area. No fighter opposition was met en route. A small percentage of gliders released prematurely owing to slipstream trouble, but most of them were staggered a few hundred feet either above or below the briefed height of 2,500 feet in order to try and avoid slipstreams.

"On running up to the RHINE, one could see that the general area was enveloped in a thick haze.

"Three check points were marked on our maps; points A, B and C all five minutes flying apart, check point C being the release point. A predetermined release point is not strictly adhered to, but acts as a guide to the Glider Pilot.

"We were flying at roughly 2,900 feet (to avoid slipstream) and point A was easily seen; from there on, nothing could be distinguished on the ground. The flak was extremely heavy and concentrated and flying in position behind the tug became harder as the surrounding air was more than a little bumpy.

"As we could not see our own LZ or anybody else's, we remained on tow.

"Suddenly we saw the autobahn below us, and as a result of careful study previously of air photographs, we knew where we were.

"We released and did a tight 270° turn to port and saw the church spire of HAMMINKELN in front of us.

"Owing to the immediate vicinity being rather crowded with gliders we applied full flap, which results in a very steep dive and went down on to the LZ as briefed. The five members of 1 RUR were none the worse after their unorthodox approach and proceeded to unload the jeep and trailer containing petrol and ammunition. Suddenly there was a loud hissing and one of the main wheels was hit. This stopped the unloading temporarily and we returned the fire. At this period we saw a Horsa in flames and when about 50 feet from the ground the starboard main plane was blown off. The glider landed a little roughly, but the occupants were unhurt except for a few minor bruises. This episode says a lot for the strength of construction and manoeuvrability of the Horsa glider.

"The load was removed from the glider via the nose and a quick survey made of the glider, which was found to have been holed considerably. We were not aware of any personal attention in the air except for a continuous bumping underneath. After some opposition we reported to the 1 RUR RV— the farmhouse in the orchard, across the road to your Right front.

"Three hours later, there was a pleasant smell of bacon and eggs from Sqn HQ (a Wehrmacht stores by the level crossing East of HAMMINKELN) and we carried on with a variety of jobs, such as retrieving an American and his Auster aircraft which had been shot down, and dispersing and controlling PWs and civilians. We remained at the disposal of Commander 6 Airlanding Bde."

SECTION IV

NOTES FOR THE GUIDANCE OF CONDUCTING OFFICERS

Some notes are given below on the preliminary work and administrative detail which will have to be carried out by the Conducting Officer before and during the running of the Battlefield Tour. They are based on experience gained in running Battlefield Tours during 1947 with about one hundred Senior Officer spectators.

Preliminary Reconnaissance

The Conducting Officer should try to have at least three or four clear days on the ground before the Tour starts (exclusive of days spent in briefing the Transport Officer, Provost Officer etc.). This time is necessary to write up the description of the ground appropriate to the time of year and weather conditions, and to become fully conversant with the whole battle area. Binoculars are indispensable for this purpose, and a prismatic compass will be found to be most helpful.

On the 1947 Tour, when speakers had still to write up their accounts, they required one day on the ground for preparation and extra time for rehearsal.

Stands

It is often advisable to tape the limits of the Stands so that the spectators may be kept in a position from which they can all see the ground; this will make the task of the Conducting Officer and speakers in describing the ground very much easier.

Introductory Lecture

A large scale wall diagram will be required to illustrate the Introductory Lecture.

Use of ground

It may be thought advisable to go round the Stands a day or two before the Tour with an interpreter, and warn the local inhabitants of the ground which it is required to use. This enables cattle to be moved, gaps to be made in the fences, etc.

Provost

A detachment from the Corps of Royal Military Police should be made available. A preliminary reconnaissance should be carried out to indicate the route for the day, what signing is required, and what signs are required at each stand.

Loudspeaker Equipment

A detachment from the Royal Signals is required to operate the Loudspeaker Equipment. There should be two jeeps, each a complete station, which can be leap-frogged from stand to stand. It is as well for at least one set of loudspeaker equipment to be portable independently of the jeep, in case a jeep cannot be driven to the exact place at which the speaker is to be sited. A reconnaissance is necessary to show the operators the route between stands and the exact positions for the loudspeakers and microphone. Care must be taken in the siting of the microphone and loudspeakers to avoid "screaming", as certain speakers like to face the spectators and others to face the ground about which they are speaking.

Transport

Buses may be used to convey spectators and again a reconnaissance is necessary with the transport officer or NCO to indicate the route, ensure that the buses can get down the lanes, and find turning places where necessary.

Conduct of the Tour

(a) It was arranged that the Conducting Officer was the first away from each stand, so that he could confirm that arrangements were complete at the next stand. The interpreter should travel immediately behind him, to clear away any farm waggons or obstacles which may be blocking the route.

(b) In the summer months, if the weather is dry, it may be possible to move from Stand 1 to Stand 2 via the track through the DIERSFORDTER WALD and road and track junction 169462. This is *NOT* the route shown on Map 13 or the one for which time is allowed in the Itinerary; it would require previous reconnaissance.

(c) The Conducting Officer should carry the following equipment in his car :—
>   Megaphones
>   Wire Cutters
>   Barbed wire—for mending fences (or, Provost may do this).

Lunch

A buffet lunch was provided ; in the Itinerary (Part III, Section II) it has been included at Stand 4, where a suitable shady site is likely to be available. A 3 ton lorry is required, and a tent was taken in case of inclement weather.

Alternative Speakers

Should some of the speakers whose accounts are printed in Part III not be available for a particular Tour, a few alternative speakers are given below :—

Introductory Lecture

> Brigadier R. H. BELLAMY, DSO (Comd 6 Airlanding Bde) } in place of Major
> Colonel W. McC. T. FAITHFULL, DSO, (CRA 6 Brit Airborne Div) } General BOLS.

Stand 1

> Major G. S. FENTON, Royal Signals (2 IC 6 Brit Airborne Div Sigs), in place of Lieutenant Colonel BRADLEY.

Stand 2

> Brigadier S. J. L. HILL, DSO, MC (Comd 3 Para Bde), now a civilian, in place of Lieutenant Colonel HEWETSON
>
> Lieutenant Colonel N. CROOKENDEN, DSO, Cheshire Regiment (CO 9 Para Bn) could describe the action of his battalion.

Appendices

APPENDIX "A"

ORDER OF BATTLE

SECOND ARMY
(Lieutenant General Sir Miles C. Dempsey, KCB, KBE, DSO, MC)

FIRST ALLIED AIRBORNE ARMY
(Lieutenant General Lewis H. Brereton, US Army)

12 CORPS
(Lieutenant General Sir Neil M. Ritchie, KBE, CB, DSO, MC)
(CCRA—Brigadier G. W. E. Heath, CBE, DSO, MC)

7 ARMD DIV (Major General L. O. Lyne, CB, DSO)

15 (S) DIV (Major General C. M. Barber, CB, DSO)
    44 (L) INF BDE (Brigadier Hon H. C. H. T. Cumming-Bruce, DSO)
        8 RS
        6 RSF
        6 KOSB
    In Support:
        11 R TKS (LVsT)
    46 (H) INF BDE (Brigadier R. M. Villiers, DSO)
        9 CAMERONIANS
        2 GLAS H
        7 SEAFORTH
    227 (H) INF BDE (Brigadier E. C. Colville, DSO)
        10 HLI
        2 GORDONS
        2 A & SH
    In Support:
        E RIDING YEO (LVsT)

52 (L) DIV (Major General E. Hakewill-Smith, CB, CBE, MC)
    155 INF BDE (Brigadier J. F. S. McLaren, DSO, OBE)
    156 INF BDE (Brigadier C. N. Barclay, CBE, DSO)
    157 INF BDE (Brigadier E. H. G. Grant, DSO, MC)
        5 KOSB
        7 CAMERONIANS
        5 HLI
    RA (CRA—Brigadier L. B. D. Burns, CBE, DSO, MC)
        79 Fd Regt
        80 Fd Regt
        186 Fd Regt
        1 Mtn Regt
        54 A Tk Regt
        108 LAA Regt
    Under command (from 8 AGRA):
        63 Med Regt
        146 Med Regt (with under command one battery 108 HAA Regt)

53 (W) DIV (Major General R. K. Ross, CB, DSO, MC)
    RA (CRA—Brigadier J. C. Friedberger, DSO)
        81 Fd Regt
        83 Fd Regt
        133 Fd Regt
        71 A Tk Regt
        25 LAA Regt
    Under command (from 8 AGRA):
        77 Med Regt (with under command one battery 108 HAA Regt)

4 ARMD BDE (Type A)   (Brigadier R. M. P. Carver, CBE, DSO, MC)
    4 RHA
    GREYS
    3/4 CLY
    44 R TKS (DD)
    2 KRRC

31 ARMD BDE   (Brigadier G. S. Knight, DSO)
(From 79 Armd Div)

34 ARMD BDE (Type B)   (Brigadier W. S. Clarke, CBE, DSO)

1 CDO BDE   (Brigadier D. Mills-Roberts, DSO, MC)
    3 Cdo
    6 Cdo
    45 (RM) Cdo
    46 (RM) Cdo
    1 CHESHIRE (under command from 115 Inf Bde)

115 INF BDE   (Brigadier E. L. Luce, DSO, TD)

3 AGRA   (Brigadier F. C. F. Cleeve, CBE, DSO, MC)

8 AGRA   (Brigadier A. P. Campbell, DSO, OBE)
    25 Fd Regt
    61 Med Regt
    53 Hy Regt

    Under command :
    40 US Fd Arty Group (36 × 155 mm)
        547 US Fd Arty Bn
        548 US Fd Arty Bn
        549 US Fd Arty Bn

9 AGRA   (Brigadier C. H. M. Brunker, DSO)

XVIII US CORPS (AIRBORNE)

(Commander—Major General Matthew B. Ridgway, US Army)
(Deputy Commander—Major General R. N. Gale, DSO, OBE, MC),
(Commander 1 Brit Airborne Corps)

17 US AIRBORNE DIV   (Major General William M. Miley, US Army)
    507 Para Inf Regt
    513 Para Inf Regt
    194 Glider Inf Regt
    17 US Airborne Div Arty
        464 Para Fd Arty Bn
        466 Para Fd Arty Bn
        680 Glider Fd Arty Bn
        681 Glider Fd Arty Bn

6 BRIT AIRBORNE DIV   (Major General E. L. Bols, CB, DSO)
    3 PARA BDE   (Brigadier S. J. L. Hill, DSO, MC)
    5 PARA BDE   (Brigadier J. H. N. Poett, DSO)
    6 AIRLANDING BDE   (Brigadier R. H. Bellamy, DSO)
    RA   (CRA—Brigadier W. McC. T. Faithfull, DSO)

	Airborne	*Seaborne Tail*
HQ	Main Div HQ	Det Main Div HQ
	Det Rear Div HQ	Rear Div HQ
Inf	HQ 3 Para Bde	
	8 Para Bn	
	9 Para Bn	
	1 Cdn Para Bn	
	HQ 5 Para Bde	
	7 Para Bn	
	12 Para Bn	
	13 Para Bn	
	HQ 6 Airlanding Bde	
	12 DEVON	
	2 OXF BUCKS	
	1 RUR	
	Dets 22 Indep Para Coy	22 Indep Para Coy

	Airborne	*Seaborne Tail*
Armd	Two tk tps 6 Airborne Armd Recce Regt 4.2″ Mortar Tp 6 Airborne Armd Recce Regt	6 Airborne Armd Recce Regt (less two tk tps and 4.2″ mortar tp)
Arty	HQ RA 53 (WY) Airlanding Lt Regt RA 3 Airlanding A Tk Bty RA 4 Airlanding A Tk Bty RA Dets 2 FOU	2 Airlanding A Tk Regt (less two batteries) 2 FOU (less dets)
Engrs	HQ RE One tp 3 Para Sqn RE Two tps 591 Para Sqn RE	3 Para Sqn RE (less one tp) 591 Para Sqn RE (less two tps) 249 Fd Coy RE (Airborne) 286 Fd Pk Coy (Airborne)
Sigs	6 Airborne Div Sigs	Det 6 Airborne Div Sigs
ST	Two pls 716 Comp Coy (Airborne Lt) RASC	HQ RASC 398 Comp Coy (Airborne Hy) RASC 63 Comp Coy (Airborne Hy) RASC 716 Comp Coy (Airborne Lt) RASC (less two pls)
Med	224 Para Fd Amb 225 Para Fd Amb 195 Airlanding Fd Amb	Det 224 Para Fd Amb Det 225 Para Fd Amb Det 195 Airlanding Fd Amb
Ord		HQ RAOC 6 Airborne Div Ord Fd Pk
REME		HQ REME 6 Airborne Div Wksps
Pro	Det 6 Airborne Div Pro Coy	6 Airborne Div Pro Coy
Postal		Div Postal Unit
Int	Dets 317 FS Sec	317 FS Sec
AAC	Sqns Glider P Regt	

6 GDS ARMD BDE (Type B) (Brigadier W. D. C. Greenacre, DSO, MVO)
    4 Tk GREN GDS
    4 Tk COLDM GDS
    3 Tk SG

ROYAL AIR FORCE

38 GROUP (Air Vice-Marshal J. R. Scarlett-Streatfield, CBE)

190 Squadron	298 Squadron
196 Squadron	299 Squadron
295 Squadron	570 Squadron
296 Squadron	620 Squadron
297 Squadron	644 Squadron

46 GROUP (Air Commodore L. Darvall, CB, MC)

48 Squadron	437 Squadron
233 Squadron	512 Squadron
271 Squadron	575 Squadron

UNITED STATES ARMY AIR FORCE

IX US TROOP CARRIER COMMAND (Major General Paul L. Williams, US Army)

    50 WING
        439 Group
        440 Group
        441 Group
        442 Group
        Pathfinder Group

    52 WING
        61 Group
        313 Group
        314 Group
        315 Group
        316 Group

    53 WING
        434 Group
        435 Group
        436 Group
        437 Group
        438 Group

APPENDIX "B"

EQUIPMENT AND ORGANISATION
(Allied and German)

The following tables give the main details of the organisation of British and German formations at the time of Operation VARSITY, and the principal data about certain tanks and equipments in use at the time.

Table 1—ALLIED TANKS

Type	Crew	Weight (tons)	Armament	Amn carried (rounds)	Max Speed (m.p.h.)	Radius of action (miles)
Churchill IV	5	38.5	1 × 6 pr 2 × 7.92 mm BESA MGs	84 6975	16.9	123
Churchill V	5	38.5	1 × 95 mm 2 × 7.92 mm BESA MGs	47 6525	16.4	123
Churchill VII	5	39.5	1 × 75 mm 2 × 7.92 mm BESA MGs	83 6525	13.5	142
T.9 ("LOCUST")	3	7.6	1 × 37 mm 1 × .300" Browning MG	38 4250	26.7	135

Table 2—OTHER ALLIED EQUIPMENTS

1. **HORSA Glider** (See photos following page 109)

    Two types of HORSA were in use on Operation VARSITY :—

    Mark I — tail unloading ; the tail was blown off after landing by an explosive charge.

    Mark II — nose unloading ; the nose of the glider, including the cockpit, was swung away to one side on landing.

    Both types carried one platoon or a jeep and trailer or a jeep and 6 pounder anti-tank gun.

    Each glider required one tug aircraft ; speed on tow was 130–150 knots ; landing speed was about 70 knots, and normally 100 yards was required in which to land, although 50 yards was enough f the skid and not the undercarriage was used.

    Intercommunication between the tug and the glider was by a cable which ran through the tow rope.

    The two pilots in the glider sat side by side. Controls were similar to those in a powered aircraft, but without a throttle and with a Cable Angle Indicator, which showed the pilot, in bad visibility or at night, whether or not he was flying in the correct position behind the tug.

2. **HAMILCAR Glider** (See photos following page 109)

    Larger than the HORSA, and with nose unloading. The cockpit was above the part of the nose which swung aside.

    The load was a jeep and 17 pounder anti-tank gun, or a LOCUST tank, or other load of stores of equivalent weight.

3. **WACO Glider**

    Used by 17 US Airborne Div. One tug aircraft could tow two WACOs, but the load of each glider was half that of the HORSA, i.e. half a platoon or a jeep or a 6 pounder anti-tank gun.

4. **Landing Vehicle, Tracked (LVT) (BUFFALO)**

    An amphibious vehicle, carrying light armour in front only. Maximum load was 4 tons and maximum speeds were 30 m.p.h. on land and 5.9 m.p.h. in the water. Used for either personnel or equipment. Main disadvantages were :—

    (a) Tracks quickly damage road surfaces.
    (b) Vehicle requires frequent maintenance.
    (c) Presents a vulnerable target when out of the water.

    LVsT were organised in regiments each of two squadrons each squadron having 36 LVsT—enough to lift an assault battalion.

Table 3—GERMAN TANKS

Particulars of the two principal German tanks in use at the time of this operation are given below:—

Type	Crew	Weight (tons)	Armament	Amn carried (rounds)	Max Speed (m.p.h.)	Radius of action (miles)
Pz Kw V "PANTHER"	5	45	1 × 75 mm 2 × 7.92 mm MGs	79 4500	34	125
Pz Kw VI "TIGER"	5	56	1 × 88 mm 2 × 7.92 mm MGs	87 5700	·23	73

Table 4—EQUIPMENT OF BRITISH UNITS

6 Gds Armd Bde — Churchill IV — 10 ⎫
                            Churchill V — 6 ⎬ per battalion
                            Churchill VII — 45 ⎭

6 Airborne Armd — T.9 (LOCUST)   8
    Recce Regt   Cruiser tanks   8

ORGANISATION OF FORMATIONS

Organisations of British and German formations ar the time of operation VARSITY are shown in Tables 5, 6, 7, 8.

Table 5—OUTLINE ORGANISATION

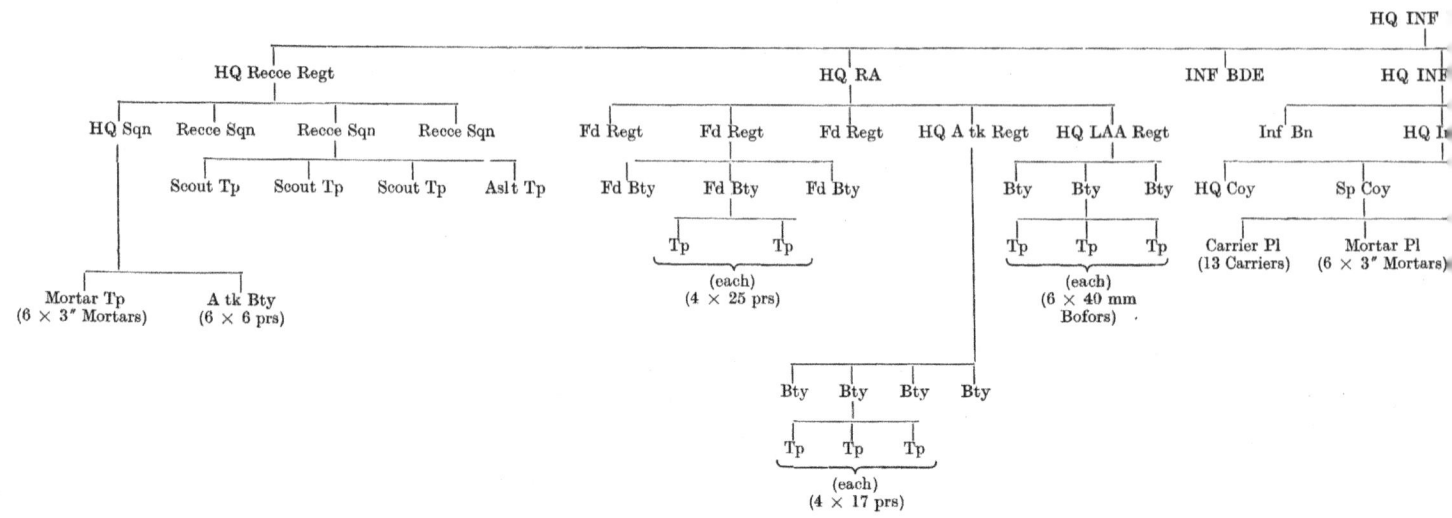

NOTES

1. Total strength of part of Inf Div show
   i.e. div less Sigs and Services
2. No weapon smaller than a MMG is sh

Table 6 — OUTLINE ORGANISATION OF A GERMA

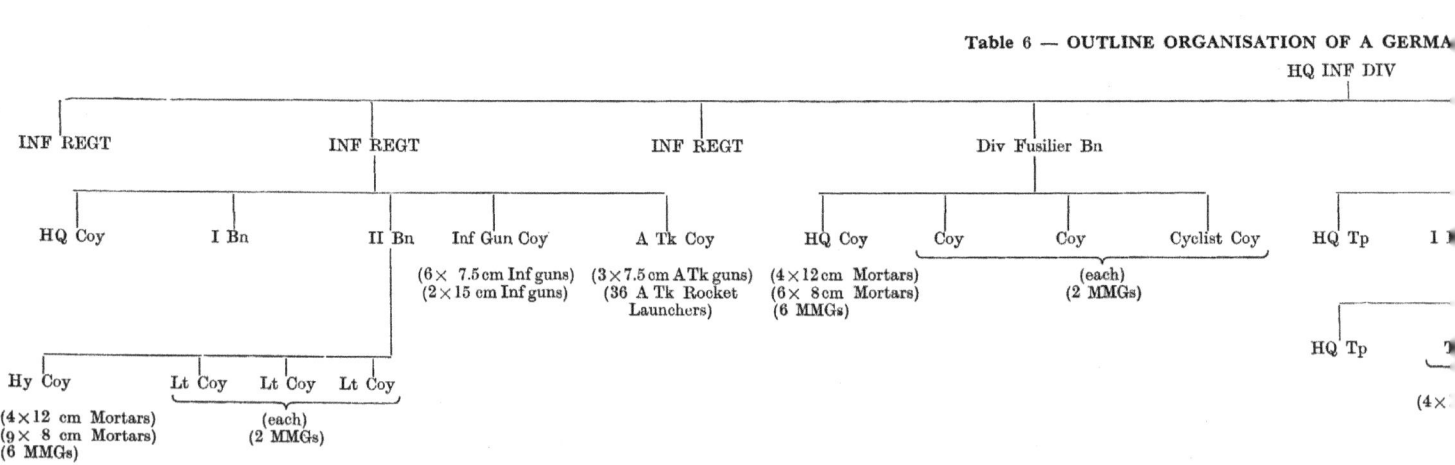

N

1. Total strength of part of German Inf
   (i.e. Div less Sigs a
2. No weapon smaller than a MMG is s

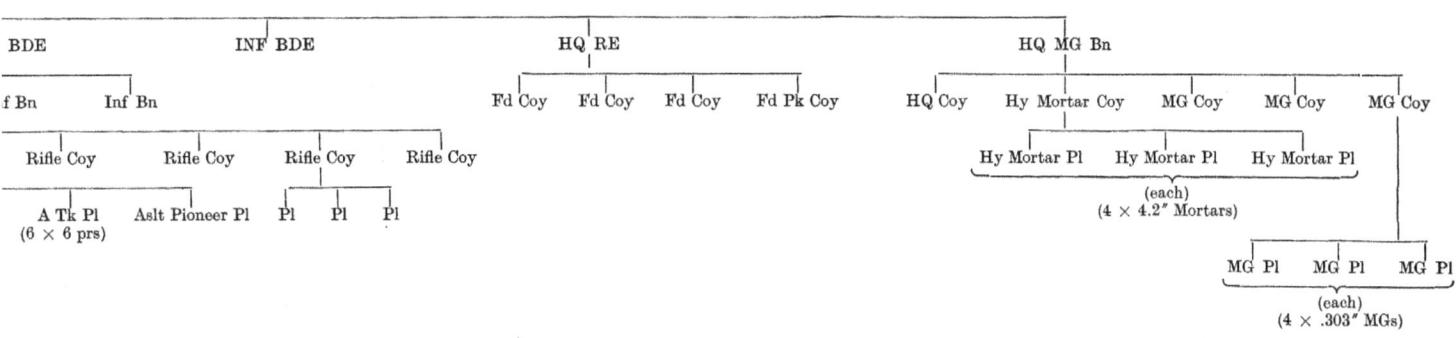

OF A BRITISH INFANTRY DIVISION (1945)

N INFANTRY DIVISION (1945)

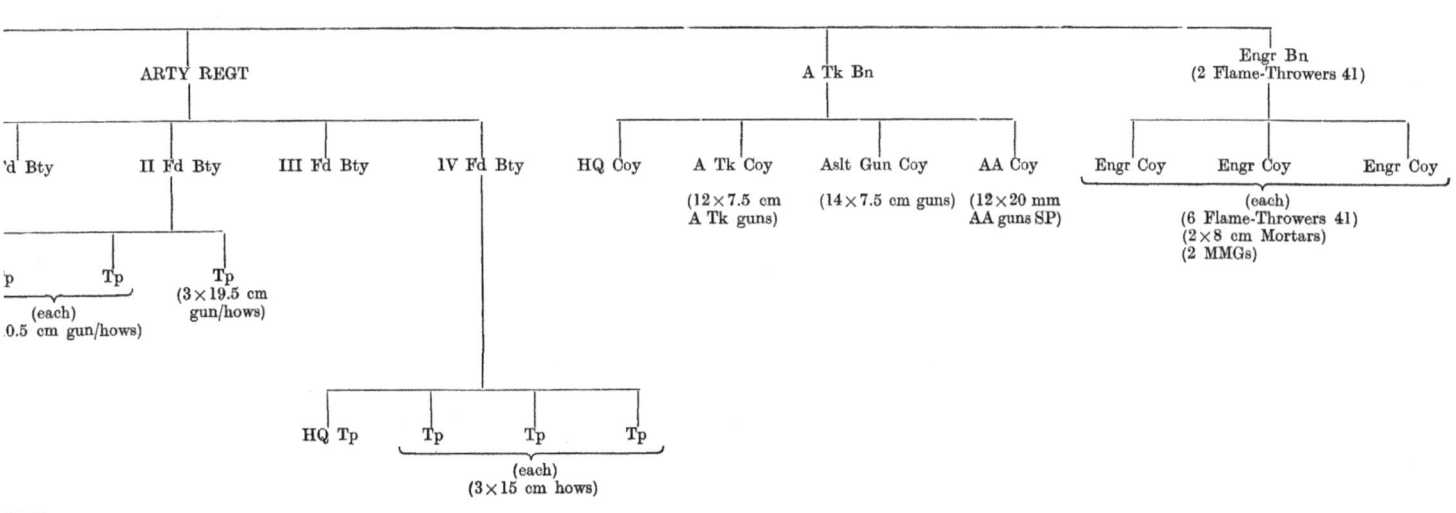

Table 7—OUTLINE ORGANISATION OF

HQ AIRBO[RNE]

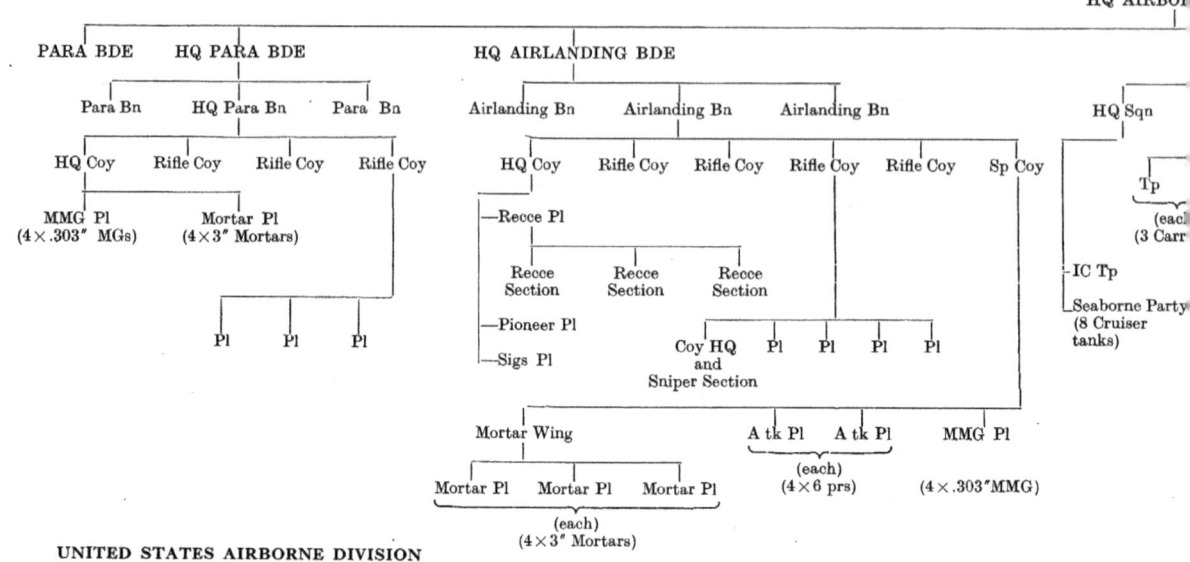

UNITED STATES AIRBORNE DIVISION

The US Airborne Division had two parachute regiments and one glider regiment, the regiment being approximately equivalent to a British brigade. It had two parachute field artillery battalions and two glider field artillery battalions.

Table 8 — OUTLINE ORGANISATION O[F]

HQ P[ARA]

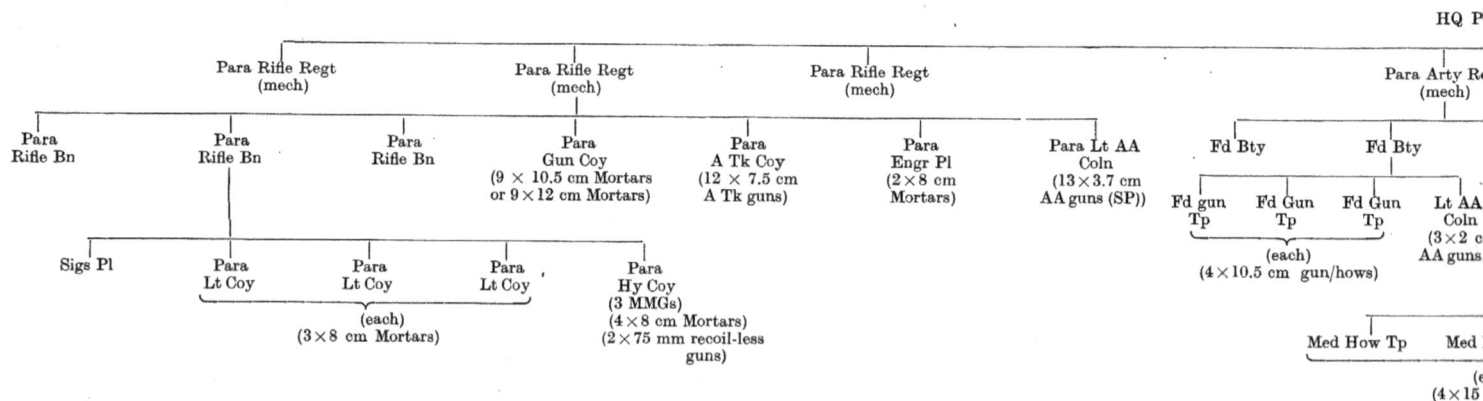

1. The German Parachute Division was designed for employment in an airborne role.
2. The division was fully mechanised.
3. It is almost certain that no parachute divisi[on] table, owing to shortage of equipment.
4. The total strength of the parachute division i[s]

BRITISH AIRBORNE DIVISION (1945)

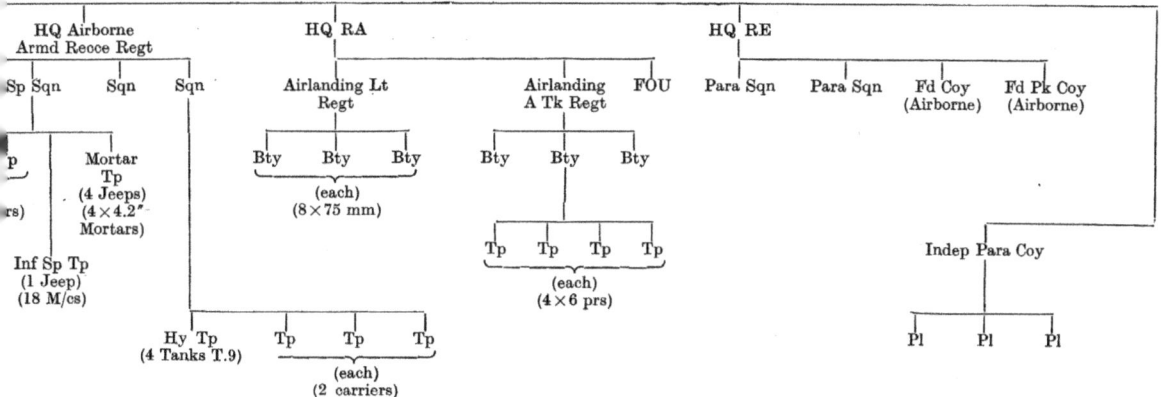

NOTES

1. **Airlanding Bn** — Recce Pl was commanded by a Captain; each Recce Section was commanded by a Lieutenant. The Platoon had its own 18 Set wireless net, with a 22 Set link to Bn HQ.
2. **Airlanding A tk Regt** — Two of the batteries had an increment of 4×17 prs.
3. **Indep Para Coy** — Organised as a normal infantry company; but usually had the special role of landing ahead of the main force to mark DZs and LZs with flares etc.
4. Total strength of the Airborne Division as shown above i.e. less Sigs and Services (approx) — Offrs 685 / ORs 11,022

A GERMAN PARACHUTE DIVISION (1945)

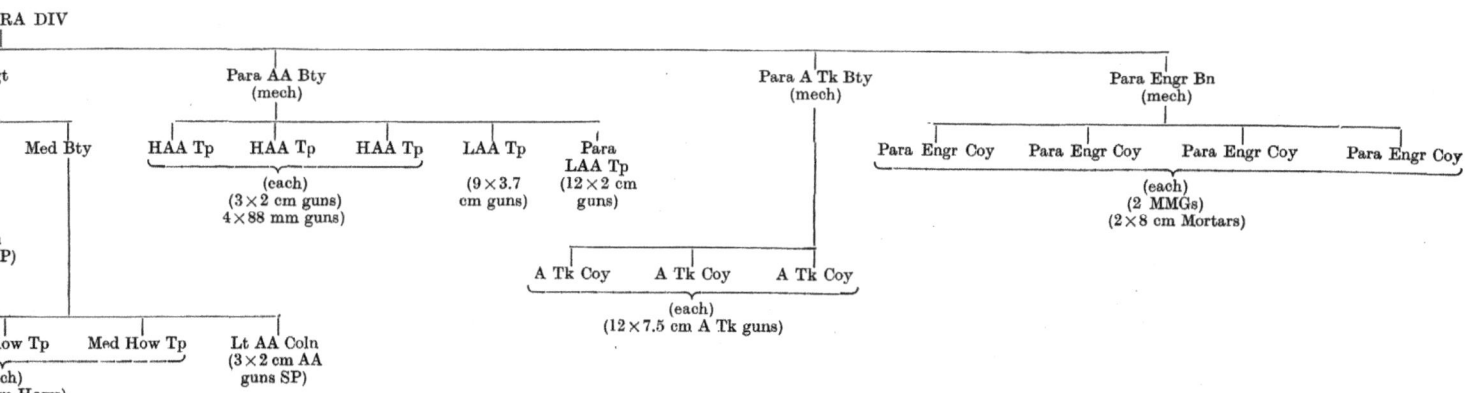

NOTES

to fight in an ordinary ground role, and to be readily available

was ever equipped up to the scale of AA guns shown in this

not known.

APPENDIX "C"

LIST OF REFERENCE MAPS

1 : 250,000   North West Europe : GS GS 4042
                    Sheets 2 A and 3 A, 3

                Germany : GS GS 4346
                    Sheets K. 52, K. 53

1 : 100,000   Central Europe : GS GS 4416
                    Sheets P. 1, Q. 1

1 : 50,000   Germany : GS GS 4507
                    Sheets 6, 7, 16, 17, 36, 37

1 : 25,000   Germany : GS GS 4414
                    Sheets 4204, 4205, 4206,
                        4304, 4305, 4306.

APPENDIX "D"

ORGANISATION OF THE AIRBORNE BASE

6 BRIT AIRBORNE DIV

This Appendix is intended to describe the organisation by which units of 6 Brit Airborne Div were moved from their initial locations in ENGLAND, to the airfields from which they were to take-off for Operation VARSITY, and to give some idea of the arrangements made to ensure that this process went smoothly, and that final preparations were completed by the time of take-off.

1. **Movement**

On return from HOLLAND at the end of February 1945, 6 Brit Airborne Div was located in the BULFORD (Wiltshire) area. Between 18 and 20 March all troops taking part in Operation VARSITY, less those in the Divisional Seaborne Tail, moved to Transit Camps in ESSEX, situated within reasonable distance of the airfields from which they were to take-off. The allotment of units to Airfield Transit Camps, and the locations of Camps and Airfields are shown in the following table, and on Map A 1.

Transit Camp	Unit	Approx Str Offrs	Approx Str ORs	Airfield
HILL HALL	HQ 3 Para Bde	15	150	CHIPPING ONGAR
	8 Para Bn	32	565	
	1 Cdn Para Bn	32	565	
	Det 224 Para Fd Amb	4	32	
		83	1312	
MUSHROOM FARM	Div HQ } Div Sigs }	70	250	RIVENHALL
	9 Para Bn	32	560	WETHERSFIELD
	3 Para Sqn RE	4	65	WETHERSFIELD
	Det 224 Para Fd Amb	4	32	WETHERSFIELD
	591 Para Sqn RE	5	85	BOREHAM
	Armd Recce Regt	2	26	DUNMOW
	Det 53 Airlanding Light Regiment RA	10	45	DUNMOW
		127	1063	
GOSFIELD AIRFIELD	12 DEVON	50	790	RIVENHALL / DUNMOW / MATCHING
BIRCH AIRFIELD	2 OXF BUCKS	50	800	GOSFIELD / BIRCH
WIMBUSH	12 Para Bn	32	605	BOREHAM
	7 Para Bn	32	605	BOREHAM
		64	1210	
SHUDY CAMP	HQ 5 Para Bde	22	170	WETHERSFIELD
	13 Para Bn	30	555	WETHERSFIELD
	225 Para Fd Amb	7	65	BOREHAM
	Det 2 Airlanding A Tk Regt RA	11	157	DUNMOW / EARLS COLNE
		70	947	
CHADACRE	53 Airlanding Light Regt RA	25	240	{ EARLS COLNE / SHEPHERDS GROVE
	HQ 6 Airlanding Bde	19	95	EARLS COLNE
	195 Airlanding Fd Amb	9	80	EARLS COLNE
	3 Para Bde Horsas	1	50	SHEPHERDS GROVE
	5 Para Bde Horsas	1	40	SHEPHERDS GROVE
	1 RUR	50	760	GOSFIELD / BIRCH
		105	1265	

89

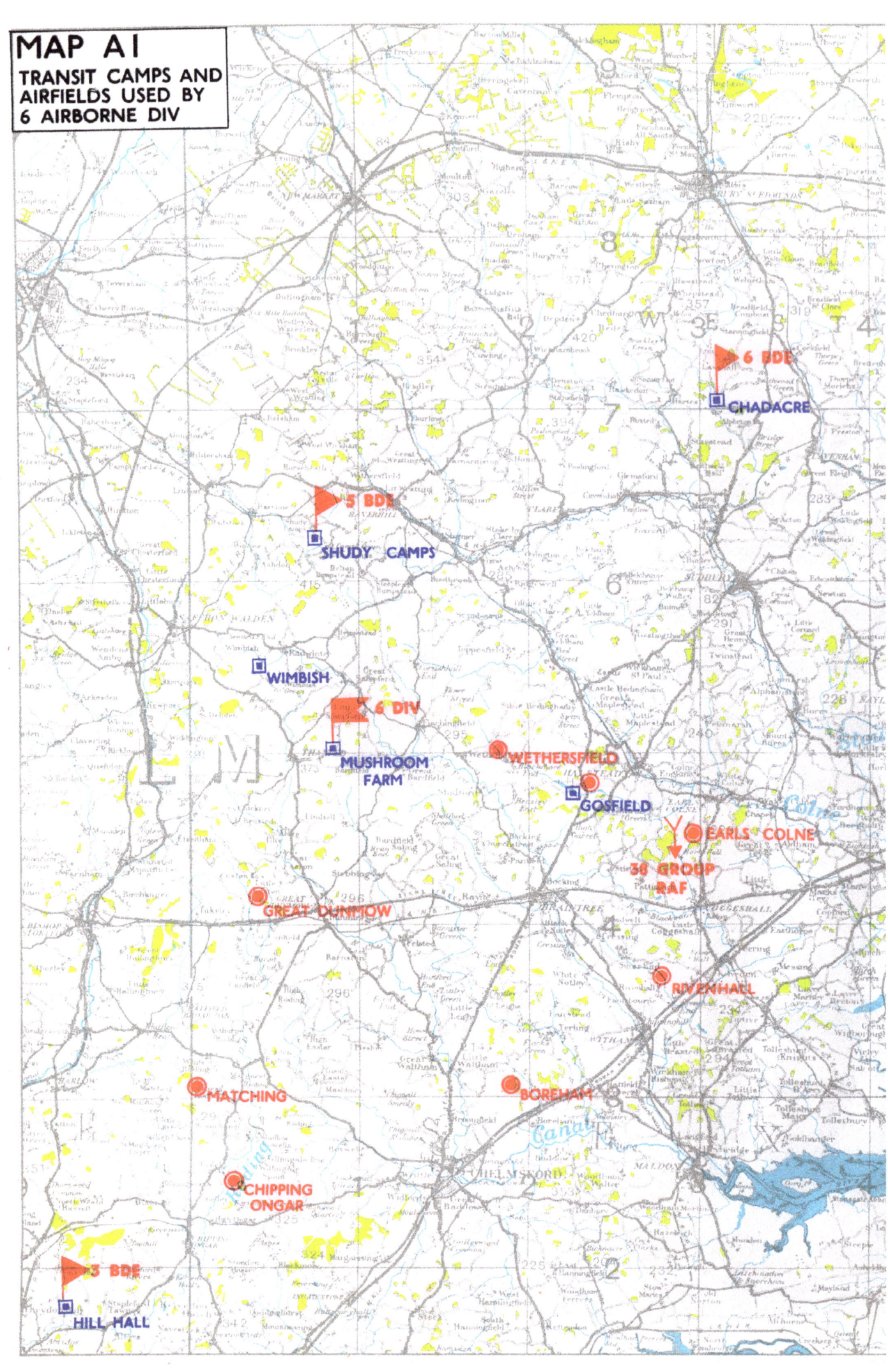

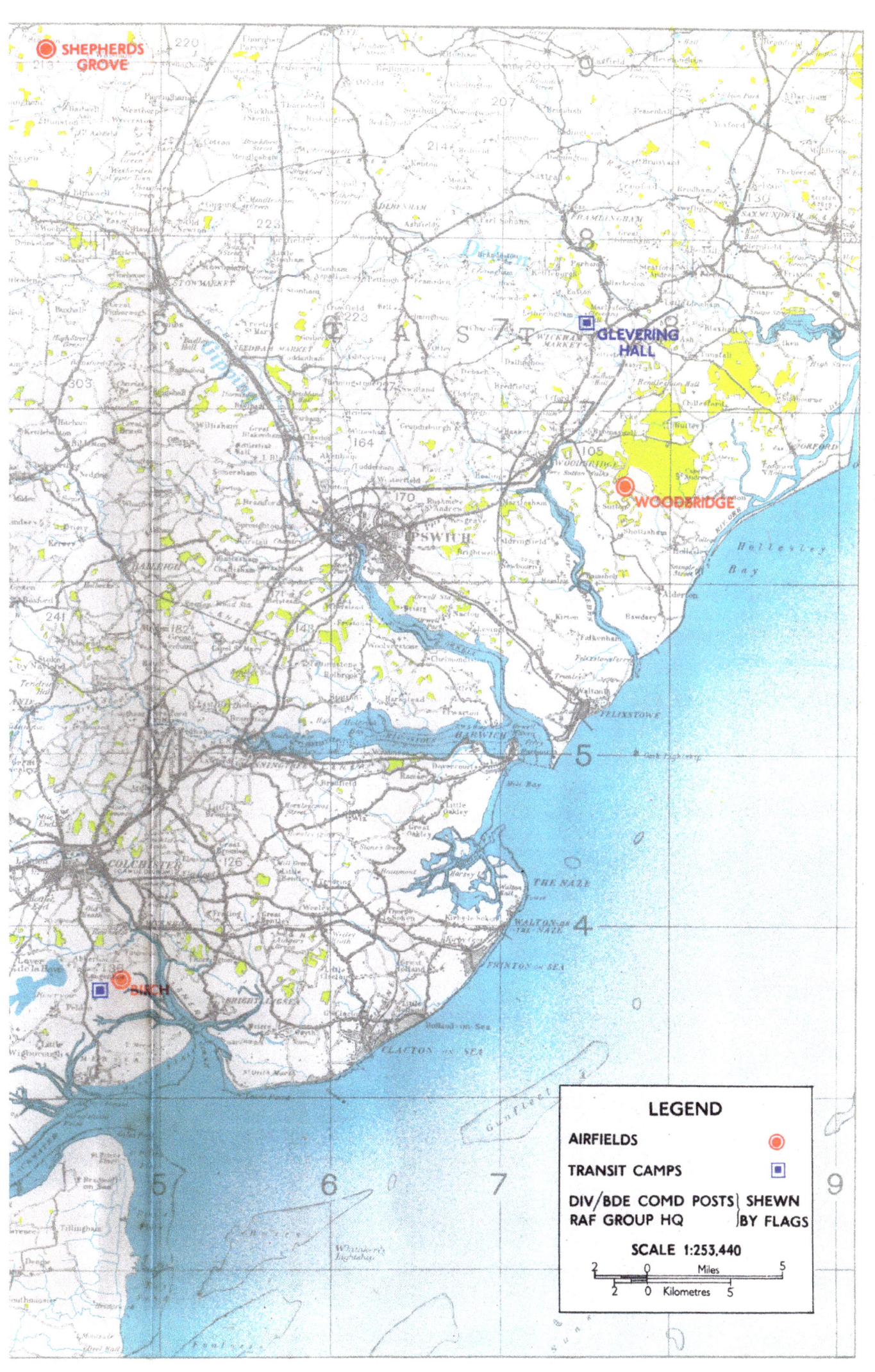

Transit Camp	Unit	Approx Str Offrs	ORs	Airfield
GLEVERING HALL	Det 2 Airlanding A Tk Regt RA	8	192	WOODBRIDGE
	Det 53 Airlanding Light Light Regt RA		16	WOODBRIDGE
	RE		4	WOODBRIDGE
	3 Bde Hamilcars	1	29	WOODBRIDGE
	5 Bde Hamilcars	1	19	WOODBRIDGE
	RASC	6	86	WOODBRIDGE
	Armd Recce Regt	3	24	WOODBRIDGE
		19	370	

COMMAND POSTS

	Transit Camp	Airfield
Div HQ	MUSHROOM FARM	RIVENHALL
3 Para Bde	HILL HALL	CHIPPING ONGAR
5 Para Bde	SHUDY CAMP	WETHERSFIELD
6 Airlanding Bde	CHADACRE	EARLS COLNE

Fifteen platoons of transport (30 TCVs per platoon) were allotted to the Division for moving troops to transit camps: these were allotted on the scale of one per aircraft in the case of parachute units, and one per twenty men in the case of airlanding units. Transport reported to units on the evening of 18 March, and remained attached until D-Day.

2. **Transit Camps**

Eight Transit Camps were arranged by HQ 1 Brit Airborne Corps. Responsibilities for their organisation were allotted as follows :—

(a) *1 Brit Airborne Corps*

Provision of :—
Camp Commandant and small staff.
NAAFI.
Accommodation, accommodation stores and bedding.
MI Room.
REME Repair facilities.
Supplies of POL.

(b) *6 Brit Airborne Div*

Arrangements for pay and exchange of currency (one Cashier per camp).
Collection and delivery of mail, by means of a mobile APO.
Fatigue and guard duties.
Provision of Security Personnel.
(Laundry had to be done by troops themselves from 19 March onwards).

(c) *HQ Eastern Command*

Traffic control and marking of routes between transit camps and airfields.

Communications are covered in paragraph 4 below.

3. **Final preparations in Transit Camps**

Petrol, Oil and Lubricants

Vehicles going on the operation were topped up before loading, and each Jeep carried an extra jerrican of petrol.

Jettison Drop Containers

These containers which had been packed by the divisional services, were issued to parachute units on a scale of four per aircraft on 19 March. It then became a unit responsibility to ensure that they were correctly loaded on to the aircraft.

Rations

The following operational rations (each man) were issued to units on 19 March :—

24 Hour Pack Ration
Hexamine Cooker
Tin Hexamine Tablets
Cigarettes (10)
Chewing Gum
Boiled Sweets (2 oz)
Emergency Ration.

Loading of Gliders

This began at 0800 hours D—2 and had to be completed by 1800 hours D—1.

4. **Communications**

The layout of telephone communications in the Airborne Base is shown on Diagram 7. The switchboard of MUSHROOM FARM was manned by 1 Brit Airborne Corps operators: formations or units occupying other camps had to be prepared to provide operators for their own exchanges.

1 Brit Airborne Corps provided a DR Service to all Camps, with two runs per day.

5. **Move of Seaborne Tail**

When 6 Brit Airborne Div returned to ENGLAND from HOLLAND at the end of February, 1945, certain detachments of administrative units (mostly transport) were left in BLA; these troops were known as the "Land Elements".

Of that part of the division which returned to ENGLAND, all units and detachments which were not to be flown in Operation VARSITY were known as the "Seaborne Tail".

The Seaborne Tail was divided into three parties, and was transported to the Continent via TILBURY and OSTEND under arrangements made by the Build-Up Control Organisation.

The first party left BULFORD on 15 March and was due to join the land element in BLA before the operation; it consisted of those complete units which played only a very small part in the actual airborne operation.

The second party left BULFORD on 19 March and rejoined the division on 26 and 27 March; it included the bulk of the administrative transport of the airborne units.

The third party leaving ENGLAND on D-Day (24 March) and rejoining the division on 29 March included a small number of men and vehicles required by the division in ENGLAND up to the time of take-off.

DIAGRAM 7

AIRBORNE BASE TELEPHONE COMMUNICATIONS

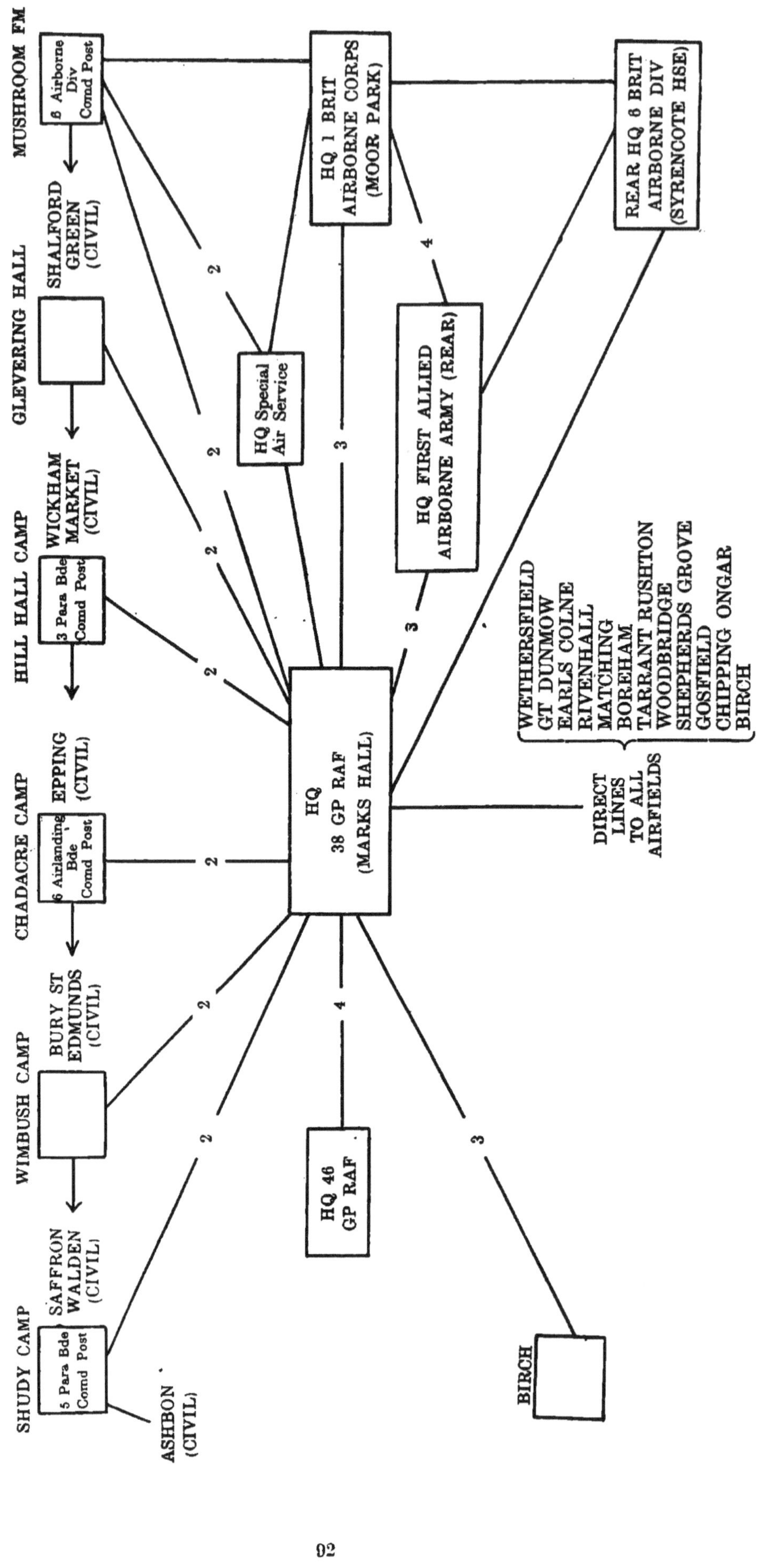

APPENDIX "E"

CASUALTIES - EQUIPMENT AND PERSONNEL

LOSSES IN VEHICLES AND GUNS IN OPERATION VARSITY

1. 6 BRIT AIRBORNE DIV

	Taken by air	Lost during 24 March	% Lost
Cars 5 cwt 4×4 (Jeeps)	323	140	46.4%
Trailers	283	125	44.2%
Carriers, Universal	18	8	44.4%
Tanks T9	8	4 (2 lost after landing)	50%
Guns, 75 mm Pack Howitzer	24	7	29.2%
Guns, 25 pounder	2	1	50%
Guns, 17 pounder, anti-tank	16	9	56.2%
Guns, 6 pounder, anti-tank	34	10	29.4%
Dodge, ¾-ton weapon carriers	16	9	56.2%

2. RASC HAMILCAR GLIDERS

Number of Gliders flown in	12
Gliders landed in divisional area	8
Number of Gliders from which Carriers were recovered	7
Number of Gliders from which trailers were recovered	5
Number of Gliders from which stores were recovered	3

BATTLE CASUALTIES
1. 6 BRIT AIRBORNE DIV

	24 March		25 March		26 March	
	Offrs	OR	Offrs	OR	Offrs	OR
Killed	39	208	—	1	—	6
Wounded	48	683	1	6	5	24
Missing	Offrs 19				OR 300	

2. RAF AND GLIDER PILOT REGIMENT

	38 Group	46 Group	Glider Pilot Regiment	Total
Killed	7	—	38	45
Wounded	—	—	77	77
Missing	16*	4*	135	155
Total Casualties	23	4	250	277

* 13 members of aircrew, previously missing, later returned to UK and are not included in these figures.

APPENDIX "F"

6 BRIT AIRBORNE DIV OPERATION ORDER NO. 1

This operation order is reproduced below, less the following items:—

Distribution
Appendix A — Order of Battle
Part of Appendix B
Appendix C — 12 Corps Plan
Appendix D — Air Support Plan
Appendix F — Codewords and Passwords
Appendix G — Diagram of Communications (other than RA)
Appendix H — Diagram of RA Communications
Appendix K — Base organisation
All Traces.

NOT TO BE TAKEN IN THE AIR

TOP SECRET
6 ABD/568/G (Ops)
12 Mar 45
VARSITY-PLUNDER
Copy No.

6 AIRBORNE DIV OO NO. 1

Ref Maps : GS GS GERMANY : 1/250,000 Sheets 2A, 3A, K52
1/100,000 Sheets P1, Q1
1/25,000 Sheets 4204, 4205, 4206
4304, 4305, 4306

INFM

1. **Enemy**

   See latest Int Summaries and ISUMS.

2. **Own Tps**

   (a) *12 Corps* :—

   (i) 15 (S) Div is aslting on a two bde front in the gen areas BISLICH 1442 and MEHR 1248–HAFFEN 1149 at H hr on D-Day. Subsequently 15 (S) Div will capture the brs over the ISSEL West of DINGDEN 2253 and relieve 6 Brit Airborne Div in area HAMMINKELN 2048.

   (ii) 1 Cdo Bde is to aslt in the area of GRAV INSEL 1841 at H—2 hrs D-Day and capture WESEL 2240.

   For further details of 12 Corps Plan see Appx C and Trace Q.

   (b) 30 Corps is aslting in the vicinity of REES 0752.

   (c) Ninth US Army is co-operating South of WESEL 2240 especially as regards fire sp.

   (d) RAF BOMBER COMD are bombing WESEL 2240 prior to H hr. 2 TAF and 12 Corps arty are harassing and destroying flak posns East of the RHINE on the 12 Corps front from H hr. For further details of air sp see Appx D.

   (e) XVIII US Corps (Airborne) with under comd 6 Brit Airborne Div and 17 US Div (Airborne) is to land at P hr D-Day East of the RHINE on 12 Corps front.

   (f) 17 US Div (Airborne) is ldg on the LZs and DZs shown on Trace S. Details of this plan will be issued later as Appx "L".

3. **Additional Tps**

   (a) The following units are coming under comd 6 Airborne Div after link up with ground forces in the following priority :—

   One sqn 44 R Tks (less 17-pdr tks) equipped with DD tks.
   One SP A tk bty (twelve SP M10 17-pdrs).
   One fd regt RA (approx D+1).

(b) The following are in sp 6 Airborne Div from P hr :—
  52 (L) Div arty gp consisting of :—
    Three fd regts
    Two med regts
    One HAA bty.

(c) The following are in sp XVIII US Corps (Airborne) from P hr :—
  8 AGRA consisting of :—
    One med regt
    One hy regt
    US 155 mm gun gp (36 × 155 mm).

INTENTION

4. 6 Airborne Div will seize, clear and hold the SCHNEPPENBERG feature 1646 and the village of HAMMINKELN 2048 together with the brs over ISSEL at 223485, 217497 and 216500.

METHOD

5. **Gen Outline**

   (a) See att Trace P.
   (b) Right — 6 Airldg Bde Gp.
       Centre — 5 Para Bde Gp.
       Left   — 3 Para Bde Gp.

6. **Grouping**

   (a) *3 Para Bde ;—*
   Comd : Brig S. J. L. HILL, DSO, MC
   Under comd :—
     One 6 pdr tp 3 Airldg A Tk Bty RA.
     One tp 3 Para Sqn RE.
     224 Para Fd Amb.
   In sp :—
     Three fd regts—52 (L) Div arty gp.

   (b) *5 Para Bde :—*
   Comd : Brig J. H. N. POETT, DSO
   Under comd :—
     4 Airldg A Tk Bty RA (8 × 17 pdr, 8 × 6 pdr).
     One tp 591 Para Sqn RE.
     225 Para Fd Amb.
   In sp :—
     One med regt RA—52 (L) Div arty gp.
     One bty (12 × 75 mm) 53 (WY) Airldg Lt Regt RA.

   (c) *6 Airldg Bde Gp :—*
   Comd : Brig R. H. BELLAMY, DSO
   Under comd :—
     3 Airldg A Tk Bty RA (less two 6 pdr tps and one 17 pdr sec—total in sp—6 × 17 pdr).
     Det 591 Para Sqn RE.
     195 Airldg Fd Amb.
   In sp :—
     One med regt RA—52 (L) Div arty gp.
     One bty (12 × 75 mm) 53 (WY) Airldg Lt Regt RA.

   (d) *Div Res :—*
     Two lt tk tps 6 Airborne Armd Recce Regt.
     Two para pls 716 Comp Coy (Airborne Lt) RASC.
     One tp 6 pdr 3 Airldg A Tk Bty RA.
     One sec 17 pdr 3 Airldg A Tk Bty RA.
   After link up of land elt :—
     6 Airldg A Tk Bty RA.
     One sqn 44 R Tks (less 17 pdr tks).
     One SP A Tk Bty.

   (e) For further details see Order of Battle (Appx A).

7. **Definitions**

   (a) H hr is the time for the aslt of 12 Corps.
   (b) P hr is the time XVIII US Corps (Airborne) commence dropping on DZs/LZs.

8. **Landing Areas and Timings**

   (a) LZs and DZs—see Trace R.

   (b) Para and glider ldgs will start simultaneously, order of ldg is as follows :—

	Para	Glider	
(i)	3 Para Bde		Note.—Order of landing later amended to :
(ii)		6 Airldg Bde	3 Para Bde, 5 Para Bde,
(iii)	5 Para Bde		6 Airlanding Bde
(iv)		Div HQ Gp	
(v)		RA Gp	
(vi)		Para Bdes Glider Elt	
(vii)		Hamilcar loads.	

   For detailed timings see Appendix B.

9. **Tasks**

   (a) 3 Para Bde Gp will :—
   - (i) Clear and hold the area rd junc 154478–rd junc 168473–rd junc 168462–feature 157461 –rd junc 158465—br 154470.
   - (ii) Patrol out to and be prepared to hold area rd and rly crossing 185476–rd and rly crossing 189474–rd and track junc 182467–cross rds 179473.

   (b) 5 Para Bde Gp will :—
   - (i) Clear and hold the area rd junc 197499–rd junc 197496–rd junc 201492–bldgs at 187493 –rd junc 187497.
   - (ii) Patrol out to and be prepared to hold area rd junc 169493–bldgs 177488–rd and rly crossing 174486–bldgs 170486–rd junc 167490.

   (c) 6 Airldg Bde Gp will seize and hold the following areas in order of priority :—
   - (i) Brs over River ISSEL at :—
       rly br 216500–rd br 217497–rd br 223485.
   - (ii) To clear the area required for Div HQ vicinity 189479.
   - (iii) Rd junc 212495–rd and rly crossing 217486.
   - (iv) HAMMINKELN 2048.

10. **Bdys and Junc Pts**

    (a) See att Trace P.

    (b) *Bdys*
    - (i) Between 6 Brit Airborne Div and 17 US Div (Airborne) :—
        Incl to 6 Brit Airborne Div, BRUNEN 2748–x rds 253482–rd to junc 229481– rly crossing 219477–excl bldgs 207473–rly crossing 196468–track junc 182465– incl x rds 169462–excl rd to bldgs 155458–thence line of water ditch to br 144447.
    - (ii) Between 5 Para Bde and 6 Airldg Bde :—
        Incl to 5 Para Bde, track junc 214533–dyke junc 213527–to bend in R ISSEL 213522–excl br 213514–excl br 209507–incl x rds 207506–incl line of rd to rd junc 201486–incl rd to junc 191481–rd junc 188482–br over rly 183478.
    - (iii) Between 5 Para Bde and 3 Para Bde :—
        Incl to 3 Para Bde, junc of LANGE RENNE and BISLICHER LEY at 138478– line of LEY to 154477–excl edge of wood to rd junc 167479–excl rd to cross tracks 173481–br over rly 177483–excl rly to 183478.
    - (iv) Between 3 Para Bde and 6 Airldg Bde :—
        Incl to 3 Para Bde, br over rly 183478–line of rly to 196468.

    (c) *Junc Pts*
    - (i) Between 6 Airldg Bde and 513 RCT–br over rly at 219476.
    - (ii) Between Div Res and 513 RCT–br over rly at 196468.
    - (iii) Between 6 Airldg Bde and 5 Para Bde–x rds 207502 and x rds 203491.
    - (iv) Between 5 Para Bde and 3 Para Bde–rd junc 167479 and x rds 172481.
    - (v) Between 3 Para Bde and 513 RCT–x rds 159458 and x rds 169462.
    - (vi) Between 3 Para Bde and Div Det Pl–br over rly 186476.
    - (vii) Between 3 Para Bde and 15 (S) Div–corner of wood 155477.
    - (viii) Between 3 Para Bde, 17 US Div (Airborne) and 15 (S) Div–track junc 155454.

11. **Patrolling**

    (a) Bdes will carry out active patrolling within their bdys to maintain contact with the enemy and harass mov of res.

    (b) If situation permits patrolling will be carried out to bdy shown on att Trace P.

12. **Arty**

   (a) 2 FOU will provide three FOOs and rep for each bde.

   (b) CRA's reps at 5 Para Bde and 6 Airldg Bde will be BCs of 53 (WY) Airldg Lt Regt in sp. A third BC of 53 (WY) Airldg Lt Regt will be flown in to act as CRA's rep for 3 Para Bde.

13. **CM**

   2 FOU will provide a listening post and A/CMO for each bde. In addition each bde will provide one listening post.

14. **4.2" Mortars**

   (a) 4.2" mortar pl 6 Airborne Armd Recce Regt will be under comd CRA.

   (b) Calls for fire will be made through 53 (WY) Airldg Lt Regt and HQ RA.

15. **RE**

   (a) CRE will coord the laying of A tk minefds as soon as possible after ldg.

   (b) CRE will be prepared to lay A tk mines to block approaches to the forest from North and East on gen line shown on att Trace P.

16. **Demolitions**

   (a) Brs over ISSEL will be prepared for demolition. They will not be blown unless their capture by the enemy appears certain. Comd 6 Airldg Bde is responsible for giving the order to blow the brs which responsibility may be delegated to an offr on the site.

   (b) Rds leading into div area from East and North will be blocked. Blocks will be capable of removal at short notice.

17. **Mines**

   (a) Particular care in laying mines, will be taken as another div is likely to take over 6 Airborne Div area at a later stage.

   (b) A pers minefds will not be laid.

   (c) Only necklaces of mines will be used for blocking rds and tracks.

   (d) 75 Grenade necklaces will only be placed in posn when the approach of enemy vehs appears imminent. They will not be left down without a gd.

   (e) Minefds will be laid primarily to deny the enemy egress from rds.

   (f) All minefds will be fenced and marked in usual manner and their posn reported to Div HQ as soon as laid.

   (g) Gaps cleared in enemy minefds will be marked in the normal manner.

18. **Glider Ps**

   (a) Glider Ps flying bdes will report to Bde HQ as soon as the situation permits. They will be formed into sub-units under their own offrs and given a role which, except in an emergency, does not involve anything more than static def.

   (b) All other Glider Ps will report to Div HQ as soon as possible after ldg. The senior offr will org them into sub-units and assume responsibility for the close def of Div HQ and the gun area.

19. **Recognition**

   (a) Recognition sign between air tps and ground forces will be the displaying of yellow celanese triangles. These will be carried by all tps of 6 Brit Airborne Div, aslting tps of 15 (S) Div, 1 Cdo Bde and 17 US Div (Airborne).

   (b) Red berets may be worn after the initial drop as an aid to recognition.

   (c) Ground to air—fluorescent panels.

20. **Pyrotechnics**

   (a) Lt sigs may be used during the aslt phase to indicate unit RVs etc.

   (b) Time, area and colours to be used will be notified to this HQ forthwith.

   (c) Lt sigs other than above will not be used.

21. **Postponement**

   In event of postponement when tps are on airfds infm will be passed through RAF channels and not through normal chain of comd.

ADM

22. Adm instrs will be issued separately.

INTERCOMN

23. **Location of HQ**

HQ 6 Airborne Div	— Bldgs 189479
HQ 3 Para Bde	— Vicinity 1646
HQ 5 Para Bde	— 195495
HQ 6 Airldg Bde	— 204486
Tac HQ 12 Corps	— Vicinity GRINSDICK 1037
Main HQ 12 Corps	— Vicinity 0732
Rear HQ 12 Corps	— WINKELSCHER BUSCH 0633
Tac HQ XVIII US Corps (Airborne)	— In 17 US Div (Airborne) area.

24. **Liaison**

The following LOs will be provided as shown below :—

From	To	Detail	Required for	When required	Remarks
3 Para Bde	15 (S) Div	Wrls team with 52 set netted to 6 Airborne Div comd net	Comn with aslt div	D—7	Set provided by 1 Brit Airborne Corps
HQ 6 Airldg Bde	17 US Div (Airborne)	Wrls team and two 52 sets — one to one	Lateral comn with 17 US Div (Airborne)	D—7	One set spare.
HQ 6 Airborne Div	Tac XVIII US Corps	Wrls team and 52 set to 6 Airborne Div	Comn with Tac XVIII Corps	D—7	

25. **SOS**

When comns have been est SOS sigs will be passed by wrls only.

26. **Wrls**

   (a) As per Appendices G and H att.
   (b) Airborne sets will open immediately on ldg. Sets with the ground forces will open as ordered by the ground fmn comd.
   (c) On arrival at RVs, listening watch will be kept on the 'Common Recognition' channel of the SCR 300, down to bn level. This watch is also kept in other airborne fmns and in the ground aslt fmn.
   (d) All operators will carry full particulars of every link which can be operated by their type of set. These particulars can be rolled up and concealed in the largest rod of the F type aerial. It can be recovered by pushing the smallest rod through.

27. **Line**

   (a) Line comn will be est as soon as practicable. Line parties will not be despatched before the proposed route is declared clear of enemy.
   (b) Initially all lines in the div area will be considered liable to interception. Necessary security measures will be taken.
   (c) No existing enemy routes will be taken into use without reference to CR Sigs, or a Bde Sig Offr. The necessary instrs regarding such routes are being issued through Sig channels.
   (d) Comds at all levels ensure that early infm of enemy comn installations is passed to Div HQ through Sig channels.
   (e) Other than the cutting of enemy cables, no destruction of enemy comns eqpt will be carried out without reference to a R Sigs offr who will ensure that it is carried out in a scientific manner, as ordered through Sig channels.

28. **DRs**

As soon as practicable DRLS will be est.

29. **Pigeons**

Will not be used.

30. **Sig Time**

Official time will be BST (designated by letter A). Time will be checked from BBC broadcasts Time sigs are radiated every hr at the hr on 6195 Kcs.

31. **Codes and Sig Security**

   (a) Codes will be issued normally through Sig channels. Ground fmns hold Airborne code keys.

   (b) Codes carried by air will be strictly limited to those for D to D+2. The codes will be written on special nitrate paper by offrs specially detailed, who will be responsible for their destruction in an emergency. Special destructor tubes will be issued. Detailed security instrs for the carrying of codes and frequency lists will be issued through Sig channels.

   (c) Slidex cursors will not be made out before ldg, unless carried in destruction tubes.

   (d) Any compromise of codes will be reported immediately to CR Sigs by secure means.

32. **Cipher**

   (a) Necessary orders will be issued through Sig channels.

   (b) No cipher will be available below bde HQ. An 'Emergency Slidex Procedure' will be used within the div as a method of passing infm in an emergency only. This method requires 24 hrs security. Necessary instrs have been issued through Sig channels.

   (c) Any compromise of ciphers will be reported immediately to CR Sigs by secure means.

33. **Passwords**

   Common passwords and replies for use by airtps and tps of 12 Corps will be issued separately. Passwords other than above will not be used by fmns and units of this div.

   17 US Div (Airborne) will be using passwords. These will be notified later and must be known to all concerned.

34. **Code Names**

   A list of place code names is being issued later by 12 Corps.

ACK

Time of signature 2345 hrs	Lt Col,
Issued to Sigs ....hrs	GS,
Method of Despatch	6 Airborne Div.

DISTRIBUTION: See separate sheet

THIS ORDER WILL NOT BE TAKEN INTO THE AIR ON D-DAY.

PART I
Op VARSITY-PLUNDER
TOP SECRET
APPENDIX "B"

6 AIRBORNE DIV OO No. 1

AIR INSTRUCTION

1. **SOP**

    Attention is drawn to SOP Brit Airborne Forces.

2. **Form A, etc**

    See Part II att.

3. **DZs, LZs, SDPs**

    See Trace 'R' att.

    Detailed tac ldgs will be arranged between fmns or units and OCs of glider sqns concerned.

4. **Aids**

    (a) No pathfinder tps.
    (b) 22 Indep Para Coy are providing aids with our own fwd ground tps. Aids are being arranged direct with IX TCC.
    (c) SDPs (for subsequent re-supply — see para 19).
      White T in centre.
      Violet Smoke (alternative White).
      Eureka Channel Transmit .... Receive .... Coded ....

5. **Re-supply**

    (a) Alternative SDPs are located in Div HQ and Bde Areas (see Trace 'R').
    (b) 22 Indep Para Coy will provide two parties of five men each with necessary eqpt to proceed with 716 Coy RASC and each Bde to mark SDPs.
      These parties will travel in separate aircraft or gliders from Bde and 716 Coy allotments. Personnel will join units before proceeding to Transit Camps.
    (c) HQ 38 Gp are being requested to arrange for all pilots to know locations and numbers of all SDPs in order that they can be diverted in emergency by VHF sets.

6. **Para Despatching Signals**

    20 min Verbal.
    5 min Verbal.
    4 min Red Light.
    Drop Green Light

7. **Run In.**

    Approx SW — NE.
    Height of para drop 500' — 600'.
    52 Wing are being requested to do second runs if practicable and the load remaining is of sufficient importance.

8. **Release of Eqpt.** (No deviation permitted).

    (a) Jettison Containers — (by pilot operating salve switch) 2 secs prior to Green light.
    (b) Unit Containers and Eqpt — as shown on Form AA submitted by units.
    (c) Push Bicycles (to be wrapped in sacking or blanket to prevent catching in door) — after last man by crew chief.
      This is to ensure bicycle does not hold up any sticks.
    (d) ACOs are being instructed to brief aircrews on release of eqpt and despatching signals and to ensure that the eqpt of the aircraft allows no deviation from these arrangements, which might cause misunderstanding.
      Stick Comds will carry out a rehearsal with the air crew of emplaning, jumping drill, signals and release of eqpt at aircraft loading.

9. Weather Decision

Preliminary	hrs D — 1
Intermediate	hrs D — 1
Final	hrs D Day

Passed to (i) Duty Offr, Command Post, 6 Airborne Div, by Air Fmn HQ.
         (ii) Units by ACOs concerned.

10. Unit Containers

Unit containers (carrying personal weapons etc of personnel in aircraft) will be drawn from PMSU NETHERAVON in accordance with Part 3.

11. Jettison Containers

(a) Four Jettison Sup Containers will be carried on all para aircraft except those carrying unit containers. Unit and Jettison containers must not be carried on the same aircraft.

(b) Jettison containers will be drawn by units in accordance with Adm Instrs — they will be shown on Form AA. Jettison containers will be taken to airfds by units — stick comds will be responsible for seeing them loaded on to aircraft and checking up with the capt of the aircraft for their release immediately prior to paratps dropping.

    (For Jettison Drop Areas see Trace 'R').

12. Parachutes

(a) All 'chutes are being placed in aircraft on D-1 before tps arrive for container loading.

(b) 'Chutes will be fitted at aircraft loading.

(c) Names will be chalked on 'chutes and they will be left on seats in aircraft. They will be wrapped in ground sheets or gas capes.

(d) ACOs are being instructed to ensure that doors are fitted and that the "vents" are put in the windows to ensure 'chutes do not get damp.

13. Emergency Release Gear.

An emergency release gear is being placed in each para aircraft with 'chutes. ACOs at stns are instructing the crew chief in its use who in turn will instr sticks on arrival at aircraft for 'chute fitting.

14. ACOs

Each airfd has a Brit ACO (Airborne Control Offr) who is entirely responsible for all airborne airfd arrangments, loading and emplaning. He is also the med of comn on an airfd.

15. Loading/Liaison Offr

Fmns/Units will detail one Loading/Liaison offr to each airfd from which they are flying to act as Loading/Liaison offrs. Where gps of units from the same fmn are using one airfd one rep of the fmn is required.

These offrs will proceed to Transit Camps in adv.

They will report to GSO I 38 Gp at MUSHROOM FM TRANSIT CAMP at 1500 hrs 20 Mar 45 to meet the ACOs of their airfds to arrange a staggered loading programme and any other necessary details. Each LO will be in possession of a copy of the necessary Form AA and/or AB.

These instrs do not apply to HAMILCAR loads from WOODBRIDGE which will load at TARRANT RUSHTON.

16. Glider Loading

(a) Loads will be numbered with chalk with the corresponding glider No.

(b) Units will ensure that their lashing eqpt is correct in accordance with scale shown in Part 3.

(c) Any deficiencies in lashings incl special Hamilcar lashings must be drawn by units from ADOS Dumps before proceeding to Transit Camps. Hamilcar lashing eqpt will be issued at TARRANT RUSHTON by the ACO.

(d) Lashing eqpt will be issued to individual loads prior to proceeding to the gliders.

(e) All ACOs hold a small res of lashing eqpt for use in emergency only.

(f) MT will refuel before leaving Transit Camps. Necessary "topping up" pet in jerricans will be taken to airfds by units.

17. **HAMILCAR landing**

   (a) Hamilcar loading will commence at TARRANT RUSHTON at 0900hrs 17 Mar and be completed by 1200 hrs 20 Mar. Hamilcars will then fly loaded to WOODBRIDGE for final take off.

0900 hrs 17 Mar	RA	20 Hamilcars
0900 hrs 18 Mar	RASC (to incl 3 and 5 Para Bdes)	18 Hamilcars
0900 hrs 19 Mar	RE	2 Hamilcars
1000 hrs 19 Mar	Armd Recce Regt	8 Hamilcars

   (b) Forms AB for Hamilcars only to be submitted to this HQ in duplicate by 1000 hrs 16 Mar.

   (c) Each unit will detail one loading offr to report to ACO TARRANT RUSHTON (Capt Sheriffs) the day before loading is to commence, to arrange details.

   (d) 3 and 5 Para Bdes will load under supervision of 716 Coy RASC.

18. **Form AA (Parachute) and Form AB (Glider)**

   (a) (i) Form AA (Para) and /or Form AB (Glider) (less *Hamilcars*) will be prepared in duplicate by all units and submitted to this HQ by 1800 hrs 17 Mar 45 by the following :—

   Bdes
   Armd Recce Regt
   RA
   RE
   RASC
   Lt Hensman (for Div HQ)

   Separate Forms AA and AB will be prepared for each airfd. Type of load (i.e. jeep etc) will be shown in Remarks coln of Form AB.

   (ii) Mark II Horsas and their chalk numbers as allotted in Form A will be incl on Form AB. Names of Lt Cols and above will be shown in remarks coln of Form AA and AB.

   (iii) Jettison Containers will be incl on Form AA under the heading of Jettison Containers.

   (b) (i) It is suggested that Comds travel in the leading aircraft of the serial which is usually flown by the air comd concerned.

19. **Form B.**

   (a) Form B will be prepared in quadruplicate by units prior to proceeding to airfds from Transit Camps.

   (b) They will be in possession of the Stick Comd who will hand over *all* copies to the ACO who will collect them prior to take off.

   (c) Stick Comds or Senior passengers in gliders will have one of the copies of Form B available at aircraft or glider loading (names of personnel need not be inserted at this stage) in order that the load may be checked by Glider P.

   (d) GSO I 38 Gp is requested to arrange distribution of Form B as under :—

HQ Airborne Tps	1 (for passing to OC Residues).
GSO I 38 Gp RAF	1
ACO RAF Sta concerned	1
O2E (Oxford)	1

   (e) An additional copy for retention by the Senior passenger or unit may be made. It will not show unit or other security details if taken in the aircraft or glider.

20. **Payloads**

   Payloads will be entered on Form B above, not to exceed :—

Para aircraft	5,850 lbs
HORSA gliders	6,900 lbs
HAMILCAR gliders	17,150 lbs

21. **Priority Forms**

   (a) Priority Forms are not required.

   (b) Lowest priority loads will be loaded in the highest numbered aircraft of each serial or sta.

   (c) In case of dispute the highest chalk numbers at each airfd will be forfeited.

22. **MT Loading**

   Lorries will arrive at airfds with chalk numbers corresponding to aircraft number prominently displayed on the front. In the case of para aircraft each lorry will contain one stick and all the containers (incl jettison) for their particular aircraft.

23. Disposal of Non Jumpers, Army Eqpt and Glider Personnel

(a) Para aircraft are returning to bases on the Continent.

(b) ACOs with 52 Wing are being instructed to arrange for the return to OC Residues, Syrencote House, NETHERAVON, of any non-jumpers and eqpt. Statements by any witnesses and MO's reports in the case of non-jumpers is also being requested from ACOs.

(c) If gliders land prematurely in UK, senior passenger will contact GSO I (Air) 38 Gp, Marks Hall, EARLS COLNE Airfd, for instrs. If on Continent personnel will proceed to HQ 12 Corps.

24. Modification and Serviceability of Air Eqpt.

(a) Units will ensure that all necessary eqpt is modified, particularly jeeps.

(b) Containers and MC Cradles will be inspected for serviceability prior to proceeding to TRANSIT CAMPS and airfds and any deficiencies made good.

25. Salvage of Gliders, Chutes and Air Eqpt

RAF are making arrangements to salvage RAF eqpt. Army units will assist as much as possible under the circumstances to protect and preserve any eqpt in their area.

26. Record of Ldg Posns

Fmns and units will eventually be asked to produce a trace (1/25,000 map) of the ldg posn of all gliders and sticks as far as is obtainable — when circumstances permit fmns and units will compile these details.

Stick Comds and Senior Glider Passengers should be warned accordingly.

PART II
Op VARSITY-PLUNDER
TOP SECRET

APPENDIX "B" TO 6 AIRBORNE DIV OO No. 1

AIRCRAFT AND GLIDER ALLOTMENT TO UNITS

GLIDERS

		Horsas	Hamilcars	Remarks
Div HQ				
to incl				
Staff and Sigs	13			
ASSU	4			
Phantom	1			
HQ RA	6	28		
HQ RE	1			
Camp and Def Pl	2			
RASC				
716 Coy			12	
HQ 6 Airldg Bde				To be att to same air serial :—
to incl				2 RE Horsas
FOO	2	13		3 RA Horsas (OPs) from RE and RA
ASSU	2			allotment
Airldg Bns				
to incl Dets				
195 Airldg Fd		196		
Amb 6, i.e. 2 Horsas per Bn)				
RE				
(2 Horsas each Bde)		6	2	
195 Airldg Fd Amb				
(in addition 6 allotted to Bn Nos)		7		
53 Airldg Lt Regt RA		74	4	*To Bdes*
				3 *Bde* 1 Horsa (OPs)
				5 *Bde* 3 Horsas (OPs)
				6 *Bde* 3 Horsas (OPs)
				Div Gun Area
				Remainder
				67 Horsas
				4 Hamilcars
Airldg A Tk Btys		38	16	3 *Bde* 6 Horsas
				(One Tp 6-prs)
				5 *Bde* 18 Horsas
				8 Hamilcars
				(One Bty of 8 6-prs)
				(and 8 17-prs)
				6 *Bde* 5 Horsas
				6 Hamilcars
				Div Gun Area 9 Horsas
				2 Hamilcars
Armd Recce Regt				
8 Tks			8	
4.2" Mortars		6		Under Comd RA
3 Para Bde				
to incl				
FOO	1 }	12	3	{ 1 RA Horsa (OP) from RA allotment
Para Fd Amb	1 }			to be incl in same serial

			Horsas	Hamilcars	Remarks
5 Para Bde					
to incl					
FOO	1	⎫	12	3	⎰ 3 RA Horsas (OP) from RA allotment
Para Fd Amb	1	⎭			⎱ to be incl in same serial
TOTALS			392	48	
GRAND TOTAL			440		

PARA AIRCRAFT

Each Para Bde to incl ⎫	3 Bde	— 122	C47s
Para Fd Ambs ⎬			
Dets Para Sqns RE ⎭	5 Bde	— 121	C47s
TOTAL		243	

GRAND TOTAL PARA AND GLIDER AIRCRAFT — 683

DETAILS OF BUILD-UP IN PRIORITY

Amended Appx "E" dated 18 Mar
to OO No 1 dated 12 Mar 45

Serial	LVT	FERRIES Cl 9	FERRIES Cl 50/60	BRIDGES Cl 9 FBE	BRIDGES Cl 9 Bailey	BRIDGES Cl 40	ET Arrival	Units	Pers	MCs	Jeeps	Trlrs	17 prs	6 prs	Ambs	Scout Cars	Carriers	15cwt	3 Ton	Misc	Total Vehs	Remarks
3	38	8	16				⎫	17 pr SP A tk bty	170	9	13	12	12								50	Incl 17-pr guns
4	25						⎬ D Day	Div Sigs (det)	55	5	35	35										Incl CA Det
8	70	14						716 Coy RASC	60		1											Incl two jeeps from Recce Det
10	4							Div HQ	3	3	1											
								224 Fd Amb	18	3	1				4							
								225 Fd Amb	18	3	1				4							
								195 Fd Amb	18	3	1				4							
								716 Coy RASC	2			1										
12	2			25			⎫	See serial 8 above								2						
13			17					224 Fd Amb	17	3					4							
								225 Fd Amb	17	3					4							
								195 Fd Amb	17	3					4							
15	8	6		40			⎬ D+1	Armd Recce Regt			7	6										
17	154							One Sqn Armd Regt			20	30										
								249 Fd Coy RE			10	8										
								317 FS Sec			1	1										
								AW Det			8	8										
19	32							Each Bn (4 jeeps and 4 trlrs)			34	34										Two bns will send 3 jeeps and 3 trlrs
								249 Fd Coy RE				8										
								63 Coy RASC				8										
								Each Bn (one 3 Tonner)														
20			50		20			317 FS Sec											15			
			11		79			Div Sigs											15			
			38		55			REME Det											9			
23					120		⎫ 0600 D+2 to 0600 D+3	Armd Regt less Serial 15						6		20	21		4			Tanks 8 Cromwells
25					120			Remainder Armd Regt														
28					14			Armd Recce Regt														
29					80			6 A/L A tk Bty RA			29	13										
29a					504			Fd Regt														
31								Fd Regt											14			
32								Div HQ											80			
34								Two pls hy coy RASC											594			
				90				Unit tpt														
35					2	26	⎫ 0600 D+3 to 0600 D+4	317 FS Sec											2	26		
36					184			286 Fd Pk Coy											184			
37								Remainder 2nd line tpt RASC														
41					95	30		Ord Fd Pk											95	30		
42					364			Remainder Unit Tpt											364			
43								See Tail 6 A/B Div														
45					65			Div Wksps											65			
50					35			Inf Bde Wksp											35			
53					10			BLBU											10			

Op VARSITY-PLUNDER
TOP SECRET
Copy No. ....

APPENDIX "J" TO 6 AIRBORNE DIV OO No. 1

TIME TABLE OF EVENTS BEFORE Y DAY

Y — 15 days	Briefing of unit comds below rank of Lt Col
Y — 10 days	Issue of Forms A completed All air trg ceases
Y — 9 days	Early sea party moves to transit camp
Y — 7 days	Forms AA and AB rendered by units
Y — 6 days	Adv parties move to transit camp Drawing of units containers
Y — 5 days	Main sea party moves to transit camp Drawing of jettison containers, med glider requirements and pack rations HAMILCAR loading parties move to transit camp Briefing of Coy Comds
Y — 4 days	Main bodies move to transit camp HAMILCAR loading begins
Y — 3 days	Briefing of tps begins
Y — 2 days	Loading of gliders begins Packing unit containers completed Preparation of Forms B
Y — 1 day	Loading of gliders and aircraft completed Issue and fit 'chutes Complete briefing
Y Day	Late sea party moves to transit camp.

Photographs

No. 1. Airborne 75 mm stowed in glider

No. 2. 6 Airlanding Bde Gliders

No. 3. HALIFAX/HAMILCAR Combinations marshalled at WOODBRIDGE

No. 4. View of 3 Para Bde DZ.

No. 5. HORSA Gliders of 6 Airlanding Bde

No. 6. German 88 mm AA guns near HAMMINKELN

No. 7. HORSA gliders of 12 DEVON

No. 8. WACO gliders of 17 US Airborne Div

No. 9. Prisoners captured by 1 Cdn Para Bn

No. 10. HORSA gliders

No. 11. Mortar and Intelligence Sections of 9 Para Bn

No. 12. A HAMILCAR glider

No. 13. View of autobahn East of HAMMINKELN

No. 14. Part of 6 Airlanding Bde on LZ.

No. 15. HAMILCAR glider on Div HQ LZ.

No. 16. LIBERATOR bombers flying in first re-supply drop.

www.ingramcontent.com/pod-product-compliance
Lightning Source LLC
Chambersburg PA
CBHW042302010526
44113CB00048B/2776